FISKE AND MARIE KIMBALL

FISKE AND MARIE KIMBALL

Shaping Public Engagement with Architecture and the Arts

EDITED BY MARIE FRANK

UNIVERSITY OF VIRGINIA PRESS

Charlottesville and London

University of Virginia Press
© 2025 by the Rector and Visitors of the University of Virginia
All rights reserved
Printed in the United States of America on acid-free paper

First published 2025

9 8 7 6 5 4 3 2 1

ISBN 978-0-8139-5399-1 (hardback)
ISBN 978-0-8139-5400-4 (paperback)
ISBN 978-0-8139-5401-1 (ebook)

Library of Congress Cataloging-in-Publication Data is available for this title.

Cover photos: Fiske Kimball and Marie Goebel Kimball, 1913. (Courtesy of the Philadelphia Museum of Art, Library and Archives, Fiske Kimball Papers, box 62, folder 3)
Cover design: Cecilia Sorochin

CONTENTS

ACKNOWLEDGMENTS

Research and writing are traditionally solitary tasks, but they cannot happen without the help and support of many individuals and institutions. The Library and Archives of the Philadelphia Museum of Art holds the Fiske Kimball Papers (which include biographical material on both Fiske and Marie) and the Fiske Kimball Records (accounts of his work as the director of the museum). The staff of the Library and Archives have been unstinting in their support for this project, sharing their knowledge of the papers as well as facilitating my research, especially in the aftermath of the COVID shutdown. I would especially like to thank Kristin Regina, Arcadia Director of the Library and Archives, and three individuals who have served as the Martha Hamilton Morris Archivist over the past few years: Susan Anderson, Margaret Huang, and Rona Razon. I would like to particularly thank Susan Anderson for sharing her knowledge of Kimball materials and for orchestrating the library's oral interview with Anne Goebel Barkman, Marie Goebel Kimball's niece, in 2018. Anne very generously shared family stories, mementoes, and photographs that have resulted in valuable additions to the biographies of Fiske and Marie. The interview also resulted in a warm friendship with Anne—our follow-up emails and visits in Burlington, Vermont, might not have always focused on the Kimballs but did include humor and good conversation.

I was also fortunate to receive the Fritz and Claudine Kundrun Open-Rank Fellowship from the International Center for Jefferson Studies, Thomas Jefferson Foundation, Inc., in Charlottesville, Virginia. A special thank-you to Director Andrew O'Shaughnessy for sharing his copy of Fiske's *Thomas Jefferson, Architect* (1916) with me and his support throughout my time in Charlottesville; and to the staff of the library, especially Anna Berkes and Endrina Tay. Through the ICJS, I also organized a 2021 symposium on Fiske and Marie and I would like to thank Whitney Pippin for her help. We had originally planned an in-person symposium for the fall of 2020, but when COVID struck we had to backpedal and convert the entire event to online. Whitney, unflappable and organized, kept everything on track during a period when virtual conferences were still a "new" thing. I would also like to thank Susan Stein, Senior Curator, Special Projects at

Monticello, for serving as a respondent at the symposium and an insightful follow up conversation as this anthology started to materialize. Diane Ehrenpreis, Curator of Decorative Arts and Historic Interiors at Monticello, brought Marie's work as a curator into perspective, and I am so thankful she agreed to record a virtual tour for the symposium.

While in Charlottesville I also met with a number of individuals who helped me better understand the Kimballs. Robin Lee—the son of Robert Lee, who served as the contractor for Fiske's restoration work at Monticello and for the construction of his house, Shack Mountain—shared insightful family stories about Fiske and Marie. Joseph Lahendro took me on a tour of University of Virginia buildings and shared his knowledge of Fiske's work as an architect there. Garth Anderson shared his knowledge and technical expertise regarding university-owned materials. While the majority of Fiske's papers are in Philadelphia, the bulk of Marie's papers are housed in Special Collections at the University of Virginia Library, and I am grateful to the staff for facilitating my research.

I would also like to extend a posthumous thank-you to Jane Moore. Jane and her husband, Bedford, purchased Shack Mountain after the deaths of Fiske and Marie. Jane regularly invited students in the architectural history program at the university to study Shack Mountain and became a staunch advocate for the Kimballs' legacy. The house could not have been in more stalwart hands.

The work in Philadelphia and Charlottesville was interspersed with research and trips that also relied on the help of others. Kathleen Curran cheerfully shared her knowledge and enthusiasm for Fiske's accomplishments at every turn. Judy Hynson, Director of Research and Library Collections at Stratford Hall, Westmoreland County, Virginia, guided me through the overwhelming amount of material in their collection. Jonathan Olly, Assistant Curator of the Long Island Museum, Stony Brook, New York, shared his knowledge of Federal-era coach lines. David Andrews, from the South Bristol, Maine, Historical Society, arranged for me to go inside one of Fiske's first commissions, Hale Aloha. Cynthia Fuller welcomed me to Castle Park, Michigan, and invited me to stay overnight in the house designed by Fiske for the Goebel family. Ann Whitney graciously opened her doors to Moor's End on Nantucket, Massachusetts, so I could examine firsthand Fiske's restoration work there; Amelia Holmes, Director of Collections and Research Services at the Nantucket Historical Association, so helpfully followed through on the numerous requests I made. Other friends and colleagues I would like to acknowledge for their continuing support include Tom and Lisa Kenney, Beatrice and Matilda Ludvino, Keith Mitchell, Kevin D. Murphy, and Lisa Reilly.

The College of Fine Arts, Humanities and Social Sciences at the University of Massachusetts Lowell generously provided me with a grant from the UML Researchers and Scholars Investment Fund as well as a sabbatical in the fall of 2024 that gave me the unencumbered time to finish this manuscript. My editor at the University of Virginia Press, Mark Mones, always kept the many details of a manuscript submission simple and straightforward. I thank him and all the staff involved in this publication for their knowledge and eye for detail.

FISKE AND MARIE KIMBALL

An Introduction

This volume consists of a set of interdisciplinary essays examining the various ways the scholarship and activities of Fiske and Marie Kimball in the early twentieth century shaped the experience and interpretation of art and architecture in the United States. Both individuals made an indelible mark. From his pioneering publication *Thomas Jefferson, Architect* in 1916 through his thirty-year career as Director of the Philadelphia Museum of Art (PMA) from 1925 to 1955, Fiske entrenched himself as a powerful and influential voice for the arts. His scholarship established the architectural accomplishments of the past, while his criticism and involvement with contemporary public monuments guided design in the present. As a preservationist, he played a critical role in determining both institutional and national policies as well as the interpretation of specific sites (such as Monticello, Colonial Williamsburg, and Fairmount Park). At the PMA, he not only built the collection but also determined the structure and display of the objects as he steered the institution toward an international reputation. As an architect, he used his design training for residential projects, campus planning projects, and museum installations throughout his career. And Fiske was an educator—both through the academic programs he founded at the University of Virginia and reestablished at New York University and through his consistent commitment to engaging Americans with the visual arts.

Working side by side with Fiske throughout his career, and often overshadowed by his dramatic personality, was Marie Goebel Kimball. Marie had a sustained career as a scholar. Her publications ranged from work in comparative literature—she knew French and German—to detailed articles on the decorative arts and her lengthy biographical volumes on Thomas Jefferson. (For this last, she received a Guggenheim Fellowship.) Appointed the first curator of Monticello in

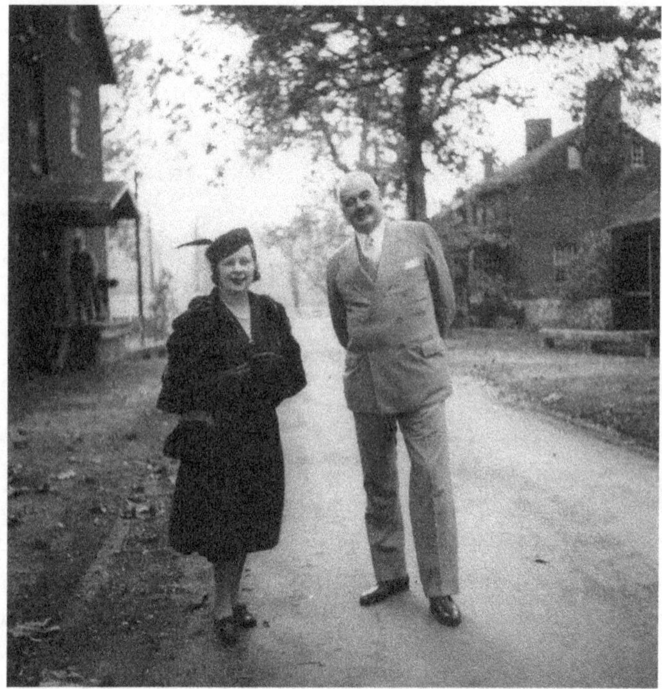

FIGURE 1. Fiske and Marie Goebel Kimball at Colonial Williamsburg, n.d. (Courtesy of the Philadelphia Museum of Art, Library and Archives, Fiske Kimball Papers, Box 62, Folder 12)

1944, she held the responsible position of identifying, collecting, displaying, and interpreting the objects within the house. The late date of her biographies and position as curator represent the culmination of a decades-long association with Jefferson's papers and the restoration of Monticello. As family friend Jane Moore recalled, Marie appeared more gentle and quiet than Fiske, but she "was quite a person in herself—she was not to be overlooked . . . [behind the gentleness] there was an iron woman."[1]

The essays gathered here offer a timely investigation into the Kimballs' contributions and their legacy on a number of levels. First, the current critical debates surrounding the canon of architectural history and public memorials have tasked art and architectural historians of the present to reexamine how the history of the visual arts has been written and constructed. Both Fiske and Marie created some of the initial interpretations of specific sites. Second, the essays blur the traditional disciplinary boundaries that have too frequently siloed the efforts of people like the Kimballs. As noted above, Fiske was a scholar, a critic, an architect, and a museum director. Readers familiar with Fiske's work in the historic preservation of colonial houses may not be aware of his knowledge of contemporary European painting. Indeed, as he began the restoration of Stratford Hall in Virginia in the 1930s, he also acquired paintings by Picasso and Cézanne for the museum in Philadelphia. Likewise, Marie worked as both an author and a curator and produced scholarship in comparative literature, history, biography, and the decorative arts. Her work on the decorative arts at Monticello coexisted with her skills as a biographer and historian. Exploring their simultaneous activities thus invites a much richer, cross-disciplinary understanding of the motivations to preserve and present the visual arts in the United States. And third, a consideration of Fiske's and Marie's professional careers also contributes to current reevaluations of gendered roles in scholarly production in the twentieth century.[2] Although Fiske and Marie worked independently, it should also be stressed how much they worked together. Their activities evidence a rare partnership of the mind.

This volume owes its origins to a virtual conference hosted by the International Center for Jefferson Studies at Monticello in March 2021. In addition to the revised and expanded essays included here, two virtual tours created for the conference can still be accessed and provide a critical complement to the volume. Architect Joseph Dye Lahendro produced "The Architecture of Fiske Kimball at UVa," an examination of Fiske's work as an architect and planner at the University of Virginia. In "Virtual Tour of Monticello with Diane Ehrenpreis," viewers join Ehrenpreis, Curator of Decorative Arts and Historic Interiors, on a progression through the rooms of the house to learn about Marie's research and decisions regarding objects and their presentation. The essays and the tours together offer focused studies on different areas of Fiske's and Marie's contributions. The volume is organized roughly chronologically, but the essays are also grouped thematically, with a set of essays on the Kimballs' work as historians followed by essays in historic preservation and museum studies.

Richard Guy Wilson's essay, "The Arc of American Architectural History to Fiske Kimball," provides a prolegomenon to the study of architecture that set the stage for the Kimball's publications. Wilson indicates the multiple levels of interest that Americans had coming out of the nineteenth century concerning the role of buildings and architecture—including the associational, anecdotal, and literary, among others. In particular, he notes the role of practicing architects and the implications of their goals as they produced some of the first studies of American buildings. Lauren Weiss Bricker's essay, "Fiske Kimball and His Contemporaries," focuses primarily on Fiske's survey, *A History of Architecture* (1918), to establish how his methodology transformed architectural history writing. Then, through a comparison with Talbot Faulkner Hamlin, she demonstrates how the two scholars used their interest and knowledge of architecture in the past to inform their criticism of architecture in the present. In "Domestic Architecture in Diagram: Fiske Kimball as Architect-Historian and the Case for Spatial Analysis," Danielle S. Willkens presents Fiske's *Domestic Architecture of the American Colonies and of the Early Republic* (1922) as a book that introduced readers to a new way of seeing architecture. She reminds us that Fiske was an architect-historian and she uses the current theory of spatial analysis to examine the presentation of image and text in *Domestic Architecture*. In "Marie Kimball, Scholar and Historian," Susan Kern takes the spotlight off Fiske and turns it toward Marie's scholarship. Kern's essay establishes the attentiveness that Marie brought to her research on Thomas Jefferson and the three volumes she published on his early career. Although initially well received, her work was soon eclipsed by the multivolume biography by Dumas Malone. Yet Kern posits that Marie's scholarship frequently brought something to Jefferson's biography that was lacking in Malone's: she presented Jefferson's engagement and support for the arts as part of his vision for the new country. Kern asks important questions about Marie's legacy as a historian and her position as a woman in the male-dominated discipline of history at midcentury.

The next group of essays centers on Fiske's work in historic preservation. Carl R. Lounsbury examines Fiske's advisory role at Colonial Williamsburg in the late 1920s and early 1930s in "Fiske Kimball and the Williamsburg Decalogue." The principles drawn up for the restoration in 1928, known as "the decalogue," set the standard for large-scale restoration prior to the National Secretary of the Interior's standards. Fiske was closely involved in the articulation of the decalogue, and through a series of case studies, we encounter Fiske as an advocate for its principles, sometimes succeeding and sometimes not. In "'Better to Preserve Than to Repair': Fiske Kimball and the Preservation Movement," John H. Sprinkle Jr. elevates Fiske's role as an advisor from the local to the national. Fiske served for fifteen years on the National Park System Advisory Board. The criteria and conventions established by this board later served as the foundation for the National Historic Preservation Act in 1966. Sprinkle provides three case studies to illustrate how Fiske negotiated and proposed solutions to preserve buildings based upon their aesthetic (rather than associational) merit and his early arguments for the adaptive and continued use of historic buildings within the urban fabric. In "'As It Is Accurate Historically': Fiske Kimball and the Restoration of Monticello," Gardiner Hallock in turn provides an in-depth account of one project: the restoration of Thomas Jefferson's home, Monticello. Fiske served as the chairman of the Restoration Committee for the house and grounds for over thirty years (from 1924 to 1955, during the same span of years he served as director at the PMA). Hallock breaks down the eras of restoration at Monticello and illustrates how Fiske's evidence-based approach advanced the restoration, even though his broad knowledge of historical examples could sometimes override the evidence.

The last two essays focus on museums and collections. Ann M. Lucas, in "The Monticello Image in the American Mind: Fiske and Marie Kimball Curate Thomas Jefferson's Home," examines how Fiske and Marie shaped the interiors of Monticello. Their insistence on research and the display of original artifacts set a standard for house museums in the country. Concurrent with Fiske and Marie's efforts to locate Jefferson-era objects for Monticello, Fiske also sought to fill the galleries of the PMA. In the last essay, "Architectural Imagination: Fiske Kimball's Modern Museum," John Vick draws together Fiske's skills as a director and architect as he endeavored to acquire modern art for the museum. In the 1940s he obtained the collection of Albert Eugene Gallatin, which included works by Picasso, Arp, and Mondrian. Then, into the 1950s, an intricate series of negotiations ultimately brought the Louise and Walter Arensberg collection to Philadelphia. This included works by Brancusi, Kandinsky, and Léger as well as a notable collection of pre-Columbian art. The acquisition of the Arensberg collection required Fiske to personally design the galleries into a new configuration for their display.

One of the most important themes tying the essays and tours together is the academic rigor and method that the Kimballs brought to their research. Fiske was an early proponent of scientific history in the United States. This method for constructing the history of a topic or subject is most commonly associated with German historian Leopold von Ranke (1795–1886), and it relied on primary sources—original documents from a period, such as letters, certificates, records, and inventories—that could be presented in a systematic way. As suggested in Wilson's essay, architectural history in the United States prior to Fiske took a multitude of approaches but lacked this type of consistent investigation. Fiske shared the methods of scientific history with Marie, and she became exceptionally adept at tracking down original sources. Both the tour by Ehrenpreis and the essays by Kern and Lucas underscore how Marie used letters, packing lists, and insurance records to uncover the history behind objects and, importantly, to support a discussion of Jefferson's thoughts on the arts.

The benefits of scientific history led Fiske to expand his search and to engage with other disciplines and technologies. Significantly, Fiske added original architectural drawings to his list of primary sources. Early in his career—in 1912, when he was just twenty-four—he suggested that basing the study of architectural history on built monuments alone was a mistake. Drawings, he believed, indicated creative thought, and he would make drawings, not standing structures, the focus of his first book, *Thomas Jefferson, Architect* (1916). He also turned to archaeology, a discipline well established in studies of the ancient world but only recently engaging the more immediate past of North America. As the essays by Lounsbury and Hallock demonstrate, Fiske regularly relied on archaeology to establish evidence about a site. His regard for the role it might play in architectural history initially led him to an active presence in the "other" AIA of the early twentieth century: the Archaeological Institute of America. (He was also active in the American Institute of Architects.) In 1916, the same year he published his book on Jefferson, he initiated a Committee on Colonial and National Art in North America for the Archaeological Institute, which he chaired until 1927. Realizing that architectural history relied on visual images to relay much of this new evidence, Fiske also championed photography and new printing methods. Willkens details how Fiske combined archival documentation with drawings, photographs, and his own diagrams to provide a comparative investigation of domestic architecture.[3]

Fiske's use of scientific history was not an end in itself but a tool to support a much larger vision for the history of architecture and the arts in the United States. Pockets of good evidence-based research on specific topics did exist before Fiske—he frequently praised, for example, the work of Glenn Brown on the architecture of Washington, DC, and he incorporated measured drawings of First Period houses by Norman Isham in his own publications. But he always had his eye on a more comprehensive engagement with architecture and art in America. Framing a larger history meant grappling with dates and details of periodization, but as Kathleen Curran has so aptly recognized, "What is most impressive is that Kimball dwelled less on the minutiae of nomenclature and more on the theory behind the evolution of American building. He asked why instead of when."[4] Asking why allowed Fiske to tell the story of American architecture differently from his peers and engage a wider audience. Writing about the origins of vernacular studies in the 1990s, Dell Upton nicely suggests, for example, that Fiske brought about an "intellectual reorientation" that created a place for categories such as the vernacular before the term "vernacular" had come into use: "His *Domestic Architecture of the American Colonies and of the Early Republic,* a prescient and generally accurate account of colonial vernacular building, marks a turning point in setting off the vernacular as a separate category of architecture."[5] Kern suggests that Marie also brought about a reorientation in the field of biographical writing by incorporating material culture. Through her examination of objects, she evinced a specificity of time and place that helped her convey how someone like Jefferson experienced the world. Another Jefferson scholar, Merrill Peterson, later criticized Marie's books in the 1960s for their focus on the "paraphernalia" of Jefferson's life—just as the field of material culture studies came into its own.

Establishing a history of architecture in America was not an end in itself. If Fiske had one eye on a comprehensive account of buildings and architects in the United States, he also had one foot firmly planted in Europe. It was not simply a matter of investigating the European antecedents for postcolonial architecture. His goal was much more lofty: he wanted a place for American contributions within the larger, more well-established European tradition. Willkens provides a specific example by highlighting how the calculated placement of text and image in *Domestic Architecture* was an attempt to craft a book that put the topic into conversation with the earlier treatises of Palladio and James Gibbs. As we shall see later in this introduction, European authors' neglect of architectural activity across the Atlantic spurred Fiske to some of his first published writings. It is indeed remarkable how early in his career Fiske expressed the desire to put American architecture on the international map and how consistently that desire shaped his scholarship, his efforts in historic preservation, and his commitment to museum collections. To paraphrase Daniel Burnham's well-known exhortation, Fiske "made no little plans."

If the goal was lofty, the audience was broad. Both Fiske and Marie produced scholarship that included painstaking research and details that only other scholars might appreciate. But they also reached audiences beyond the academic world through their writing and museum work. For example, Marie's early research on Monticello's objects was published in the trade journal *Magazine Antiques,* not an academic journal, and Bricker suggests that through his scholarship and his criticism, Fiske engaged with an early form of public history. Fiske certainly enjoyed knowing that his writing had wide appeal. *Domestic Architecture* received positive reviews from his peers, but he seemed just as pleased that "the public, too, seems to like it, as they have bought five hundred copies at the wretched price of $12.00 between Thanksgiving and Christmas, although there wasn't any advertising."[6] For a museum director or curator, the visitor experience always remained a priority. In her foundational study, *The Invention of the American Art Museum,* Curran pinpoints how Fiske shaped the visitor experience at both the American Wing of the Metropolitan Museum of Art in New York City and at the PMA. The experience centered on the display of original objects and a sequence of spaces that took the visitor chronologically through the various periods of art up to the present.[7] Likewise, Fiske and Marie shaped the visitor experience at Monticello. As Lucas and Ehrenpreis illustrate, Fiske and Marie insisted on the display of original objects from the Jefferson period, even if that meant leaving the rooms initially somewhat bare.

The distinct focus of each of the essays helps build a fuller picture of Fiske and Marie as individuals. Kern focuses on Marie as a historian, and Lucas takes up her curatorial work. Other essays also integrate a discussion of Marie and the respect she earned from her colleagues at Monticello, such as Milton Grigg, and curators at the PMA, such as John Canaday and Carl Zigrosser. With Fiske, we have become so accustomed to photographs of him as the accomplished middle-aged scholar and museum director that we can lose sight of the youthful aspirations that set him on that course. He had just earned his MArch in 1912 when he began work on his survey text, *A History of Architecture*; took his peers to task for their lack of method; turned to new sources and technologies; and argued for national policies to preserve the historic monuments of the country. He was a "radical" of his own generation. His attempts to formalize the discipline of architectural history served as a foundation for the efforts and achievements of future generations of young scholars, who have continued to argue for change by adding yet additional methods and technologies to better understand the built environment. We typically think of Fiske as an architectural historian, but in these essays we encounter him as an advocate and consultant for historic preservation who kept committees on task, as a museum director on constant alert for the acquisition of new collections of modern art that required skills of persuasion and negotiation, and as a staunch supporter of public art projects.

We also learn more about collaboration in scholarship, museum studies, and historic preservation. This was particularly true for Fiske, given the many activities in which he participated. Fiske worked with an impressively wide network of colleagues. He convened regularly with his sister, Theodora, and her husband, Henry Vincent Hubbard, about landscape literature and projects; he coauthored articles and books, such as *Great Paintings in America* with Lionello Venturi (1948); and his work on the French Rococo, which took place in the years leading up to World War II, required a host of French allies.[8] In architectural design, he relied on on-site architects—Milton Grigg at Monticello, Stanley Makielski at the University of Virginia, and Erling Pedersen for historic restoration projects that ranged from Moors End on Nantucket Island to Stratford Hall on the northern neck of Virginia. At the museum he worked in conjunction with Henri

Marceau and curators John Canaday, Joseph Downs, and Carl Zigrosser. And just as Fiske relied on others, others relied on him. As Sprinkle puts it, Fiske was frequently used for "heavy, quick axe work" to settle controversies or serve as the front man for committees whose members, for various reasons, wished to remain in the background.

While we learn of the ways in which the Kimballs contributed to our understanding of the built environment, we also learn of the couple's limitations. As a number of the essays make clear, neither Fiske nor Marie engaged in discussions concerning the enslaved populations at Monticello or other sites. Willkens indicates how Fiske erased spatial divisions between races in his images, and Kern states outright that Marie "failed" on the question of slavery in her discussion of Jefferson. Both also fell prey to their devotion to scientific methods and primary sources. In some of her writing, Marie simply provides a litany of furnishings or dates of travel without any interpretation. And as already mentioned, Fiske occasionally let his knowledge of colonial architecture sources override what his eyes or the archaeology of a site revealed—what has become known as a "Kimballization," as Hallock's essay relays in discussing decisions about the restoration of Monticello. And while Marie's research has stood the test of time, her writing style has not. Fiske's writing remains clear and convincing, but its very authority created a legacy and canon of American architecture with such a firm hold that certain topics and figures remain understudied to this day.

Fiske, in particular, presents us with a complex character. The impressive level of scholarly contributions, on the one hand, and his accomplishments as a museum director, on the other, suggest two lifetimes of activities for most people. He authored more than a hundred articles and a half dozen books as well as a regular stream of editorials and reviews. The work he did at the museum took place through the Great Depression in the 1930s and World War II in the 1940s. He was one of the first museum directors to utilize Works Progress Administration programs to keep people employed. As noted above, he served as a mentor and model for an entire generation of architectural historians and preservationists. Thomas Waterman coined the honorific "dean of historians of American Architecture" in his book *Mansions of Virginia* (1946), and other young historians, such as Hugh Morrison, Charles Peterson, John Coolidge, and Henry-Russell Hitchcock, would all acknowledge Fiske's impact. John Canaday, who worked with Fiske at the PMA, extended Fiske's title to the museum world when he recognized him as "the dean of American museum directors" for a generation of museum curators.[9]

Numerous European scholars, such as Leigh Ashton, Ludwig Heydenreich, and Hans Tietze, held him in high regard. Erwin Panofsky unhesitatingly included Fiske in his "Golden Age" of American scholarship, and, once settled at Princeton University, he and Fiske became personal friends as well.[10] Fiske also earned the respect of modern architects and artists, such as Frank Lloyd Wright, Erich Mendelsohn, George Howe, and Lee Lawrie. He worked resolutely to help scholars who had emigrated from Europe, such as Werner Hegemann (whose wife was a friend of Marie's) and Walter Friedländer, find positions in the United States. Further, his friendships were not all restricted to fellow academics. Memories of conversations and the exchange of gifts with Robert E. Lee, the Charlottesville contractor who carried out the restoration work at Monticello and built Fiske and Marie's home, Shack Mountain, attest to their shared humor and mutual respect. Fiske served on numerous public art committees without recompense and never charged the Thomas Jefferson Memorial Foundation a fee for his work on Monticello from 1924 to 1955, beyond his travel expenses from Philadelphia.[11]

And yet all of these accomplishments were embodied in a figure that also caused people to recoil. Canaday summed up the extremes of Fiske's character, taking note of his "grossness of language, surprising in a man who wrote so elegantly; of his bluster and rudeness, antithetical to the idea of a museum director as a courtier to wealth and influence; of his prejudices, which were appalling; of his bull-in-a-china shop technique in coping with situations that aroused his impatience, in contrast with the meticulous patience with fine points that made him a faultless scholar; of the aura of braggadocio, arrogance and even contempt that this physically huge man with the bristling Prussian brush of white hair and the heavy black eyebrows could exude as he entered a room."[12] The strength of Fiske's personality and the energy that drove his endeavors were most likely linked to the "ailment" Canaday and his peers also noted. Fiske struggled all his life with what today might be diagnosed as manic depression. There are indications of it as early as his years at Harvard, and it clearly overcame him at the end of his life.

Clearly there is more work to be done. The essays here are weighted toward Fiske and historic preservation, partly as a result of the conference that spurred the volume. Yet this also indicates the breadth of Fiske's work and the need for further research on Marie. The sheer amount of archival material available will require the concerted efforts of many individuals. The PMA holds Fiske's records as a director and his personal papers. Fiske left his scholarly materials to Harvard University, and Marie's papers are located at the University of Virginia. Each institution or house museum they worked with also has archival holdings, such as the records of the Thomas Jefferson Memorial Foundation[15] at Monticello. This volume aims to serve as a starting point for further research and discussion of two scholars who had an instrumental role in shaping our experiences of buildings, places, and objects.

Where Does Their Story Begin?

Fiske, one year older than Marie, was born in 1888 in Newton, Massachusetts, into an educated, upper-middle-class family. His father, Edwin, earned a reputation as a respected educator in the Boston public school system and traced his roots back to the seventeenth-century families of Charlestown, Massachusetts. His mother, Ellen Ripley, descended from the eighteenth-century Fullam family that had made a comfortable fortune operating stables for coach lines running out of Boston. Ellen's father, Theodore Ripley, served as a colonel in the Civil War (and later became a general). Edwin and Ellen christened their son Sidney Fiske Kimball after the Fiske family line on Edwin's side. Fiske had one older sister, Theodora, named for Ellen's father, and the small family developed strong, affectionate, and lasting bonds. When Fiske designed a house for the family in Milton in 1914, he wrote to Theodora, "One of the best features of the whole idea is the opportunity it will give you to unfold and develop your personal life. . . . I think I can do a more picturesque and personal house for us than for anyone else because of knowing the problem itself involves personalities highly individual."[13] Although not a member of the Boston Brahmins, Kimball enjoyed the history of his New England family and repeated the apocryphal tale that a Fullam coach transported the noted architect Charles Bulfinch from Boston to New York on his honeymoon.[14]

More than any genealogical roots, however, Fiske's sense of self was indelibly shaped by the Transcendentalist tradition espoused by his father. Edwin extolled both Emerson's and Thoreau's recognition of the singularity of the American landscape and their call to civic duty. He regularly took his young family out into nature, walking the Blue Hills southwest of Boston or summering on the coast at South Bristol, Maine. Although Fiske joked that his "antipathy to learning the stars was a sad trial to [his father]," the immersion nonetheless encouraged Fiske's attention to the physical spaces around him. His sister, Theodora, would notably go on to have an influential career in landscape architecture, coauthoring with her husband, Henry Vincent Hubbard, one of the first textbooks in the discipline, *An Introduction to the Study of Landscape Design* (1917).[15] Edwin regarded his own career as a form of civic duty, and Fiske recalled decades later his father's

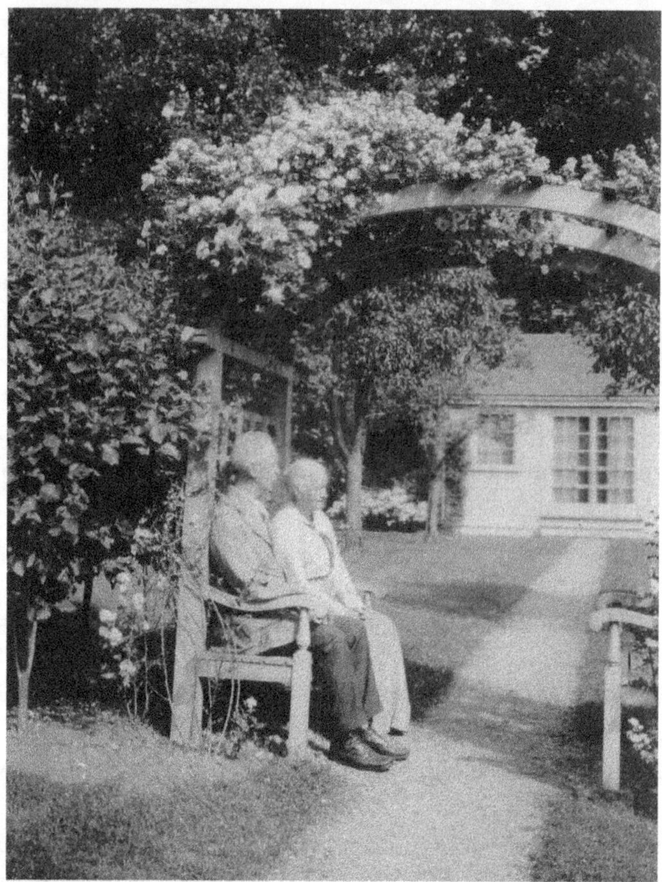

FIGURE 2. Edwin and Ellen Kimball sitting under an arbor, June 1919, at the family house designed by Fiske on Spafford Road in Milton, Massachusetts. (Courtesy of the Philadelphia Museum of Art, Library and Archives, Fiske Kimball Papers, Box 63, Folder 3)

singular passion for education: "[Edwin's] devotion to American history and institutions, his belief in the democracy of the public schools were equally deep [*sic*]."[16] Edwin had high hopes that his son would also contribute in a meaningful way to American institutions and the democracy of education. He made those hopes crystal clear in a letter on Fiske's twentieth birthday: "I look to you to accomplish some high and noble service through your disciplined powers,—to become a leader in America's renaissance, not only in art but in all civic improvement. If you can discipline your will as well as your intellect you must surely succeed. My heart is bound up in your future. Do not disappoint me or us who know

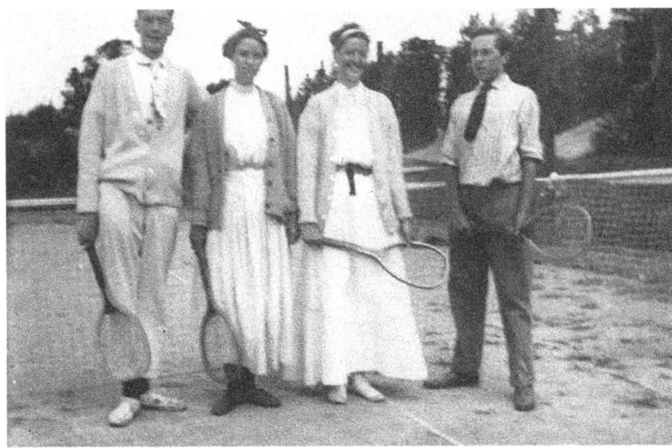

FIGURE 3. The Kimball family spent many summers at Christmas Cove in South Bristol, Maine. Here, Fiske (*far left*) and Theodora (*second from right*) play tennis with two unidentified individuals, ca. 1910. (Courtesy of the Philadelphia Museum of Art, Library and Archives, Fiske Kimball Papers, Box 63, Folder 2)

you best. . . . Keep your soul untarnished, your body pure, your heart generous and sympathetic, and God will bless you. Your devoted and loving Father."[17] This heartfelt letter conveys the love but also the expectations that structured Fiske's adolescence. Ultimately, Fiske's civic duty took shape through a career devoted to the arts.

Edwin wrote the letter in Fiske's senior year as a student at Harvard University. Fiske received his undergraduate degree in 1909 and his MArch in 1912. H. Langford Warren, the head of the architecture program, had shaped a unique curriculum that provided Fiske with the education that made him so successful in his later career. Beyond teaching the practical skills related to architectural drafting, Warren aimed to strengthen the students' aesthetic sensibility for design and form. Nurturing formal sensibility meant broadening their coursework to include discussions of the perception of form in all the arts, not just architecture, and, importantly, recognizing how the aesthetic merit of an object worked in tandem with the construction, technology, and materials of the era. As an architectural educator, Warren felt keenly the need for a modern American architecture that incorporated the latest technology but still retained the "art" of design. This could be achieved not through a reiteration of historic styles, he argued, but through a focus on principles: "What we need is to understand more and more fully those fundamental principles of our art which underlie the best work of all times and all styles." Thus, the curriculum included studios structured on the principles of the École des Beaux-Arts system (not just the style of classicism), which included projects in the Gothic and Romanesque styles, as well as three semesters of architectural history.[18]

To strengthen students' perception of form, Warren required courses outside of the department. Architecture students took courses with psychologist Hugo Münsterberg, philosopher George Santayana, and design theorist Denman Ross. Münsterberg demonstrated how the science and principles of visual perception—for example, how the muscles of the eye reacted to certain shapes—could be applied to art in various media, including new media based on new technologies. His book *The Photoplay: A Psychological Study* (1916) is one of the earliest analyses of the new medium of cinematic film, which, he argued, was the new twentieth-century art form. Fiske developed a particularly close bond with Santayana. Santayana taught a course based upon his highly influential book *The Sense of Beauty* (1896). Fiske excelled in the course, and Santayana subsequently asked him to serve as his teaching assistant. In the book and course, Santayana outlined how the perception of form—again, in various media—strengthened the sense of beauty in a person. Further, he asserted that a person's ability to assess aesthetic merit was sharpened through wide exposure to a variety of objects. With Ross, Fiske took the infamous Pure Design course. Ross stressed the universal principles of harmony, balance, and rhythm in design that underpinned all art objects in all media from all eras (and consciously sought to abolish the traditional boundaries between the fine and decorative arts). He required his students to study textiles, ceramics, and prints as well as paintings, sculpture, and architecture. Ross himself had expertise with Japanese prints, South American textiles, and Persian painting and regularly put objects from his collection on display (first in Robinson Hall and then, in later years, in the Fogg Art Museum). In this way, students could train their eye to evaluate the formal and aesthetic merits of a work of art regardless of the medium, the place, or the era in which it was produced.[19]

Thus, between Warren, Münsterberg, Santayana, and Ross, Fiske left Harvard with an education that strengthened his understanding of the principles of good design, that prioritized the evaluation of aesthetic merit, and that focused on finding the best examples of any particular era or medium. Training in the formal elements of design (and the breadth it generated) shaped not just Fiske's eye for design but also an entire generation of curators and museum directors that came out of the Harvard program in the early twentieth century. What Fiske

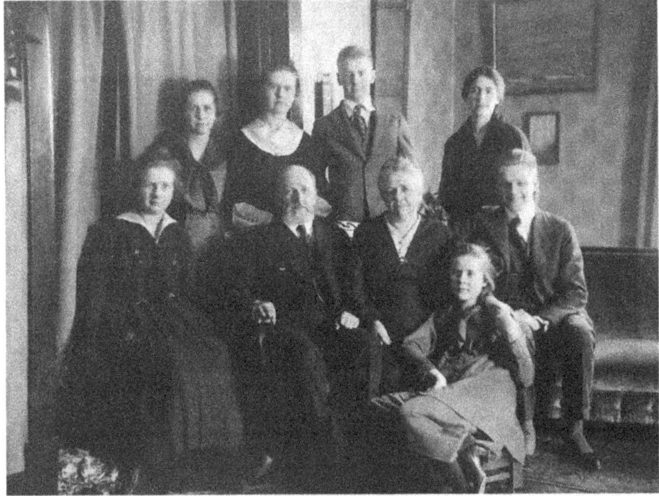

FIGURE 4. The Goebel family, ca. 1917. Marie is standing in the back row on the left. (Courtesy of Anne Goebel Barkman)

brought to it was a startling ability to absorb and remember anything he studied, a decisive temperament, and the ability to write prolific, lucid prose.

As Fiske ran through Cambridge to his classes at Harvard, he may have unwittingly passed a young Marie Goebel on the street. Marie also came from a family that prioritized education, and by 1907 she was enrolled at Radcliffe College. Her father, Julius Goebel, a professor of Germanic studies, taught at Stanford University before coming to Harvard in 1906. However, when the University of Illinois at Urbana-Champaign offered him a chairmanship, he packed up the family, and Marie completed her degree in Urbana in 1911. Both parents encouraged their children to pursue studies for careers in the public realm. Marie's brother Julius became a professor of law at Columbia University; her brother Walther worked as a chemist for the Rockefeller Institute for Medical Research; her younger sister, Irma, without a doubt the most audacious of the bunch, toured as a professional pianist and spearheaded the study of South American Indigenous music.[20] Like Fiske, Irma thrived on drama, and the two of them together no doubt enlivened many family vacations. As Walther's daughter Anne later recalled, the siblings were all very smart, but they also enjoyed a shared sense of humor: "[T]hey had a lot of fun together."[21]

Although Fiske and Marie's paths crossed but diverged in Cambridge, the pair seemed destined to meet. After graduating from Harvard and failing to win a

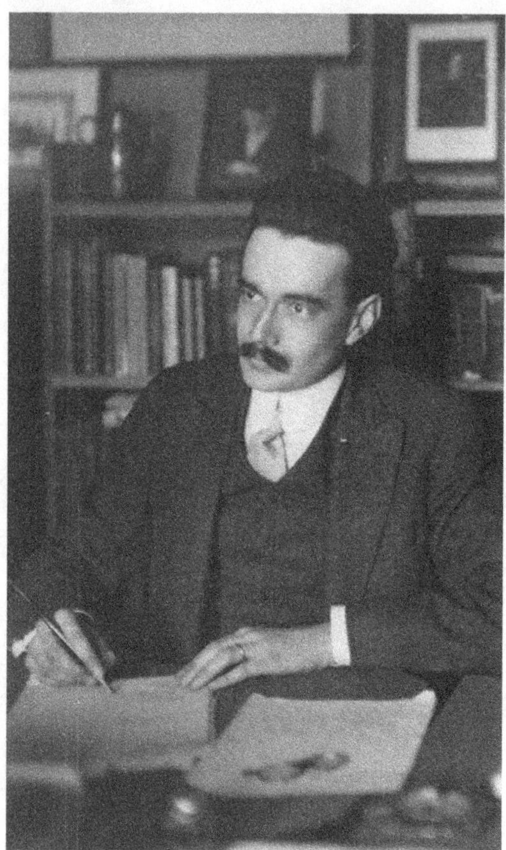

FIGURE 5. Fiske Kimball, 1913. (Courtesy of the Philadelphia Museum of Art Library and Archives, Fiske Kimball Papers, Box 62, Folder 3)

series of design fellowships, Fiske accepted a faculty position in architecture at the University of Illinois at Urbana-Champaign in 1912. He met Marie that fall, and a storybook whirlwind romance ensued: they were engaged by March 1913 and then married on Marie's birthday, June 7, 1913. Letters between the pair and Fiske's family capture their palpable elation at discovering one another; over a year into the marriage, Fiske still reveled in his good fortune, telling his parents, "A modern girl like Marie is really what I need."[22] From the beginning, an essential part of Marie's "modernity" centered on her own career ambitions. Just a month before their wedding, she completed an edited volume of the Austrian author Peter Rosegger's story *Das Holzknechthaus* for use in German-language programs in American schools. Fiske wrote proudly to his parents when Radcliffe College adopted the volume for their curriculum and the plans they had to spend the royalties.[23] The pair never had any children, and there is little evidence of any lament in their letters; indeed, Marie more than once archly commented

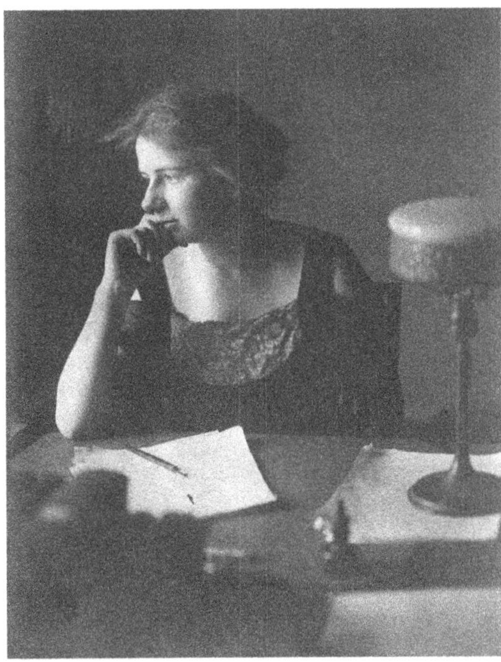

FIGURE 6. Marie Goebel Kimball, 1913. (Courtesy of the Philadelphia Museum of Art Library and Archives, Fiske Kimball Papers, Box 62, Folder 3)

on women who "dropped everything but babies."[24] In two photos taken shortly after their marriage, both are shown with pen and paper as scholars and writers.

The first summer of their marriage, 1913, stands out as a critical one for both of their careers. Fiske, eager to publish, had signed a contract to write a history of architecture for Harper Collins and planned to include a lengthy section on American architecture. This decision may not seem noteworthy today, but other major surveys of the time, such as James Fergusson's *History of the Modern Styles of Architecture* of 1902, did not mention architecture in the United States at all. This neglect by European authors was an affront to young Fiske. From the outset, therefore, he aimed to put the study of art and architecture in America on an equal footing with the scholarship and collections of Europe. This aim cannot be overstated: it explains his focus on the major monuments and the people who designed them in his first books and articles. Yet Fiske's ambitions did not end there; with the bravado of youth, he not only wanted recognition for American architecture within the European tradition but also argued ceaselessly for its leading role in the modern period. He notably ended the American section in his *History of Architecture* with Frank Lloyd Wright's Unity Temple. Thus, at the very inception of his career, Fiske already had the road map that guided his scholarship and activities for the next decades.

To establish the study of American architecture on an equal footing with that of Europe, Fiske imported European methodologies—specifically, scientific history. As already noted, the methodology is associated with Ranke, but Fiske claimed that reading Charles-Victor Langlois and Charles Seignobos's *Introduction aux études historiques* (1898; translated as *Introduction to the Study of History,* 1904) while a graduate student at Harvard transformed his approach. He roomed with two history students, Lawrence Packard (who later taught at Amherst College) and Dexter Perkins (later the secretary of the American Historical Association), noticed Langlois and Seignobos's book in their rooms, and "devoured it": "This book . . . was an illumination. All that had been implicit by example, in the books Langford Warren had referred to in his courses in architectural history like those of Burckhardt and Guymüller was here made explicit. All my own intellectual instincts and ambitions were sharpened and stimulated."[25] Only through a scientific methodology could American scholarship begin to catch up with European accomplishments. In a letter of 1914 to the *Journal of the American Institute of Architects,* Fiske baldly stated that the inability to even date important buildings was "a confession of our historical incompetence unthinkable in any other country. . . . There has been too much shirking of obligation to go to the sources, too much inconsequent fantasy spinning, in writings on the history of American architecture. . . . If the subject is to be discussed at all, let us have a more conscientious search for evidence."[26]

Thus, between his embrace of scientific methods and his object-oriented training in the fine arts at Harvard mentioned earlier, Fiske believed he had the tools to tell the story of American architecture. It is important to recall that the academic discipline of architectural history did not exist in American universities at this time. The methodological approaches employed by scholars today—social history, material culture, vernacular, race and gender studies—did not exist. Kimball is often credited with a founding role in establishing the discipline, because in 1915, he earned the first PhD on an American postcolonial subject from the University of Michigan with his dissertation on Thomas Jefferson's Virginia State Capitol. Kimball's accomplishment holds significance not because it was "first" but because it placed the study of American architecture under the broader umbrella of the arts and sciences and the methods of historical research and writing found there. Frequently, other "architect historians," such as his own mentor, Warren, operated out of schools of architecture. Indeed, Kimball's advisor for the dissertation was not a colleague with a background or area of expertise in American architecture at all; he worked with Francis Kelsey, a Latin scholar and archaeologist who had earned renown for his work on Pompeii (and later in the Near East and Egypt). What united the two was method: Kelsey was also a proponent of scientific history and the person with whom Kimball determined the approach and scope of his dissertation.[27]

Fiske shared the methods of scientific history with Marie, and in the summer of 1913, while they lived with his parents outside of Boston, they turned their attention to the Jefferson materials at the Massachusetts Historical Society (MHS). The brunt of the work fell to Marie, because Fiske unexpectedly lost his position at Urbana-Champaign. A nepotism clause in the university's by-laws forbade the employment of multiple members of any one family, and his marriage to Marie made him a son-in-law to Julius Goebel. In addition to applying for other jobs, he also had to continue working on his *History of Architecture* volume, and he had a deadline to finish designing a set of summer cottages in Onekama, Michigan; when he secured a position in the architecture program at the University of Michigan, he then also had to prepare his classes. Each day, as Fiske set off to Harvard's library to work, Marie set off to the MHS and painstakingly went through Jefferson's correspondence for any references to architecture. By the end of 1913, Marie was probably the one person who was most familiar with the contents of Jefferson's letters at the MHS—and it was Marie who realized from references in the letters that drawings might exist.

Fiske recalled the start of their Jefferson research in his memoirs. In that summer of 1913, Marie "effectively ran down various allusions which indicated Jefferson had undoubtedly made drawings, some of which might well survive among his manuscripts."[28] Initially, Marie planned to write up her findings on Jefferson, but when Worthington Ford from the MHS informed them that a collection of drawings did exist, owned by the Coolidge branch of Jefferson descendants in Boston, the pair agreed that the task of assessing the drawings was better suited to Fiske. Ford arranged for the drawings to be brought to the MHS's reading rooms, and Fiske got his first look. He immediately recognized their significance: "I know of no equal opportunity ever likely to occur in the field of the history of American architecture."[29]

The outcome of Fiske's study of the Jefferson drawings and Marie's study of the letters was the publication of *Thomas Jefferson, Architect* in 1916, the book that established Jefferson's reputation as an architect and Fiske's as an architectural historian. He was twenty-eight years old, and Marie was twenty-seven. The book is a testament to the methods of scientific history, specifically the use of original drawings, to establish an architect's standing. Fiske's clear writing in some ways makes the results seem so obvious, but the amount of work that went into the volume was enormous. Marie wrote to Edwin as they prepared to send off the manuscript: "Thomas Jefferson is progressing famously. We both feel greatly encouraged and confident of a great and glorious finish. We have a great file of manuscript ready to send off and more is being produced every minute. How I hope people will appreciate this book! And the amount of careful and exacting work that has gone into it. It is really a monumental thing—the first and greatest of its kind in English."[30] Marie largely took on the task of identifying the watermarks for the paper used by Jefferson (which was generated as an appendix at the end of the volume and drew Kelsey's particular admiration) in order to help date the drawings. The almost obsessive interest in pinning down the dates of Jefferson's drawings did not stem from mere antiquarianism but, in fact, supported Fiske's larger goal of putting American architecture on the international map. He would use the primary sources related to Jefferson's efforts at the Virginia Capitol to argue that it preceded the major monuments of neoclassicism in Europe. In the "Note of Acknowledgment" for the volume, Fiske credited Marie with initiating the study of Jefferson and her integral role in the project: "Her self-sacrificing collaboration is a debt I can never repay." Acknowledgments can often easily be glossed over, but Fiske meant every word—he would support and promote Marie's scholarship for the rest of their lives.

The Kimballs' choice to study Jefferson in 1913 should give us pause. It was a far from obvious topic for the history of American architecture. First, Jefferson existed on the periphery of architectural discussions, and second, the largely New England–centric focus of Fiske's peers meant that regional biases against southern contributions ran strong. For any Harvard-educated and Boston-bred aspiring historian looking to establish the significance of early American architecture, the logical choice was Charles Bulfinch. Bulfinch's granddaughter had recently published *The Life and Letters of Charles Bulfinch, Architect* in 1896, which drew attention to existing drawings and letters at nearby MIT; in 1907 the proposed removal of the Bulfinch façade of the Massachusetts State House generated heated debate that drew further attention to Bulfinch's significance and, in turn, prompted the publication of *The Georgian Period* in 1908.

Thomas Jefferson's reputation as an architect, on the other hand, was shrouded in ambiguity. In *The Georgian Period,* the essay "Old Colonial Work of Virginia and Maryland" did not include any illustrations of Jefferson's buildings and casually remarked that "Mr. Jefferson . . . was a tremendous critic in architectural matters, though perhaps not always successful in the application of his theories to practice." As late as 1913, both Montgomery Schuyler and Glenn

Brown, two established writers on American architecture, still attributed Monticello to Robert Mills. Also in 1913, Brown began to question Jefferson's authorship of the one complex usually safely attributed to him, the University of Virginia, which Brown suggested really owed its design to William Thornton. Other publications, such as William Lambeth and Warren Manning's *Thomas Jefferson as an Architect and Designer of Landscapes* (1913), brought scathing criticism from Fiske for their belletristic approach. Some sense of the uncharted ground Fiske faced emerges in his matter-of-fact comment in 1914 on Jefferson's second home, Poplar Forest: "No photographs of this have ever been published but I have assurances the house is still standing." In 1913, therefore, there was no established history of Jefferson as an architect, let alone a concrete trail to suggest what buildings he had designed or that a collection of drawings by him even existed.[31]

Fiske's interest in Jefferson began before he and Marie discovered the drawings. To construct a history of American architecture meant isolating the pivotal moments and the individuals responsible for change. For Fiske, Jefferson's real distinction "was to introduce the classic style of antiquity." Fiske was certainly aware of Bulfinch—and he methodically followed up on him and others, such as Peter Harrison and William Thornton—but the subsequent discovery of the drawings provided the evidence to separate Jefferson from his peers. As Fiske wrote in the introductory essay for *Thomas Jefferson, Architect,* Jefferson had the advantage over them in both drawing ability and constructive ingenuity: "In draughstmanship Bulfinch never surpassed him; in extent of practice Thornton fell far behind."[32]

Thomas Jefferson, Architect set in motion a burst of research. Fiske became the first incumbent of Harvard's Sachs Fellowship in 1916 and spent the spring of 1917 traveling to archives and sites in the South and then up the eastern seaboard. This research unearthed the contributions of Benjamin Henry Latrobe, in whom Fiske found Jefferson's counterpart—to Jefferson's Roman classicism Latrobe added the Greek tradition, and he was a professionally trained architect with sophisticated rendering and engineering skills to boot. Fiske penned four articles on Latrobe between 1917 and 1918 and intended to write a book. But the wealth of new material he kept finding on other individuals and projects took him from topic to topic. For example, through Ford at the MHS he learned of drawings and materials related to Samuel McIntire and started research for a book similar in format to the one on Jefferson; while doing research in Washington, DC, he focused on the design of the White House and the plan of the city; in New York City he discovered drawings and materials related to the architect John McComb Jr.

He also reached beyond architecture: he wrote articles on landscape gardening, portraits, and sculpture. Interspersed with articles on specific topics, Fiske continued to write provocative assessments of the study of colonial architecture or the development of American architecture for mainstream architecture magazines such as the *Architectural Review* or *Architectural Forum.*[33]

While the book on Latrobe did not materialize, he did funnel all the new research into two larger projects. The survey he had started in 1912, *History of Architecture,* was published in 1918 with a section on American architecture equal in length to the section on ancient Greece. More importantly, it generated his seminal publication of 1922, *Domestic Architecture of the American Colonies and Early Republic,* a book that is discussed in more detail by Willkens in this volume and is notably still in print to this day. In the books and articles, Fiske's focus on the formal merits of a work and his reliance on primary sources allowed him to structure a history of the major monuments, or canon, with an emphasis on the finest examples. By the 1920s, Fiske had secured his reputation as the "dean of historians of American Architecture."[34]

Fiske relished his title and would remain an authority for the rest of his career. But the publication of *Domestic Architecture* also signaled the decline of his focus on American topics. The intensity of study that produced the wealth of articles and books between 1913 and 1922 had burned out: "After nearly ten years of work in the American field, I was beginning to get tired of it." He realized he could put the same amount of research and effort into a study on Michelangelo as he could on McIntire (and indeed his interest in McIntire waned to such a low level that it took until 1943 for him to publish the book). He turned his attention to art and to Europe. The painters of the Urbino school piqued his interest while he was teaching at the University of Chicago in the summer of 1921, and the result was the article "Luciano Laurana and the 'High Renaissance'" for *Art Bulletin* in 1927. When his good friend Ogden Codman wrote in 1923 to congratulate him on *Domestic Architecture,* he again spoke of his European interests: "I think there is still a splendid opportunity for a good work on Palladio and the later Palladians." (James Ackerman would ultimately pursue that opportunity with the publication of *Palladio* in 1966.) And again, in the early '30s, when Codman wrote to ask Fiske for photostats of some Bulfinch drawings, Fiske replied that he was happy to send them because "I never plan to do anything more with them, for, as you know, I am wholly seduced by the study of French interiors."[35] By the 1930s, Fiske and Marie had already traveled to France a number of times as he began the work for his study of the Rococo.

Fiske made one return in the 1920s to his American research—the publication of his survey text *American Architecture* in 1928. But as he himself readily admitted, he wrote the book quickly (over the summer, in just six weeks) as a synthesis of his earlier articles when he heard that Rexford Newcomb and Thomas Tallmadge had both started work on their own survey texts. Any new research in 1928 was geared toward France, such as his 1928 article for the *Gazette des Beaux-Arts* on the paneling of the Hôtel de Soubise, which he cowrote with Edna Donnell.[36] He was also far more occupied with the museum. In 1928 Fiske started negotiations to secure the Edmond Foulc collection of Renaissance decorative arts; its cost of over one million dollars made it the most expensive single purchase by any museum at that time.[37]

Beyond Writing Architectural History

Fiske had earned his reputation as an architectural historian by the 1920s, but it is important to remember that he never held an academic position solely as an architectural historian—he was always employed to accomplish other duties. Fiske balanced his scholarship with an equal amount of effort setting up programs and policies, and it is in these years that he emerges as an adept administrator. His work in architectural history had in fact caused friction with Emil Lorch, the chairman of the architecture program at Michigan. Fiske attempted to appease him by taking on the design of a half dozen residences for the Scottwood development in Ann Arbor—work done between 1914 and 1916, the exact time he and Marie were producing the Jefferson volume—but Lorch did not relent, and in 1919 Fiske left to establish the McIntire School of Fine Arts at the University of Virginia. As with his choice of Jefferson in 1913, choosing a state university in the South was not a typical career path for a New Englander. However, he saw it as an opportunity to champion the importance of the region's art and architecture. In 1918 he wrote of his intentions to make the department a center for the study of southern arts and soon after participated in the exhibitions of the American Federation of the Arts (a decision that resulted in the acquisition of notable contemporary paintings for the university). In 1924 he followed up with the article "Recent Architecture in the South," in which he urged southern schools of architecture to look at their own past: "It has scarcely been realized that the South has also its own traditions, which offer an individual point of departure." He named not just the Jeffersonian tradition but the Spanish in Florida and Texas as well as the French and West Indian traditions in Louisiana.[38]

In 1920 he gave a series of lectures at the Metropolitan Museum of Art in New York City (which served as the basis for *Domestic Architecture*). This event, in conjunction with his growing reputation as an administrator, soon led to an invitation from New York University (NYU) to serve as the F. B. Morse Professor of the Literature of the Arts of Design and to reestablish their fine arts department. Fiske and Marie moved to New York City in 1923—a move that reunited them with Marie's brothers, Julius and Walther—and Fiske began laying the groundwork for what later became known as the Institute of Fine Arts. His training in architecture also resulted in an appointment as a consulting architect for the NYU campus plan, a position he retained until his death.

Parallel with his work in higher education, Fiske devoted his energy to raising awareness of and establishing policies for America's historic buildings and landscapes through professional and public entities. He initially worked through the Archaeological Institute of America and the American Institute of Architects. In 1916, he initiated and chaired the Committee on Colonial and National Art for the Archaeological Institute, a position he held until 1927. In 1920, he agreed to oversee the American section of the Thieme-Becker publications. From 1922 to 1925 he chaired the AIA Committee on the Preservation of Historic Monuments and Scenic Beauties, and in 1928 he joined the advisory board at Colonial Williamsburg. Sprinkle's essay in this volume connects these efforts to Fiske's later instrumental role in forming policies at the National Park Service. In 1924, Fiske accepted the position as the chairman of the Restoration Committee at Monticello (a position he held until his death). Lack of funds prohibited any significant changes to the building itself in the late 1920s, so Fiske and Marie turned their attention to the interiors. Marie focused her research on decorative arts within Monticello and began to publish her findings, including her seminal article of 1929, "Thomas Jefferson's French Furniture," for *Magazine Antiques.*

Fiske's professional positions and affiliated activities attest to his administrative abilities as well as his ambition to put programs and institutions in place that educated Americans about the arts. These efforts culminated in the offer that would define the second half of his career: the invitation to serve as Director of the Pennsylvania Museum and School of Industrial Art (later the PMA) in 1925.

In Philadelphia, Fiske encountered a situation similar to the state of architectural history when he began his Jefferson studies: he literally arrived to find a shell of a building. The imposing classical edifice at the terminus of the Benjamin Franklin Parkway had started construction in 1919, but by 1925 only the exterior walls were completed. When the building officially opened in March 1928 it was immense, grand, and largely empty. Fiske's energies were focused on raising its endowment, negotiating for collections, and determining the layout of the galleries. In his thirty years as director of the museum, he initiated the acquisition of the works of art that serve as the basis for the museum's international reputation today. And just as he turned to European methods of scientific history for a scholarly methodology, he also turned to European methods to structure the layout of the works of art within the museum, as Curran has so ably demonstrated. The period rooms Fiske installed in Philadelphia did not elevate one period over another but provided a sequence of spaces that represented the best work of each era. The training he received at Harvard gave him the confidence to collect for both breadth and depth and to validate the significance of representing modern art of the twentieth century. He initially hoped to end the sequence of period rooms with an ensemble in the Art Nouveau style by Alphonse Mucha (though he lost that battle to conservative members of the museum's board).[39] Nonetheless, as Vick's essay in this volume demonstrates, Kimball continued to collect contemporary art, courting both Albert Gallatin and Louise and Walter Arensberg for the range and quality of their collections, which included modern painting and sculpture and pre-Columbian art.

Modern Art and Architecture

Fiske's pursuit of the Gallatin and Arensberg collections signals an often-overlooked aspect of his career: his continued interest and support for modern art and architecture. Because of his work on Jefferson, Fiske is frequently pigeonholed as an ardent classicist. However, Fiske had the skills to assess the aesthetic merit of any work, regardless of style; what mattered was the quality. His breadth of interest is perhaps best seen in three projects for which he served as a committee member and that all generated controversy: the public art program at Rockefeller Center in New York City, the Thomas Jefferson Memorial in Washington, DC, and the Jefferson National Expansion Memorial in St. Louis, Missouri.

In 1932, architect Harvey Corbett invited Fiske to serve on the committee for the public art program at Rockefeller Center. At the initial meetings, Fiske and the other committee members discussed a list of potential artists to invite, both American and European. For the Americans, Kimball ranked Thomas Hart Benton and Reginald Marsh the highest, with John Sloan and Charles Sheeler as strong seconds. Sloan and Sheeler were both over fifty but had each earned their reputations with the avant-garde a few decades earlier (Sloan with the Ashcan School and Sheeler as a Precisionist). Benton, now associated with American Regionalism, had not yet painted his murals for the Missouri State Capitol, but he had just painted *America Today* (1930–31), a series of murals that focused on everyday activities in American life, for the New School of Social Research in New York City. What united these artists for Fiske was, in fact, their focus on the everyday: he noted that they had demonstrated their ability to capture American types and urban scenes.

For the Europeans, his choices may seem even more surprising: he selected Henri Matisse, underscoring and starring his name, and Pablo Picasso. He then added to the list the Japanese artist Yasuo Kuniyoshi and tried to talk the committee out of considering Welsh artist Frank Brangwyn, who was in his mid-sixties. Indeed, when Kimball got labeled for favoring "modernistic work" by other members of the committee, he responded, "I am not keen about anything 'istic.' I hope (against hope) to find someone alive and modern and not just following this or that 'ism.'"[40] His argument for assessing the artistic merit of a work seems to be one he made regularly with the committee. A few months earlier, a few committee members must have raised questions about keeping Diego Rivera or other politically left artists on the list, because Kimball again returned to merit: "I may say that the question whether a man is a 'radical' or a 'conservative' does not interest me; all I care about is that he should be a figure of real significance in American art, who has something to say and whose work shows personal creative power."[41]

In the two Jefferson projects, Fiske contended with the chairman of the National Commission of Fine Arts, Gilmore Clarke. In the late 1930s, he served on the committee for the Jefferson Memorial in Washington, DC, and in the late '40s on the Jefferson National Expansion Memorial in St. Louis, Missouri. Both memorials generated controversy—the Jefferson Memorial because it was too classical and the St. Louis arch because it was too modern. In both cases, Fiske effectively pushed through the final choice and defended it in print.

The disputes surrounding the Jefferson Memorial ran the gamut from the number of lanes of traffic approaching it, to the methods of keeping birds off it, to the number of cherry trees taken down for it. Without a doubt, though, the major issues centered on location, scale, and style. From the start, Fiske wanted the site at the Tidal Basin and a building in scale with the Washington Monument and Lincoln Memorial. Clarke argued equally strongly against that, favoring instead a site in the middle of the Mall that would therefore necessitate a low and open monument (the opposite of the Pantheon-derived form of John Russell Pope's design). Additionally, a number of architects, including Frank Lloyd Wright, petitioned for a modern design. Fiske, spokesperson for the Jefferson Memorial Commission, successfully defended their case in a letter to the *New York Times* by framing it within the larger historical context of the L'Enfant and McMillan plans: "Let us complete the central group in Washington with a building in harmony with its neighbors and with Jefferson's ideas, and then turn the architecture of the capital, in its new areas, in a modern direction. The Jefferson Memorial is not the place to begin this change."[42]

Just as Fiske objected to being labeled "modernistic" in the Rockefeller project, however, he also distanced himself from the classicist camp. In a letter to his friend Charles Moore, he praised Pope's design for the Jefferson Memorial as competent and very dignified but added, "The classic style cannot make now the same pristine appeal which it had on its revival at the hands of McKim; any examples of it now are inevitably the work of epigoni. . . . You know I am a great exponent of a truly creative modernity, but I always took the view that, in this southwest section, we were merely completing the execution of a great plan adopted and pursued consistently through many years. Even Leonardo da Vinci, when asked to design a façade for Milan Cathedral, felt it must be Gothic, and I think this analogy is a true one."[43] When Fiske wrote his defense of Pope's design in 1938, he noted that the modernists had yet to design a successful public monument—that they were "lamentable failures, with nothing of the eternal."[44] Yet ten years later, he saw the opportunity to champion a successful modern memorial.

Fiske's friend the architect George Howe chaired the competition for the National Expansion Memorial in 1947 and invited Fiske to serve on the jury, which also included Richard Neutra. In the blind competition that followed, Eero Saarinen's parabolic arch emerged as the winner, and the jury announced its decision: "The entire concept, full of exciting possibilities for actual achievement, is a work of genius, and the memorial structure is of that high order which will rank it among the nation's greatest monuments."[45] As images of the design circulated, Gilmore Clarke raised an outcry because the arch resembled a proposed Fascist monument in Italy associated with Mussolini. Publicity increased, and the jury asked Fiske to draft a response. The parabolic arch, he wrote, was in the public domain and not invented by Fascists. Moreover, the form was characteristic of modern architecture: "[I]t repeats none of the types of existing memorials either in this country or abroad. . . . The jury welcomed the fact that [it] was not an adaption of classical or historical motifs, but one specially characteristic of modern architecture and engineering." He closed the statement by underscoring the opportunity it provided to put American memorial architecture at the forefront of design: "It is left for us in this country to make the first great commemorative monument in this beautiful and inspiring form, so suitable in its symbolism as a Gateway to the West." And to the director of the Monument Association, he wrote privately: "Gil Clark's [*sic*] attack boomeranged. I was delighted that, on the morning after, I could give the whole matter several good bumps."[46]

Fiske's interest and support for modern design resulted in friendships with a number of contemporary architects. He and Frank Lloyd Wright bonded immediately. Fiske's good friend and architectural collaborator Erling Pedersen introduced the pair around 1926 and vividly recalled that first meeting: "[Y]ou never saw such good fellowship in all your life. . . . [The dinner] went on almost all night long—a battle of conversation and wit, and both very sympathetic to the other."[47] When Fiske wrote to Wright for photographs to include in his forthcoming survey, *American Architecture* (1928), he referenced one of Wright's jibes that classicism had corrupted his principles: "While we do not always see eye to eye with one another, I do not think you will dislike what I say of your work. In spite of my corrupt principles, I am really one of your greatest admirers!" Wright responded in kind, "You are a friendly enemy. They make ultimately the best friends." Wright admired the way that Fiske wrote, and Fiske in turn admired Wright's formal sensibility. For Fiske, there was no need to take sides. He parried Wright's invitation to forsake "The Classic" by replying, "I wish you would understand that my own interest is not at all in prophecy or polemics, but is merely the historian's view which tries to take for its motto that of Ranke, 'I only wish to show what actually happened.' The march of events ever turns the present into the historical past and thus adds a new chapter to the story." And he added in his own memoirs, "Only Wright, among the moderns, has realized that form does not 'follow' function but that form and function are fused simulateanously [*sic*] in the artistic crucible, to be crystalized as one and inseparable."[48] Over the years, Wright asked to add Fiske's name to the prospectus for the Taliesin Fellowship, and Fiske wrote letters in 1941 to stop the demolition of the Robie House and to support an honorary degree for Wright from the University of Wisconsin.[49]

Fiske and Wright shared another mutual modernist friend, German Expressionist architect Erich Mendelsohn. Fiske met Mendelsohn through Werner Hegemann and praised Mendelsohn's *Amerika*, a copy of which he kept on his desk at the museum. Fiske used some of Mendelsohn's photographs in his *American Architecture*. Mendelsohn, like Wright, asked Fiske how he could write supportively about both classical and modern architecture, to which Fiske responded, "I hope it can never be said that I am disloyal in my treatment of the Modernists whom I admire personally, and whose work also I admire so much for its creative power, as I believe you will see in the new book [*American Architecture*]. Our difference has lain in that I admire also the work of the great classicists of the nineties and early nineteen hundreds, and the contribution these men made to return abstract unity of form, as against merely technical expression."[50] Again, for Fiske, aesthetic merit crossed stylistic boundaries; as a critic and a historian, he focused on the quality of the work, not the polemics.

That Fiske could support something as modern as the St. Louis arch may seem at odds with his work on eighteenth-century architecture and Jefferson, but in fact, both he and Marie loved the present. Photographs and portraits show them as a fashionably dressed, elegant couple—as seen in figure 1 or the portraits commissioned from Leon Makielski. Fiske had a running account with Brooks Brothers in New York City, and Marie rarely left the house without gloves and a hat. They enjoyed luncheons at the Cloud Club in the Art Deco Chrysler Building and fast, sporty cars. They owned both a Packard Convertible Roadster and a Plymouth Deluxe Club Coupe in which they raced around Philadelphia and Charlottesville, accumulating tickets and insurance quotes for fender benders. Milton Grigg, the architect with whom Fiske and Marie worked on the restoration of Monticello, stated without hesitation that Fiske was a "notoriously bad driver. He was terrible. I used to visit him quite a bit in Philadelphia and would dread when he insisted on taking me over to the train station. He was known by all of the policemen [in Philadelphia]; they sort of cleared the way."[51] Jane Moore, another Charlottesville friend of the Kimballs, recalled a picnic outing for which Marie dressed in a white dimity outfit, complete with gloves, and that Fiske, as

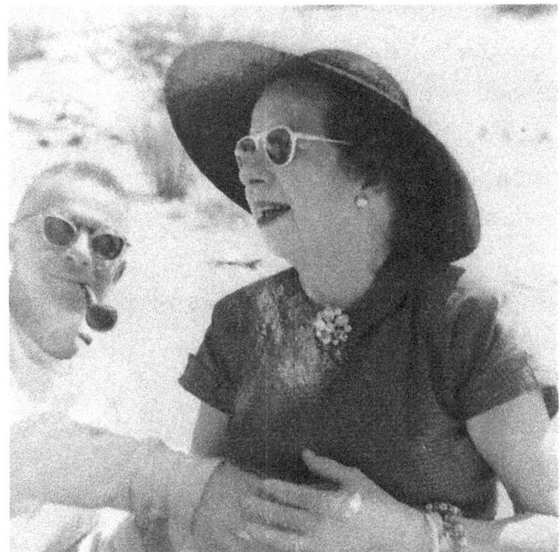

FIGURE 7. Marie Goebel Kimball on the beach at Castle Point, Michigan, with her brother Julius behind her. (Courtesy of Anne Goebel Barkman)

he drove them all out into the countryside, talked and gesticulated so energetically that "I don't think he touched the wheel. . . . [the other passengers] seemed unaware that we were about to end our life."[52]

Fiske and Marie's taste in art also included the contemporary. The works they purchased for themselves included Marc Chagall's *To My Betrothed* (1911, PMA Collection), an Expressionist work whose depiction of a bull-headed man and a beautiful woman perhaps captured some of the humor that Fiske and Marie saw in their own relationship. They also owned the Surrealist painting *The Philosopher Seated Holding Lyre and Books* by Giorgio de Chirico (private collection). Fiske relished the drama of shocking visitors who entered Shack Mountain's Jeffersonian exterior only to be confronted by the de Chirico he deliberately hung over the parlor fireplace. Jane Moore, a regular visitor to (and later owner of) Shack Mountain, recounted her own reaction to the painting of "a man with books coming out of his stomach" and Fiske's additional role in the drama: he greeted guests to the annual Christmas party at the house in a bright red waistcoat, "a huge expanse of red waistcoat and I thought 'that's the biggest waistcoat I've ever seen.'"[53]

Eschewing any scrap of antiquarian nostalgia for the simple life of bygone days, Fiske and Marie embraced new inventions. One of the events Fiske thoroughly enjoyed was his appearance in 1951 on the modern technological marvel of the television. Invited as a guest expert for the popular show *What in the World*, Fiske and other professionals in the visual arts faced the challenge of identifying a work of art placed before them. Hosted by Dr. Froelich Rainey of the University of Pennsylvania Museum, the show prefigured the popularity of *Antiques Roadshow* today: no dry excursion into analysis, the show enticed viewers with a dramatic opening introduction that paired music from Debussy's *Syrinx* with spotlights and a disembodied voice intoning, "What in the world?" The popularization of art-historical discussions such as this appealed to Fiske, who saw it as yet another opportunity to engage the public with works of art (and, undoubtedly, to compete with and best his co-panelists for the correct answer).

The 1940s marked a time of maturation for the pair. Marie published *Jefferson: Road to Glory* in 1943, the same year that Fiske published his book on the French Rococo, *The Creation of the Rococo*. Reviews of Marie's book were positive, and its success led to Guggenheim awards in 1945 and 1946 to continue work on succeeding volumes. In 1947 she published *Jefferson: War and Peace, 1776–1784*, and in 1950 *Jefferson and the Scene of Europe, 1784–1789*; in the early '50s she embarked on a manuscript for a fourth volume. As Kern so ably discusses in her essay, Marie brought to her biographies a discussion of culture and the arts that helped define Jefferson's worldview and stood in contrast to the later multivolume biography by Dumas Malone.

Fiske's book on the Rococo was also well received and praised for the methodology, mastery of the material, and clear writing that had characterized his work on American topics. He received letters from Leigh Ashton, Director of the Victoria and Albert Museum in London; Theodoor Lunsingh Scheurleer, Director of the Rijksmuseum; and art historians Hans Tietze, Erwin Panofsky, and John Coolidge, among others. Ashton said outright, "It is quite definitely one of the most important books, if not the most important, that have been published on the subject, and the amount of documentation which you have extricated from French sources is of cardinal interest." Renaissance art historian Ulrich Middeldorf wrote to Fiske to thank him for the fresh look that he brought to the Rococo: "I think it is the first book which treats my favorite period in a fashion which I like. With all due respect to our French and German colleagues, their publications are certainly always lacking something. It is very seldom that one receives a book which gives such undivided pleasure . . . and I want to thank you very much for your efforts on behalf of good art which not only has been neglected, but looked at in askance." The architectural historian Nikolaus Pevsner, however, wrote a review that suggested the thesis of the book lacked a "universal applicability" because it did not take into account the simultaneous works of the English Picturesque. Undaunted, Fiske replied to Pevsner in the essay "Rococo and Romanticism" (1946), in which he identified the differences in their approaches: "The basic question is one of method and parlance, and it has doubtless more than a single answer." Fiske then defended his reasons for restricting the use of the term "Rococo" with one of the clearest distillations of his rationale regarding periodization and style.[54]

Following the publication of *Road to Glory,* Marie was officially named the first curator of Monticello in 1944. In the following years she would work simultaneously on the collections of the house as she penned her second and third volumes of her Jefferson biography. Marie's work as an author and curator commanded the respect of her colleagues at Monticello. Grigg spoke of Marie's accomplishments with an awed reverence and specifically noted how she grounded decisions through research: "She was always writing. . . . She comes in without any prejudice or preconceptions of this very thing we were talking about [the tendency to make interiors in house museums 'pretty']. She is the first to admit the homeliness of some of the things she was writing about. No, I think she was basically a historical writer. Very thorough. He [Fiske] relied on her—much of the scholarship that he used in his works Marie had produced. She did the research." And when it came to decisions about the placement of furniture in Monticello, Grigg stated unequivocally that Marie's recommendations were followed "altogether."[55]

In these same years, Fiske continued to stretch himself beyond his duties as director at the PMA. In addition to his continuous stream of articles, in 1944 he was asked by the American Institute of Architects to chair the restoration of their headquarters at The Octagon in Washington, DC. He served on the St. Louis arch project in 1947, as already mentioned; in 1949 he was elected to the council of the Institutions of Early American History and Culture; and he received the Jefferson Presidential Medal from the Thomas Jefferson Memorial Foundation "for his services in the restoration of Monticello." In 1950, he was elected president of the Association of Museums and Art Museum Directors, energetically orchestrated the Seventy-Fifth Jubilee anniversary for the museum he had such a critical role in expanding, and received Philadelphia's prestigious Bok Award for his contributions to the city.

But the expenditure of energy also started to take a toll on the pair, and the cosmic activity and alignment of their lives turned earthward. Marie had struggled with her health since the mid-1930s, and in 1946, just prior to the publication of her second volume on Jefferson, she suffered a severe heart attack. The couple spent lengthy periods in California and Europe to help her recover, but when Marie had another heart attack in 1951, Fiske did not hesitate to install an elevator in their historic home, Lemon Hill, in Fairmount Park. More problematically, by the late 1940s, Fiske himself started to exhibit intense swings in mood—the strong but fair character that had marked his earlier interactions now gave way to a strong and overbearing, volatile personality. Carl Zigrosser, the curator of the print department at the museum, wrote a brief but insightful account of Fiske's final years. When Fiske exhibited moods of depression or lashed out at his colleagues for little reason, the staff had relied on Marie to help control his behavior. But after her heart attack in 1951, that task fell to the associate director, Henri Marceau. In 1953, the frequency of incidents rose sharply. There is every indication that Fiske's growing "manic-depressive psychosis," as Zigrosser referred to it, was itself tied to Marie's failing health and his own role in precipitating it.[56]

In March 1953, Fiske's long history of driving too fast caught up with them both—he ran a red light near the museum, and a car crossing the intersection crashed into the front of Marie's side of their Buick sedan.[57] Fiske initially expressed relief that Marie was not thrown from the car, but she never fully recovered from the accident. Fiske's grief, anger, and feelings of helplessness all unfurled. His close friend of decades, Milton Grigg, articulated the pivotal effect of the accident on

Fiske's mental and emotional state: "Those of us who were close to Fiske agree that he had a sense of guilt [from the accident] that permeated the rest of his life. . . . The accident—that was the catalyst."[58] Through 1953 and 1954, Fiske's ability to run the museum or carry on with the restoration of Monticello vacillated between periods of capability and incapacity. For example, one set of letters to Grigg in 1953 exhibits a remarkably detailed and clear understanding of the complex issues related to a new HVAC system at Monticello; then, for a lengthy period, he would simply ignore Grigg's questions and finally abruptly reply, "I have no interest in Virginia."[59] A similar pattern occurred at the museum. Zigrosser relates that through the spring of 1954, Henri Marceau had to quietly "undo the mischief [Fiske] caused" and yet, after spending the summer in Europe, Fiske returned "reasonably sane" for the Arensberg opening in October 1954. But when Marie became ill yet again in December 1954, Fiske plummeted. Sturgis Ingersoll, president of the museum board, asked Fiske to resign on January 21, 1955.[60]

In the next months, Fiske rode out a roller-coaster of emotions. Pedersen had to rescue him from one of the clubs in Philadelphia because the other patrons claimed he was drunk. Pedersen, ever loyal, took them to task: "You know he's not drunk . . . he's not well. The man is not well."[61] Fiske began firing off hostile letters to friends and colleagues. Both Pedersen and another close friend, art historian John Canaday, tried to get him to seek treatment. Canaday was particularly concerned about the impact on Marie, "a tiny woman who collapsed under the strain of trying to cope with Fiske's gargantuan affliction."[62] Marie did finally reach the end of her ability to cope. In a letter to her brother Walther, she confided just how difficult life with Fiske had become: "He refuses all psychological aid and goes around bragging that he is a hypo maniac—they are the only people in the world who get anywhere. It is just too terrible."[63] Marie died on March 2, 1955, just three days after writing this letter.

A memorial service for Marie was held in Philadelphia, and then a funeral at Shack Mountain in Charlottesville. After her heart attack in 1951, Marie had drawn up instructions for her funeral. She did not want "any service, any prayers, or any preaching" but instead an opportunity for friends and family to come together and say good-bye. She urged her siblings to look back at their happy memories together—their parents, their home, and their music—and she paid tribute to Fiske, "my dearly beloved husband, the best and truest man who ever lived." And then she asked that everyone listen to two works by Wagner, "Wotan's Farewell" and "Magic Fire" from *Die Walküre*.[64] Her choice of Wagner had unintended ramifications, because her death threw Fiske into a depression of Wagnerian dimensions. He followed Marie's instructions and gathered friends of the family, but the depth of his grief all but swallowed the exchange of happy memories for which Marie had hoped. Grigg remembers that Fiske played the Wagner very loudly, no one could speak, and they stood around the dining room of Shack Mountain awkwardly. About twenty people attended, mostly friends from the University of Virginia and Charlottesville. Fiske insisted the casket be left open and, after carrying the casket through the house, everyone filed out behind it to a grave dug behind the house. After the burial, Fiske retreated back inside, and everyone departed. Jane Moore described it simply as a "tragic funeral."[65]

Fiske did not recover. Grigg remembered, "He really did go to pieces . . . his mind was not at all normal."[66] At the urging of friends, he made plans to spend the spring and summer in Europe amid the art and architecture that he enjoyed. He traveled first to Amsterdam, then Munich, and then Florence in early July. His letters to colleagues seem jovial and in good humor, but he did not rebound. In Ravenna, he suffered a stroke and partial paralysis; Richard Offner and John Coolidge both helped get him medical care. German art historian Ludwig Heydenreich played a particularly critical role: he transported Fiske to Munich and into the care of a specialized clinic, where he visited Fiske every day. But Fiske suffered a second stroke and then a heart attack. In his last days he could not speak but remained conscious. Henry Clifford, a curator from the PMA, had joined Heydenreich in the room and, recognizing that Fiske was failing, held up a picture of Marie: "I don't know what made me do it but I held up before his eyes two small photos of Marie that were in a sort of old-fashioned frame on his night table. . . . This was definitely the last thing he saw as he never opened his eyes again."[67] Fiske died on August 14, just four months after Marie.

The volatility of Fiske's last years, and the heightened drama of his own passing, initially seemed to color or even eclipse the achievements of both his and Marie's long careers. Many close friends spoke out in response to the book on Fiske and Marie by George and Mary Howland Roberts, *Triumph on Fairmount* (1959), which concluded with a cinematic retelling of his last days that portrayed Fiske as a fallen god of the Götterdämmerung. Pedersen exploded when he learned that the couple initially intended to title the book "The Mad Man of Fairmount" and told them to "get the hell" out of his office. Canaday wrote one of the most succinct yet incisive responses. Fully acknowledging all of Fiske's faults and his madness, he contested that Fiske was never pitiful or absurd. For Canaday, Fiske's madness was more Shakespearean tragedy than Wagnerian: "The word 'madness' has connotations of grandeur and tragedy. . . . Anyone who lived with him through his last years felt as much as ever the man's stature and his power. But no one could help him. He was not a big man who became little, but a big man who entered wild places where he could not be reached."[68]

Fiske and Marie had prepared detailed wills, and after their death their estate was dissolved. Family members received a number of items (Marie left her grand piano to her brother Walther), but the Kimballs left the majority of their art collection, and their house, Shack Mountain, to the PMA. The museum sold Shack Mountain to Jane and Bedford Moore in 1956. Marie's body was removed from the grounds, and both she and Fiske were interred in Monticello Memorial Park, a cemetery located at the base of Monticello. Fiske designed the minimalist rectangular grave marker that included only their names and dates. The decision to be buried there—and not Philadelphia, where they had lived for thirty years, or in New England with Fiske's family or the Midwest with Marie's—closed the loop of their scholarly lives together. They began with *Thomas Jefferson, Architect* in 1916, in which Marie had supported Fiske's writing with her own research, and ended in the months following her death with Fiske determinedly editing Marie's manuscript for her fourth volume on Jefferson.[69]

Notes

1. "Jane Moore Interview Conducted by William L. Beiswanger," 11:03, William L. Beiswanger Papers, Thomas Jefferson Foundation Archives, Jefferson Library, Thomas Jefferson Foundation, Inc. (hereafter Moore interview).

2. See, for example, Kathryn Brush's excellent discussion on the photography of Lucy Wallace Porter that supported the scholarship on medieval art by her husband, Arthur Kingsley Porter, in "Medieval Art Through the Camera Lens: The Photography of Arthur Kingsley Porter and Lucy Wallace Porter," *Visual Resources* 33, nos. 3–4 (2017): 252–94, or the recent biography in literature by Camille Peri, *A Wilder Shore: The Romantic Odyssey of Fanny and Robert Louis Stevenson* (New York: Viking Press, 2024).

3. For Fiske's suggestion about the role of drawings, see Fiske to Herbert Langford Warren, September 28, 1912, Fiske Kimball Papers, PMA Library and Archives (hereafter FKP), box 2, folder 6. For his work with the Archaeological Institute, see FKP, box 93.

4. Kathleen Curran, *The Invention of the American Art Museum: From Craft to Kulturgeschichte, 1870–1930* (Los Angeles: Getty Research Institute, 2016), 159.

5. Dell Upton, "Outside the Academy: A Century of Vernacular Architecture Studies, 1890–1990," in *The Architectural Historian in America: A Symposium in Celebration of the Fiftieth Anniversary of the Founding of the Society of Architectural*

Historians, edited by Elisabeth Blair MacDougall, Studies in the History of Art 35 (Washington, DC: National Gallery of Art, 1990), 205. See also the valuable overview of American architectural history in Keith Eggener, ed., *American Architectural History: A Contemporary Reader* (London: Routledge, 2004), 1–22.

6. Fiske Kimball to Ogden Codman, January 31, 1923, FKP, box 11, folder 10.

7. See Curran, *Invention*, 157–61 and 187–201.

8. On Fiske's network for his Rococo studies, see Demetra Vogiatzaki, "'America Is Broke': Sidney Fiske Kimball and His French Allies (1933–1945)," in *Polytechnos: Essays in Honor of Panayotis Tournikiotis*, ed. Kostas Tsiambaos (Athens: Melissa, 2024), 218–35.

9. For the "dean of historians" phrase, see Thomas Tileston Waterman, *The Mansions of Virginia, 1706–1776* (Chapel Hill: University of North Carolina Press, 1945), 403. For "dean of directors," see John Canaday, *Culture Gulch: Notes on Art and Its Public in the 1960s* (New York: Farrar, Straus and Giroux, 1969), 139.

10. See Erwin Panofsky, "Epilogue: Three Decades of Art History in the United States; Impressions of a Transplanted European," in *Meaning in the Visual Arts* (1955; repr., Chicago: University of Chicago Press, 1982), 326. See also the correspondence between Fiske and Panofsky, FKP, box 21, folder 12.

11. On Lee, author's oral interview with Robin Lee (Robert's son), March 30, 2018. Fiske presented the Lees with his own personal annotated copy of *Thomas Jefferson, Architect*. On waiving recompense at Monticello, see Fiske Kimball to Stuart Gibboney, May 17, 1924, Thomas Jefferson Memorial Foundation Archives, box 14, folder 1.

12. Canaday, *Culture Gulch*, 140.

13. Fiske Kimball to Theodora Kimball, July 4, 1914, FKP, box 48, folder 7.

14. See Fiske Kimball, "Harvard in Transition," FKP, box 159, folder 3. Fiske stopped using his first name, Sidney, in 1913, with the start of his professional career.

15. On Theodora, see Heidi Hohmann, "Theodora Kimball Hubbard and the 'Intellectualization' of Landscape Architecture, 1911–1935," *Landscape Journal* 25, no. 2 (2006): 169–86, and Sarah Allaback, "Theodora Kimball: Defining a New Field—City Planning," *View* 23 (2023): 15–21.

16. Kimball, "Harvard in Transition," 3–4.

17. Edwin Kimball to Fiske Kimball, December 8, 1908. The following year, Edwin's birthday letter congratulated Fiske for being "on the road to even higher usefulness"; see Edwin Kimball to Fiske Kimball, December 8, 1909. Both letters in FKP, box 44, folder 1.

18. See Maureen Meister, *Architecture and the Arts and Crafts Movement in Boston: Harvard's H. Langford Warren* (Hanover, NH: University Press of New England, 2003), and Joseph Lahendro, "Fiske Kimball, American Renaissance Historian" (master's thesis, University of Virginia, 1982).

19. Marie Frank, *Denman Ross and American Design Theory* (Hanover, NH: University Press of New England, 2011).

20. See Anna Berkes, "Marie Kimball: Pioneering Scholar and First Curator of Monticello," in *Virginia Women: Their Lives and Times,* vol. 2, edited by Cynthia A. Kierner and Sandra Gioia Treadway (Athens: University of Georgia Press, 2016), 202–21; on Irma specifically, see "Ambassador for South American Music: Irma Goebel Labastille," *Special Collections Mosaic,* University of Miami Libraries, March 23, 2021, https://uml-mosaic.org/2021/03/23/ambassador -for-south-american-music-irma-goebel-labastille/.

21. Interview with Anne Goebel Barkman, July 19, 2018, p. 4, Oral History Collection, Philadelphia Museum of Art Archives.

22. Fiske Kimball to Edwin Kimball, January 15, 1915, FKP, box 44, folder 4.

23. Fiske Kimball to Edwin Kimball, March 16, 1914, FKP, box 44, folder 2.

24. Marie Kimball to Theodora Kimball, February 5, 1914, FKP, box 49, folder 3. Marie wrote, "Emily is a nice girl—and she would be nicer if she had only *not* dropped everything but babies." Marie's brother Walther suggested to his daughter Anne that she ask Marie to be her godmother in part because Marie and Fiske had no children of their own, but Anne and her sister don't recall seeing them much growing up, because "they were too busy with their professional lives." See Interview with Anne Goebel Barkman, pp. 5–6.

25. Kimball, "Harvard in Transition," 24–25.

26. Fiske Kimball, "Jefferson's Place in Our Architectural History," *Journal of the American Institute of Architects* 2, no. 7 (1914): 329. Fiske may have had contemporary European publications in mind, such Austria's catalogue of monuments, edited by Hans Tietze between 1908 and 1914.

27. On Kelsey, see John Pedley, *The Life and Work of Francis Willey Kelsey* (Ann Arbor: University of Michigan Press, 2011).

28. Fiske Kimball, "Scholarship," 4, FKP, box 159, folder 5.

29. Fiske Kimball to his parents, March 6, 1914, FKP, box 44, folder 2. See also Marie Frank, "Fiske Kimball and the Genesis of *Thomas Jefferson, Architect,*" *Classicist* 13 (2016): 56–64, for a full account of the discovery of the drawings.

30. Marie Goebel Kimball to Edwin Kimball, November 23, 1915, FKP, box 46, folder 5.

31. For the reference to Poplar Forest, see FKP, box 44, folder 3. See also Frank, "Fiske Kimball and the Genesis."

32. Fiske Kimball to his parents, December 20, 1913, FKP, box 44, folder 2, PMA; Kimball, *Thomas Jefferson, Architect,* 82.

33. See the list of Fiske's articles in Mary Kane, *A Bibliography of the Works of Fiske Kimball* (Charlottesville: University of Virginia Press, 1959), 4–5.

34. Waterman, *Mansions of Virginia.*

35. See Kimball, "Scholarship," 24–25. See also Fiske Kimball to Ogden Codman, January 31, 1923, and Fiske Kimball to Ogden Codman, April 23, 1934, both in FKP, box 11, folder 11.

36. See Kimball, "Scholarship," 28a.

37. See Jack Hinton, *Renaissance Treasures from the Edmond Foulc Collection* (New Haven, CT: Yale University Press).

38. Fiske Kimball, "Recent Architecture in the South," *Architectural Record* 55 (March 1924): 212. See the excellent discussion of Fiske's first years with the museum in Curran, *Invention,* 190–99. See also Marie Frank, "Emil Lorch, Pure Design, and American Architectural Education," *Journal of Architectural Education* 57, no. 4 (2004): 28–41, and Marie Frank, "Fiske Kimball and the University of Virginia Architecture Program in the 1920s," *ARRIS* 18 (October 2007): 15–27.

39. See Curran, *Invention,* especially the illuminating exchange of letters in 1928 with Charles Russell Richards (190–99).

40. Fiske Kimball to Harvey Corbett, September 17, 1932, FKP, box 107, folder 5. Box 107, folder 3, contains the list of artists considered by the committee, with Fiske's annotations.

41. Fiske to Harvey Corbett, April 7, 1932, FKP, box 107, folder 4.

42. Fiske's letter to the *New York Times* was reprinted with a group of letters from Clarke in the May 1930 issue of *Architect's World* (224–37). FKP, box 72, folder 1.

43. Fiske Kimball to Charles Moore, October 31, 1941, FKP, box 72, folder 6.

44. Fiske Kimball, "The Jefferson Memorial Commission Speaks," April 10, 1938. Fiske sent the statement to the *New York Times;* the quotation used here is from the copy Fiske sent for publication to *The Architect's World: A Monthly Digest,* edited by Henry Saylor, May 1938, 235.

45. "Summary of Comments of Jury of Award on Winning Designs," p. 3, FKP, box 82, folder 6. Note that Fiske's association with the National Expansion Memorial in St. Louis began in 1937, when a National Parks subcommittee sent him and a few others out to review the site.

46. Fiske Kimball, "Statement by the Jury of Award on the Winning Design," and Fiske Kimball to Edward Dail (Executive Director of the Jefferson National Expansion Memorial Association), March 8, 1948. To Clarke he wrote personally, "The resemblance you mention does not disturb me." Fiske Kimball to Gilmore Clarke, February 26, 1948. All quotations from FKP, box 82, folder 4.

47. Erling Pedersen to Charles B. Hosmer, oral interview transcript, p. 30, "Interviews Conducted by Charles Hosmer Relating to Historic Preservation, 1969–1976," Archives of American Art, Smithsonian Institution, Washington, DC.

48. Fiske Kimball to Frank Lloyd Wright, October 27, 1928, FKP, box 26, folder 12; Fiske Kimball, "Architecture at the Turn of the Century," FKP, box 159, folder 4.

49. Fiske Kimball to Frank Lloyd Wright, November 14, 1927, and Frank Lloyd Wright to Fiske Kimball, April 30, 1928, FKP, box 26, folder 12. For an assessment of the "classical" qualities in Wright that Kimball might have appreciated, see Patrick Pinnell, "Academic Tradition and the Individual Talent: Similarity and Difference in the Formation of Frank Lloyd Wright," in *Frank Lloyd Wright: A Primer on Architectural Principles,* edited by Robert McCarter (Princeton, NJ: Princeton Architectural Press, 1991), 18–58.

50. Fiske Kimball to Erich Mendelsohn, January 9, 1928. In 1929 Kimball facilitated an introduction for George Howe to meet Mendelsohn, who, he wrote, was "throwing himself heart and soul into the modern movement." Fiske Kimball to Erich Mendelsohn, June 12, 1929. Fiske wrote to Mendelsohn: "It is not the least of my prides that you and Wright care what I think." Fiske Kimball to Erich Mendelsohn, December 18, 1929. All FKP, box 19, folder 12.

51. "Milton Grigg Interviews Conducted by William L. Beiswanger," tape 11, 42:00, Milton Grigg Monticello Restoration Papers, 1934–1957, box 83–10, folder 1, Thomas Jefferson Foundation Archives, Jefferson Library, Thomas Jefferson Foundation, Inc. (hereafter Grigg interview). See also Marie Frank, "Fender Benders in Philadelphia's Built Environment: The Insurance Records of Fiske and Marie Kimball," *Pennsylvania Magazine of History and Biography* 145, no. 3 (2021): 364–65.

52. Moore interview, 8:30.

53. Moore interview, 7:00.

54. For the letters Fiske received regarding his book, see Leigh Ashton to Fiske Kimball, September 13, 1945, and Ulrich Middeldorf to Fiske Kimball, November 8, 1943, both in FKP, box 159, folder 18. See also [Nikolaus Pevsner], "Rococo to Romanticism," *Times Literary Supplement,* March 23, 1946, 133–34; Fiske Kimball, "Rococo and Romanticism," in *To Dr. R: Essays Here Collected and Published in Honor of the Seventieth Birthday of Dr. A. S. W. Rosenbach,* edited by Percy E. Lawler and John Fleming (Philadelphia, 1946), 12–123. For more on Kimball and Pevsner, see the opening paragraphs of Lauren Bricker, "The Writings of Fiske Kimball: A Synthesis of Architectural History and Practice," in MacDougall, *Architectural Historian,* 215.

55. Grigg interview, tape 11, 39:25.

56. See Carl Zigrosser, "Fiske Kimball," in *A World of Art and Museums* (Philadelphia: Art Alliance Press, 1975), 218–38.

57. The accident occurred on March 22, 1953; see FKP, box 57, folder 5, for letters and documentation on the accident and follow-up with Marie's doctors.

58. Grigg interview, tape 11, 42:00.

59. For example, see letters between Kimball and Grigg about the new HVAC in Milton Grigg Monticello Restoration Papers, 1934–1957, box 2, folder 2, Thomas Jefferson Foundation Archives, Jefferson Library, Thomas Jefferson Foundation, Inc.; for Kimball's quote that he "has no interest in Virginia," see Grigg interview, tape 11, 39:00.

60. Zigrosser, *World of Art*, 235.

61. Erling Pedersen to Charles B. Hosmer, oral interview transcript, p. 34.

62. Canaday, *Culture Gulch*, 143.

63. Marie Goebel Kimball to Walther Goebel, February 27, 1955, personal collection of Walther's daughter, Anne Barkman, Montreal, Canada. I am very grateful to Anne for permission to publish an excerpt from this letter.

64. "Marie Goebel Kimball," funeral pamphlet, FKP, box 53, folder 20.

65. Moore interview, 28:00.

66. Grigg interview, tape 11, 42:00.

67. Henry Clifford to Henri Marceau, August 28, 1955, p. 3, Henri Marceau Records, PMA, box 2, folder 18.

68. Canaday, *Culture Gulch*, 143.

69. Ludwig Heydenreich wrote to one of Marie's brothers after Fiske's death that "he [Fiske] had *finished* Marie's book here in Munich and had sent the last chapters to the publisher, before he went with us to Italy. I think it is a wonderful and consoling fact, that Fiske could complete so really the life-work [*sic*] of Marie, just before he had to die himself, too!" Ludwig Heydenreich to Mr. Goebel [either Julies or Walther], August 21, 1955, Henri Marceau Records, PMA, box 5, folder 21. The manuscript, however, remained unpublished. It is now located, with a foreword by Fiske, in the Marie Goebel Kimball Papers, Special Collections, University of Virginia Library, Charlottesville, VA.

THE ARC OF AMERICAN ARCHITECTURAL HISTORY TO FISKE KIMBALL

RICHARD GUY WILSON

Tracing the development of the discipline of architectural history in America prior to the twentieth century evokes being lost in a vast library's endless stacks; you grab one book, then pick another, and still more, but what do you find? How does it come together? Buildings represent the past; they can provide identity and can tell stories. But when does their history, from either the scholarly or popular side, develop in the United States? The answer is complex, but the central figure on the academic side was Fiske Kimball. His articles and early books, including *Thomas Jefferson, Architect* (1916), *A History of Architecture* (1918), and *Domestic Architecture of the American Colonies and of the Early Republic* (1922), helped set the stage for scholarly pursuit. But what preceded him?

The arc of American architectural history is not a smooth, rising curve but contains many fluctuations, reflecting changes in what was defined as "American." America, of course, changes, and it is not just the English heritage that plays a role but also the Spanish, French, Dutch, and Native American. Does "American architecture" only encompass grand structures, such as large houses, public buildings, and churches, or the vernacular as well? Is the setting of a building—either rural or urban—important? What about its surroundings, such as gardens? And what about a building's contents, such as furniture or decorative arts? Or the people who built it, designed it, or occupied it initially (and since)? The history of what is considered American architecture constantly evolves.

The issues that shaped the background to Kimball's place in the emergence of American architectural history are complex. In the nineteenth century, the definition of architecture and the profession of the architect began to change. In addition, interest in the history of architecture in the United States grew out of multiple levels of awareness of the role of buildings in the quickly developing landscape.[1] The interwoven connections among these issues will soon become apparent.

Defining Architecture and the Architect

For Fiske Kimball and most of his contemporaries, "historic architecture" essentially referred to buildings that made a visual impression. They were significant structures, whether public or private, and they were often monumental. But architecture can be defined in many ways. The complexity of defining architecture goes back to the first surviving Western treatise: Vitruvius's *De architectura* (or *Ten Books on Architecture*), written ca. 30 BCE–15 BCE in Rome. It existed only in manuscript form until it was published in 1486—and then in illustrated form in the early sixteenth century. For Vitruvius, architecture was very broad. *De architectura* treated not just buildings and construction but included sections on city planning and the design of military camps, with structures both large (aqueducts, buildings, harbors) and small (machines, measuring devices, instruments). However, the broad inclusion of all this could be narrowed, as in book 3, where Vitruvius claimed that "architectura" contained three elements: "utilitas," "firmitas," and "venustas," or utility, strength, and beauty. This definition remained the rule in the nineteenth century.

The *Oxford English Dictionary* (initially published in 1884) keeps Vitruvius's breadth: "The art or science of building or constructing edifices of any kind for human use." The *OED* then expands and divides the concept of architecture into different categories, such as "*civil, ecclesiastical, naval, military,* which deal respectively with houses and other buildings (such as bridges) of ordinary utility, churches, ships, fortification." Hence, architecture in this definition encompasses the entire built environment. Increasingly in the nineteenth century, however, construction (or "firmitas") was separated from architecture, and another definition also appears in the *OED* that speaks to Kimball's period: "But *architecture* is sometimes regarded solely as a fine art."[2]

Without a doubt, John Ruskin helped steer nineteenth-century definitions toward the art of architecture. One of the most popular and influential writers in the English-speaking world, Ruskin was read by those who considered themselves intelligent. In his *The Seven Lamps of Architecture* (1849, reprinted many times and quoted in the *OED*), Ruskin claimed, "Architecture is the art which so disposes and adorns the edifices raised by man . . . that the sight of them contribute to his mental health, power, and pleasure."[3] Following this line of thinking is yet another definition by a leading English architect, George Gilbert Scott, in the *OED*: "Architecture, as distinguished from mere building, is the decoration of construction."[4]

Elements of Vitruvius and these other definitions of architecture can be found in the book Fiske Kimball wrote with George Edgell, *A History of Architecture* (1918). The book opens with this sentence: "From the beginning of its history architecture has had a threefold problem or aim: to build structures at once commodious, strong, and satisfying to the artistic sense."[5]

The idea of the architect—and the architect's role—also changed in these years. Vitruvius defined the architect as both creator and builder. Construction was part of an architect's role, but that disappeared with time. The architect, as initially defined in the *OED*, was: "A master-builder. *spec.* A skilled professor of the art of building, whose business is to prepare the plans of edifices and exercise a general superintendence over the course of their erection. A builder." However, succeeding definitions added: "One who so plans, devises, contrives, or constructs, as to achieve a desired result (especially when the result may be viewed figuratively as an edifice)." And then the *OED* includes a quote from Ruskin: "No person who is not a great sculptor or painter *can* be an *architect*. If he is not a sculptor or painter, he can only be a *builder*."[6] Architects certainly provided the specifications and lists of materials, but the builder or contractor became a separate occupation, with the "art" of architecture reserved for the architect. This shift took place slowly but persistently in the nineteenth century—the architect became an artist, a designer of important buildings that made a statement and stood out. Similarly, for many writers in the nineteenth century and most of the twentieth, "architecture" meant the creation of important buildings that appealed to the artistic side. Sir Nikolaus Pevsner echoed this definition in his very popular declaration of 1943: "A bicycle shed is a building; Lincoln Cathedral is a piece of architecture. Nearly everything that encloses space on a scale sufficent for a human being to move in is a building; the term architecture applies only to buildings designed with a view to aesthetic appeal."[7] In other words, architecture was not junk, the buildings that dot the landscape and are easily torn down. Beginning in the 1960s, this definition of architecture began to change, and interest in "roadside architecture" and "vernacular architecture" grew. In a sense, for scholars, architecture became the entire man-made environment. However, in Kimball's time, the term referred to important buildings with aesthetic appeal that largely came from the Western tradition.

The Rise of Architectural History

The emergence of the academic discipline of architectural history is a murky tale mired in the development of the discipline of art history. Books that helped set the stage were Giorgio Vasari's *The Lives of the Most Excellent Painters, Sculptors, and Architects* (1550) and Horace Walpole's *Anecdotes on Painting* (1762). Just two years after Walpole's *Anecdotes,* Johann Joachim Winckelmann published *The History of the Art of Antiquity* (1764). Winckelmann was part of a German academic group that tried to provide a scholarly, scientific basis for the study of art and architectural history with the systematization or division of the past into periods such as "Ancient," "Egyptian," "Classical," "Medieval," and "Renaissance." For these authors, a work of art comes from a specific time and place. More periods and styles were added, stretching from France to England and then to the United States. An integral part of this academic approach was the concept that the study of the history of art and architecture could be subjected to a quasi-scientific method that G. W. F. Hegel applied to history, overall, but also to the arts, which he saw as part of an evolution. The word "evolution" also reminds us of Charles Darwin's *On the Origin of Species* (1859). How many actually read Darwin remains a question, but people certainly knew of his idea of evolution. Systematized and comparative methods soon made their way into architectural books such as Sir Banister Fletcher's *A History of Architecture on the Comparative Method* (1896, with nine later editions). The frontispiece of the 1901 edition, "The Tree of Architecture," is well known in the Western world and illustrates their argument. The center of the trunk is Greek and Roman. Only in the sixth edition, of 1921, did the "tree" include another branch at the top with American contributions (notably the Flatiron Building in New York City).

In the United States, the teaching of architectural history to architects was largely derived from the École des Beaux-Arts in Paris, which had a tremendous impact upon American architects.[8] At the École, the history of architecture, or precedents in architecture, played a seminal role, and history was part of the students' curriculum. Significantly, although classicism dominated in the nineteenth century, students at the École took courses in materials and could make designs that drew upon different stylistic sources.

By the 1840s, some separate courses in the history of architecture were taught. Then, in 1863, Eugène Emmanuel Viollet-le-Duc (1814–1879), a prominent Gothic revival and restoration architect, became an instructor for a short time at the École. Viollet-le-Duc's books *Dictionnaire raisonné de l'architecture française du XI au XVI siècle* (1854–68) and *Histoire de l'habitation humaine* (1875) legitimized approaches to architecture that were different from classicism. His most important book, *Entretiens sur l'architecture* (1863–72), was translated as *Discourses on Architecture* (1875) by Henry van Brunt, a Boston-based architect. Van Brunt's architectural partner, William Robert Ware, founded the first architectural program in the United States at the Massachusetts Institute of Technology in 1865.

A flood of young Americans attended the École, beginning with Richard Morris Hunt in 1846 and then H. H. Richardson, Charles Follen McKim, Louis Sullivan, and many more (perhaps as many as eight hundred). One of the consequences is the so-called Beaux-Arts style, a term widely used today to refer to the classicism of the 1880s–1920s period in America, but there were many styles taught at the École. The École's model of a studio as the center of education, supplemented by other courses, came to the United States through programs at MIT, the University of Pennsylvania, Harvard University, and others.

The architectural history that evolved in American colleges and that Fiske Kimball experienced in his years at Harvard was thus also dominated by the study of the great and beautiful buildings of the European past through formal and quasi-scientific analysis. Harvard differed slightly from some of the other academic programs in its emphasis on training the formal sensibility of its students. Several eminent scholars taught courses for the architecture curriculum, such as George Santayana and Denman Ross.[9] In addition, the school's founder, Herbert Langford Warren—whom Kimball greatly admired—believed that a knowledge of history was as important as technical training and taught elements of the German method. (Warren, it might be noted, was also one of the founders of the Arts & Crafts Society of Boston.) Kimball took a three-year course taught by Warren on the history of architecture that included reference to American examples.

Knowledge and treatment of American architecture at the academic level existed on the back burner for most teachers, but Warren's classes inspired Kimball to try to make sense of it. Only later, after leaving Harvard, did Kimball discover Heinrich Wölfflin's *Principles of Art History*, published in German in 1915 and translated into English in 1932.[10] Kimball read it in German, and Wölfflin's five pairs of precepts for analyzing art (and architecture) had an impact on his later work in architectural history.

America's Architectural Past

The emergence of an interest in the architectural history of America outside of schools of architecture was, then, complex and had several components. From the early eighteenth century on, there was an awareness of architecture as an expression of identity and values, as seen in the various colonial governmental structures and churches erected under the British in Philadelphia, Newport, Boston, and elsewhere. In Newport, the notable buildings included the large, seven-bay red brick Colony House (1739), with a giant pediment, and the tall spire on Trinity Church, built between the 1720s and the 1740s. Individuals who had wealth and hubris expressed themselves with large houses, too, such as Drayton Hall in Charleston, South Carolina; Stratford Hall in Virginia; or the MacPheadris-Warner House in the large trading city of Portsmouth, New Hampshire. The money to build these mansions came from different sources, though slavery and the "triangle trade" were major contributors. And of course, a continuation of this can be seen in two of the most famous American house mansions, by two of the nation's founders: George Washington's Mount Vernon and Thomas Jefferson's Monticello.

The leaders of the young breakaway republic that became the United States viewed architecture as an expression of identity and therefore essential to the future of the country. Jefferson's design in 1785 for the Virginia State Capitol in Richmond was based upon a Roman temple in Nîmes, France. Up in Boston, Charles Bulfinch created an identity for the city and the state with the giant portico and dome of the Massachusetts State House (1795–98). And nationally, the elaborate design for Washington, DC, by Major Pierre Charles L'Enfant—and then the work of William Thornton, Benjamin Henry Latrobe, and others on the various buildings, including the Capitol and the President's House—created a national image. This would continue with succeeding architects, such as Robert Mills, William Strickland, Thomas U. Walter, and others.

Publications that drew attention to American architecture were also important. William Dunlap's three-volume *History of the Rise and Progress of The Arts of Design in the United States* (1834) focused on painting, although architecture received some attention. Dunlap devoted one chapter to a brief history of architecture from the ancients to Washington, DC, with specific mention of Robert Mills and his drawings for Monticello. Dunlap noted Jefferson's work at the University of Virginia and quoted directly from Mills: "[The] drawing of the details Mr. Jefferson reserved to himself; and it is surprising with what minuteness he entered into these . . . so that nothing was left for the workmen to conjecture," adding, "Mr. Jefferson was altogether Roman in his taste and continued so to the end of his days."[11] In 1848 the first architectural history book published in the United States appeared: *History of Architecture from the Earliest Times; Its Present Condition in Europe and the United States,* by Louisa Caroline Huggins Tuthill, a very successful author of children's books and an advocate for great architecture. Her book was well illustrated and quite up to date with recent buildings in the United States. However, it was dedicated to "The Ladies of the United States of America, the Acknowledged Arbiters of Taste."[12] Whether the dedication alienated men from reading the book remains unknown, but Tuthill was forgotten for many years.

Works of fiction also played a role in drawing attention to architecture and early efforts at both historic preservation and the Colonial Revival. In Newport, Rhode Island, early restoration efforts included Touro Synagogue in the 1820s and then, in the 1850s, the restoration of the portico of the Redwood Library and the saving of the notorious "Viking Tower." The tower was the inspiration for Henry Wadsworth Longfellow's 1841 poem "Skeleton in Armor," but in reality, the tower was the remnant of a mill dating to the 1680s.[13] Longfellow's various poems about the American past point to another element of the developing interest in American architecture: fictional creations where buildings appear. Examples are Washington Irving's "Rip Van Winkle" (1819) and "The Legend of Sleepy Hollow" (1820), Nathaniel Hawthorne's *The House of Seven Gables* (1851), and Harriet Beecher Stowe's *Uncle Tom's Cabin* (1851). These popular books emphasized different aspects of the architectural past, and of course Stowe's book about slavery helped make the log cabin an integral part of the American mythology. Historical fiction passed into architecture through examples such as Washington Irving's Sunnyside in Tarrytown, New York, in the 1830s and 1840s; it drew upon Dutch Colonial architecture and is one of the first Colonial Revival houses in the country.

If Tuthill was initially overlooked, one group of women did take on the role of arbiters of taste. In 1853 Ann Pamela Cunningham founded the Mount Vernon Ladies Association, which in 1858 purchased George Washington's house—which had fallen into bad disrepair—and restored and preserved it. Mount Vernon was, of course, very well known. It had appeared in paintings and prints by Edward Savage in 1789–91, on Chinese export ceramics in 1805, and in many other places. The house had become a national symbol and not simply Washington's home. In 1859, Benson Lossing published a book on Mount Vernon, which may be the first book on an American house (though it is not as much focused on the architecture as on the stories connected with the site).[14]

After the Civil War and with the approach of the 1876 Centennial, interest in earlier American buildings strengthened, especially among the younger architects. Charles Follen McKim, who had attended the École and then worked for H. H. Richardson, began to sketch the colonial buildings of Newport, Rhode Island, and then commissioned John Appleby Williams to photograph them. The result was twenty-nine plates bound as a portfolio and titled *Old Newport*

Homes (1875). It represents the first photographic record of America's colonial architecture. McKim published one image in the December 1874 issue of *The New-York Sketch Book of Architecture,* of which he was an editor. Shown was the rear of the 1729 Bishop Berkeley house (known as Whitehall) with a long, sloping shingle-covered roof and some additions. In the short text, McKim wrote, "now let somebody write about them as 'Architecture.' The Architects are their true historians."[15] The photographs in McKim and Williams's portfolio showed both formal fronts and details of notable buildings but also included other views, displaying additions over time. The result was the creation of a "modernized Colonial," as it was labeled then, and later named the "Shingle Style" by Vincent Scully in the 1950s.[16] McKim, with his partners William R. Mead and Stanford White, and others began to design more formal Colonial Revival buildings, and the American past was exhumed—at least for architects.

Books by architects, and primarily aimed at architects, began to appear frequently—principally of photographs and some drawings. They included *Examples of Domestic Colonial Architecture in New England* (1891) and *Examples of Domestic Colonial Architecture in Maryland and Virginia* (1892), both by James Corner and Eric Ellis Soderholtz. In the opening pages of the New England volume, the authors explained their purpose succinctly: they aimed "to present [architectural examples] in a form convenient for use and reference by architects and those interested in architecture." The growing appreciation of colonial buildings led the compilers "to hope that the publication of these plates may be the means of stimulating closer study in their adaptation to modern domestic work."[17]

Others followed, composed almost exclusively of photographs, which emphasized the more formal, classical, and embellished architecture of the latter half of the eighteenth century. Between 1898 and 1902, William Rotch Ware's magazine *American Architect* (originally *The American Architect and Building News*) published twelve portfolios entitled *The Georgian Period: A Collection of Papers Dealing with "Colonial" or XVIII-Century Architecture in the United States,* which provided measured drawings of the early work. These efforts became a mantra for a subsequent wave of books that appeared over the next century as the American architectural past was increasingly documented and reproduced.

The focus on photography and architects continued, but some authors started to appeal to wider audiences. Norman Isham, a Rhode Island–based architect very interested in preservation, published a volume with Albert Brown, *Early Rhode Island Houses* (1895), which was filled with drawings of the buildings. However, it also included a more substantial text to explain the history, features, or construction of the structures. Down in Washington, DC, Glenn Brown, an architect, published a two-volume *History of the United States Capitol* (1900–1903), which brought its architectural history to light.[18] Joseph Everett Chandler compiled *The Colonial Architecture of Maryland, Pennsylvania, and Virginia* (1892), intending its illustrations to be "wholly for the use of architects." *The American Architect* praised the book but noted that the poor quality of some negatives and the printing created an effect of "impressionistic pictures." The unnamed reviewer credited Chandler with "perspicacity" in having produced a series of "artistic pictures which will interest non-professional book buyers quite as much as it will architects . . . [for the] artistic effect."[19] The book assisted in changing perspectives on American design.

A growing reverence for the past in American history and historic preservation increased greatly at the turn of the century through the founding of organizations and committees. Members of the American Institute of Architects (AIA) voiced concerns about colonial-era buildings in New York and elsewhere at their 1890 convention and set up a committee devoted to their conservation. The resolution summed up a popular sentiment: "The history of civilization and the world is traced by the character of its buildings and its architecture, and the degree of civilization of peoples is determined by the monuments they have left."[20] In Virginia, Mary Jeffrey Galt and Cynthia Coleman—upset about the decay and possible destruction of venerable buildings and sites at Jamestown and Williamsburg—formed the Association for the Preservation of Virginia Antiquities in 1888.[21] In New England, William Sumner Appleton, a colleague of Kimball's at Harvard, founded the Society for the Preservation of New England Antiquities (renamed Historic New England) in 1910 with the goal to save early colonial houses.[22] The National Society of Colonial Dames and its rivals, the Colonial Dames and the Daughters of the American Revolution, were all founded in the early 1890s. These groups had social functions (and displayed certain xenophobic tendencies), but they also helped preserve colonial structures.

America's architectural past, present, and future came together in the World's Columbian Exposition of 1893 in Chicago. The past was on full display with the Virginia pavilion, a replica of Mount Vernon; the Massachusetts pavilion, modeled on the demolished Hancock House in Boston; and the California pavilion, which was in the Mission style and designed by A. Page Brown (who had worked for McKim, Mead and White). The buildings of the Court of Honor were designed by contemporary leading École-trained architects, and the Court complex itself served as the impetus for the City Beautiful movement of the twentieth century.

Following the Exposition, several publications appeared to help widen the field of American architectural history. An attempt to surmount the anecdotal and localized histories was Montgomery Schuyler's highly illustrated, lengthy essay of forty pages for the *Architectural Record* in 1895. Written to quell the criticisms of a "popular historian" who claimed "'there did not exist in the country' in 1784 'a single piece of architecture which, when tried even by the standard of that day, can be called respectable,'" Schuyler produced a comprehensive view of colonial and post-Revolutionary buildings, finding much to praise. (He did acknowledge, however, the lack of educated architects and concluded his essay with the backhanded compliment that even the feebleness and timidity of some of the colonial carpenters' work displayed "an engaging and amiable weakness.")[23] Schuyler's grudging acceptance of colonial architecture indicates the shift taking place among architects and critics.[24]

The arc of American architectural history prior to Fiske Kimball, then, consisted of intersecting strains that sometimes, but not always, aligned. As noted in the first half of this essay, the focus in architectural education was on the monumental, primarily Western classical tradition and on the formal and aesthetic merits of design. In the second half, we have seen how activities and publications outside of the schools shaped attitudes toward America's architectural past. These activities and publications incorporated new research and new technologies, such as photography. At the same time, they remained largely local studies, or relied on anecdotes and historical associations, or were aimed at architects. The academic side of architectural history, as Fiske Kimball experienced it (and at other schools of architecture), was out of touch with the interests of professional architects and the public sector. Thus, Kimball received an education and embarked on a career at a critical moment at the turn of the century; it became his task to give academic legitimacy and create the parameters of scholarly investigations into American architecture. The ensuing essays in this volume draw out the ways Kimball hoped to insert American architecture into the European trajectory of monumental and significant architecture through the deployment of scientific history, archaeology, formal analysis, and primary research.

Notes

1. Studies of the discipline are several: see David Watkin, *The Rise of Architectural History* (London: Architectural Press, 1980), and Elisabeth Blair MacDougall, ed., *The Architectural Historian in America: A Symposium in Celebration of the Fiftieth Anniversary of the Founding of the Society of Architectural Historians*, Studies in the History of Art 35 (Washington, DC: National Gallery of Art, 1990).

2. *The Compact Edition of the Oxford English Dictionary* (Oxford: Oxford University Press, 1971), 434–35 (hereafter *Compact OED*).

3. John Ruskin, *The Seven Lamps of Architecture* (Boston: Dana Estes, 1899), 15; *Compact OED*, 434–35.

4. *Compact OED*, 434–35: "1878 G. G. Scott *Lect. Mediæval Archit.* (1879) II. 292."

5. Fiske Kimball and George Edgell, *A History of Architecture* (New York: Harper & Brothers, 1918), 1.

6. *Compact OED*, 434: "1854 J. Ruskin *Lect. Archit. Add.* 113."

7. Nikolaus Pevsner, *An Outline of European Architecture* (London: Pelican, 1943), 1. There were many later editions.

8. Arthur Drexler, ed., *The Architecture of the École des Beaux-Arts* (Cambridge, MA: MIT Press for the Museum of Modern Art, 1977); Jean Paul Carlhian and Margot M. Ellis, *Americans in Paris: Foundations of America's Architectural Gilded Age; Architecture Students at the École des Beaux-Arts, 1846–1946* (New York: Rizzoli, 2014). A few Americans did attend German schools.

9. George Santayana, *The Sense of Beauty* (New York: Charles Scribner's Sons, 1896); Denman Waldo Ross, *A Theory of Pure Design: Harmony, Balance, Rhythm* (Boston: Houghton, Mifflin, 1907). See Marie Frank, *Denman Ross and American Design Theory* (Hanover, NH: University Press of New England, 2011), chapters 3 and 5.

10. Heinrich Wölfflin, *Kunstgeschichtliche Grundbegriffe: Das Problem der Stilentwicklung in der neueren Kunst* (Munich: F. Bruckmann, 1915).

11. William Dunlap, *A History of the Rise and Progress of the Arts of Design in the United States* (1834; New York: Dover, 1969), 2:221–22.

12. Louisa Caroline Tuthill, *History of Architecture from the Earliest Times; Its Present Condition in Europe and the United States* (Philadelphia: Lindsay and Blakiston, 1848), v.

13. Charles B. Hosmer Jr., *Presence of the Past: A History of the Preservation Movement in the United States Before Williamsburg* (New York: G. P. Putnam's Sons, 1965), 31–32, 33.

14. Lydia Brandt, *First in the Homes of His Countrymen: George Washington's Mount Vernon in the American Imagination* (Charlottesville: University of Virginia Press, 2016); Benson J. Lossing, *Mount Vernon and Its Associations: Historical, Biographical, and Pictorial* (New York: W. A. Townsend, 1859).

15. *The New-York Sketch Book of Architecture* 1, no. 12 (December 1874), opposite plate 45. See also Richard Guy Wilson, "The Early Work of Charles F. McKim, Country House Commissions," *Winterthur Portfolio* 14 (Fall 1979): 235–67.

16. George William Sheldon, *Artistic Country Seats* (New York: D. Appleton, 1886–87), 1:23; Vincent J. Scully, *The Shingle Style* (originally published in 1955)

and then *The Shingle Style and the Stick Style* (New Haven, CT: Yale University Press, 1971).

17. James M. Corner and Eric Ellis Soderholtz, *Examples of Domestic Colonial Architecture in New England* (Boston: Boston Architectural Club, 1891), introduction. See also Corner and Soderholtz, *Examples of Domestic Colonial Architecture in Maryland and Virginia* (Boston: Boston Architectural Club, 1892).

18. Glenn Brown, *History of the United States Capitol* (Washington, DC: GPO, 1900–1903).

19. Joseph Everett Chandler, *The Colonial Architecture of Maryland, Pennsylvania and Virginia* (Boston: Bates, Kimball & Guild, 1892); Chandler, "Books and Papers," *American Architect* 36 (June 4, 1892): 153, 154.

20. *Proceedings of the Twenty-Fourth Annual Convention . . . Washington, D.C.* (Chicago: American Institute of Architects, 1890), 33–35.

21. James M. Lindgren, *Preserving the Old Dominion* (Charlottesville: University of Virginia Press, 1993).

22. Norman Isham and Albert F. Brown, *Early Rhode Island Houses* (Providence: Preston & Rounds, 1895); Isham and Brown, *Early Connecticut Houses* (Providence: Preston & Rounds, 1900); James M. Lindgren, *Preserving Historic New England* (New York: Oxford University Press, 1995).

23. Montgomery Schuyler, "A History of Old Colonial Architecture," *Architectural Record* 4 (January–March 1895): 366.

24. Schuyler's career and his changing viewpoint are considered in William H. Jordy and Ralph Coe, "Montgomery Schuyler," in *American Architecture and Other Writings by Montgomery Schuyler,* ed. William H. Jordy and Ralph Coe (Cambridge, MA: Belknap Press of Harvard University Press, 1961), 1:1–89, and Edward R. Smith, "Montgomery Schuyler and the History of American Architecture," *Architectural Record* 36 (September 1914): 364–66.

FISKE KIMBALL AND HIS CONTEMPORARIES

LAUREN WEISS BRICKER

Fiske Kimball was preeminent among the writers who forged the new profession of American architectural history. Other figures contributing to the growing literature on historic and contemporary architecture included Talbot F. Hamlin, Lewis Mumford, Norman Isham, and Thomas Tallmadge; however, Kimball was distinct in his ambition to create a methodology for the analysis of American architecture and decorative arts, fields he thought lacked precision. In several publications, Kimball advocated for the use of written and graphic documentation to identify and interpret the historic object. Along with documentation, he promoted the use of physical evidence as part of the process to date and authenticate the object, and he situated the work within a historic context to better understand its significance. His methodology was transformative, but the seventeenth- and eighteenth-century works he analyzed (and, by implication, those he valued) were exclusively created by European émigrés to America. This bias, which he shared with other contemporary writers to a greater or lesser extent, is currently the subject of considerable scrutiny in an effort to create a more inclusive understanding of American architecture. Kimball also produced influential architectural criticism that tended to explore a particular view of contemporary American architecture; his thesis synthesized his view of America's contribution to the history of architecture with then-current theories of art and design. The role of this essay is to create a context for a fuller understanding of Kimball's scholarly intentions, his critical analysis of architecture of his own time, and how his writing compares with the work of one of his contemporaries, Talbot F. Hamlin.

Early Scholarship

In 1916, a year after earning his PhD, Kimball wrote "The History and Monuments of Our National Art" for *Art & Archaeology*, a publication of the Archaeological Institute of America. In the article, Kimball characterized the historical practices of his predecessors as "relatively desultory and unsystematic," led by individuals "inexperienced in historical and technical matters." These predecessors were either architects "preoccupied with artistic appreciation, rather than with authentic information respecting origins or development," or local historians "preoccupied with historic associations, rather than with the form and the artistic consequences."[1] Kimball believed that historians must reform the "ways we document buildings before the nation suffers any more losses of historic works." Following the European model, Kimball saw that government could play an essential role in establishing research standards and publishing results, but he also recognized that unlike those in European nations, government agencies in the United States might be reticent to lead such efforts and that private organizations were more likely to assume that role.

Kimball believed the Archaeological Institute of America was the organization best equipped to conduct the research. Having applied a scientific approach to the study of prehistoric antiquities in America, the organization was expanding the scope of its activities by this time to include the creation of a Committee on Colonial and National Art, which Kimball led from 1916 through 1927. Kimball remained on the editorial board of *Art & Archaeology* until 1922.[2]

Kimball's Evolving Art-Historical Approach
to Historic Architecture

In the article appearing in *Art & Archaeology*, Kimball alluded to his knowledge of troves of architectural drawings and documents, most of them largely waiting to be explored by future scholars. Archival records were essential to Kimball's historical method, and one would expect him to advocate for their retention and accessibility to scholars and preservationists. Paramount among them were the Jefferson papers housed in the Massachusetts Historical Society. In citing this and other collections, Kimball observed that the buildings they documented might have been better preserved had their attribution been known, substantiated by available original construction documents. In reference to the Jefferson papers, Kimball suggested that the significant changes to Jefferson's Capitol in Richmond, Virginia, and the library at the University of

Virginia might have retained a higher level of historic integrity had the draw-ings been available.[3]

Kimball's appreciation for the importance of original documents synthesized several factors that can be traced to his formal education at Harvard College and University (BA, 1909; MArch, 1912). His generation experienced a rift with the architectural scholars who preceded them. In Kimball's unpublished memoir, he discussed the tensions that existed between the "old-guard" architectural his-torians at Harvard University, largely followers of British art and architectural critic John Ruskin and of William Morris, founder of the Arts and Crafts Move-ment, and those who espoused alternative interpretations of art and architecture. Members of the old guard included Charles Herbert Moore, Professor of the History of Fine Arts; his predecessor, Charles Eliot Norton; and Herbert Lang-ford Warren, who taught architectural history.[4] Despite philosophical differences Kimball may have had with Warren, he was deeply indebted to his history classes, which played such a dominant role within the architecture school's curriculum that its graduates "often tended to graduate into teaching, writing, and editing rather than practice."[5] Kimball had worked closely with Warren, and following the latter's death, Kimball was asked to edit Warren's unfinished manuscript and prepare illustrations for the first volume of a projected history of architecture. The published work, *The Foundations of Classic Architecture*, appeared in 1919.[6]

For Kimball and other members of his generation, the late Gothic Revival espoused by Harvard's old guard must have seemed out of step with the transfor-mational impact the French École des Beaux-Arts was having on American ar-chitectural education and practice. At MIT, William Robert Ware introduced an Americanized version of the École curriculum (1865), which he later modified for Columbia University's architectural program (1881).[7] Kimball and his con-temporaries could readily observe the impact of Beaux-Arts classicism on Amer-ican cities through the City Beautiful Movement and the influential buildings designed by American alumni of the École, including Charles Follen McKim. Harvard was slow to hire a graduate of the École as a permanent faculty mem-ber. For a period, MIT's Constant-Désiré Despradelle, a Beaux-Arts alumnus, conducted advanced design courses for Harvard students. Finally, Harvard hired E. J. A. Duquesne, a Prix de Rome recipient, in 1910, just as Kimball started his master's degree.

Outside the old guard, innovative views on art and architecture were ex-pressed by George Santayana, Professor of Philosophy, and design theorist Den-man Waldo Ross. Architecture students were required to take Santayana's courses on the philosophy of fine arts and aesthetics. He employed a "psychological" method to investigate the "origin and conditions of [aesthetic judgments]." His volume *The Sense of Beauty* (1896) was a compilation of lectures from his aesthetics course (1892–94). Ross was hired by the architecture department and later moved to the fine arts department. He was the author of *A Theory of Pure Design* (1907); his design theory class focused on basic abstract principles intended to develop a sense of beauty and the power of imagination.[8] Ross was an avid collector of Asian and Middle Eastern artifacts, which he kept on display in Robinson Hall, home of the architecture program, and later in the Fogg Art Museum.

As mentioned above, Kimball gravitated toward the notion of pure form. However, this was to evolve over the next decade, as Kimball was influenced by the writing of British art historian Roger Fry.[9] Concepts found in art history were more compelling to Kimball than were contemporary theories of architecture, and consequently they found expression as Kimball defined American modernism in his criticism of the 1920s. He began to formulate a theoretical basis for evaluating architecture. One can see its formulation as early as 1914 in a book review of Alfred Hoyt Granger's *Charles Follen McKim: A Study of His Life and Work*. There Kimball highlights the classical standards of beauty conveyed through the "purity and assonance of his architectural language, the delicate beauty of proportion and of line, the music of *forms*," adding, "McKim was the first of our time."[10]

Despite Kimball's growing confidence in his ability to critically assess the work of other architects and writers, he harbored doubts about his own abilities as a designer. In his memoir, Kimball recalled finding it challenging to learn how to see in "abstract spatial and plastic terms."[11] Fortunately, Harvard's stimulating intellectual environment buoyed Kimball while he was pursuing his master's degree. During that period, he roomed with graduate students in the history department who introduced him to Charles-Victor Langlois and Charles Seignobos's *Introduction to the Study of History* (1898).[12] So profound was the book's impact on Kimball that he noted in his memoir, "all my intellectual instincts and ambitions were sharpened and stimulated. It was in this indirect way that Harvard University did the most for me for which I can never be sufficiently grateful."[13] The central thesis of Langlois and Seignobos's volume was that there is no substitute for documentation in historical research—"no documents, no history."[14] The authors proposed a historical method dependent on primary sources.

Kimball completed his degree in 1912 and was hired to teach during the 1911–12 academic year at the University of Illinois, Urbana-Champaign, where he met and soon married Marie Goebel. The following year, Kimball took a position at the University of Michigan. Concurrent with his teaching, Kimball was invited by his former professor George Chase to writer a volume for the Harper's Fine Arts Series titled *A History of Architecture.* Kimball worked on the textbook for the next six years (bringing in a Harvard colleague, George H. Edgell, to write the chapters on medieval architecture), and it was published in 1918.[15] As soon as Kimball received the invitation to write the volume, he immediately began to collect material for his manuscript. The process made him acutely aware of what resources were, and were not, available to scholars.

Notably, Kimball planned to cover American architecture, which was minimally treated in contemporary architecture textbooks. By utilizing an architectural survey format, the book enabled Kimball to situate American architecture within a global context. In contrast, other comparable volumes of the time diminished the place of American architecture (see the discussion of A. D. F. Hamlin's *A Text-Book of Architecture* below) on the world stage or ignored it altogether.[16] Within American scholarship, there was also little consensus about the contributions of Thomas Jefferson. Although the third US president is now widely regarded as an architect, in the early twentieth century, publications attributing works to Jefferson limited them to Monticello and the University of Virginia, with no acknowledgment that he was the architect of the Virginia Capitol until Kimball's *Thomas Jefferson, Architect* (1916) was published.[17] By the time he wrote the American architecture chapter, Kimball was immersed in research on Thomas Jefferson as an architect. He credited Marie with introducing him to the topic.

While working on the survey book, Kimball learned about the existence of the Thomas Jefferson Coolidge Collection of Jefferson Papers housed at the Massachusetts Historical Society. The collection contained most of Jefferson's architectural drawings. Here was an opportunity for Kimball to employ Langlois and Seignobos's document-based research methodology. Through his study of the drawings, Kimball was able to attribute the Virginia Capitol conclusively to Jefferson. Additionally, he argued, the drawings verified that Jefferson's Virginia Capitol predated other contemporary neoclassical works found in Europe. The Capitol, which was based on the Maison Carrée constructed during the Roman Republic, allowed Kimball to reinforce Jefferson's intention to create a building whose form embodied the democratic ambitions of the new nation. So compelling was the history of the Virginia Capitol that Kimball wrote his dissertation on the building (PhD University of Michigan, 1915), published in full in the *Journal of the American Institute of Architects* the same year.[18]

At this time, Kimball also learned of other collections that were relevant to the nation's architectural development during the Federal period, ca. 1776–1825. With the support of George Chase and Denman Ross, Kimball successfully applied for the first Sachs Fellowship in the Fine Arts offered by Harvard.[19] The fellowship provided a one-year stipend to support new research in the fine arts. Kimball concentrated his work in archives located along the Atlantic seaboard. The development of Washington, DC, and its architects (e.g., Charles Bulfinch, Benjamin Henry Latrobe, Samuel McIntire, Robert Mills, William Thornton, James Hoban) were a particular focus for him. The newly gathered information provided the basis of Kimball's discussion of the "national period" in the book, which he also published as a three-part article, "The Development of American Architecture," in *Architectural Forum* (1918). By the time the book was in print, the third installment of the article had appeared in the July 1918 issue.[20] Kimball used his discoveries as the basis of other articles, covering works by Benjamin Henry Latrobe and Jefferson's role in the design development of the White House, and research that Kimball later incorporated into his volume on Samuel McIntire (1940).[21] In each case, Kimball focused on "discoveries" that became the basis of the attribution of works to specific architects and builders. Through this process, he was evolving a history of the early architectural profession in America.

The first section of Kimball's discussion of American architecture in *A History of Architecture* (1928)[22] focused on the "Colonial" period. It was organized chronologically, with specific discussion of architectural types that embodied the goals of the colonizing European nations: Spanish (including reference to Mesoamerican architecture in Mexico), French, and, most extensively, British. While his analysis provided a structure for the future study of early American architecture, there is little acknowledgment of the presence, much less contribution, of Native American people residing on the colonized lands. Emphasis is placed on the formal characteristics of buildings, with particular focus on public buildings, houses of prominent citizens, and works of known builders, where possible.

Following the discussion of the Federal or National Period, Kimball presented architecture associated with the periods stretching from the Civil War to his own time. These he captured under the subheadings of "Eclecticism" through "Modernist Forms" and "Later Developments," his reference to contemporary works by Frank Lloyd Wright. In spite of the range of works produced during this period, Kimball maintained the view that the authority of the "unparalleled heritage of classical monuments from the formative period of the nation . . . and the founders of the republic . . . achieved their aim of establishing classical architecture as a permanent national style."[23] Kimball observed that several factors coalesced in the design vocabulary of American architects during the latter third of the nineteenth century. These included an interest in the American Colonial Revival, emerging in the wake of the Centennial, and a predisposition toward classicism on the part of architects returning from the École, many of whom sought to apply the lessons from the Italian Renaissance, and more contemporary works designed by École alumni, such as Henri Labrouste's Bibliothèque Sainte Geneviève (Paris, 1851). This synthesis was notable in McKim, Mead and White's Boston Public Library (Boston, 1888), for example, as well as ensembles including their campus plan of Columbia University (New York City, ca. 1895).

Attention to form colors Kimball's treatment of twentieth-century architecture. In sections labeled "Functionalism" and "Expression of Structure," Kimball acknowledged a debt to nineteenth-century "structural purism" and the lessons of John Ruskin and Eugène Viollet-le-Duc. However, he credits "a steady development of logical planning and expression of plan [to] the leadership of the Beaux-Arts men."[24] Unlike early advocates of the structural determinism inherent in the skyscraper, structural expression is less interesting to Kimball than the aesthetic possibilities of masonry cladding, whether as fire protection, as was the case for Cass Gilbert's Woolworth Building (New York City, 1913), or for aesthetic purposes in Louis Sullivan's exploration of terra cotta cladding as a strategy to emphasize a building's height and provide organic ornament, as in the Wainwright Building (St. Louis, 1891) and the Guaranty (Prudential) Building (Buffalo, 1896). Kimball includes a discussion of several buildings by Frank Lloyd Wright, whose form embodied a set of emotional or spiritual factors. He saw the midwestern houses as echoing the "lakes and the plains" of their immediate landscape, Midway Gardens in Chicago as embodying the "spirit of gaiety in forms of exuberant yet delicate fantasy," and Unity Temple in Oak Park as "a monumental and characteristic house of worship for disciples of modern rationalism."[25] In each case, Kimball focuses on the formal qualities of a building to capture their emotional meaning and aesthetic appeal.

Kimball concludes the book chapter with an open-ended question: Will the neoclassicism that has been a long-held tendency in American architecture prevail into the future, or will the "international forces of functionalism . . . ultimately cause a wider adoption of modernist forms"?[26] In 1918, as World War I concluded, the future of architecture may have seemed murky to Kimball. "Modernism," as Kimball applied the term in his "Modern Architecture" chapter, was a label he used to cover the period from the mid-1700s to the early 1900s rather than representing a current movement. He used the term as he had applied "Post-Renaissance"—associating it with a particular time rather than narrowing it to a specific style or movement. Within the "Modern Architecture" chapter, he used the term "Functionalism" to encompass the Vienna Secession and Peter

Behrens's AEG Turbine Factory in Berlin, where the aesthetic of industrialization suggests new directions that were to emerge during the next few years.

The only connection he made between European developments and those in the United States was in the section titled "Development of Modernist Forms," where he suggests that the Arts and Crafts Movement and the Art Nouveau of Belgium pollinated the work of Louis Sullivan. Henry Hobson Richardson's architecture was credited as an influence on English architect C. Harrison Townsend, as in Bishopsgate Institute (London, 1893–94).

Throughout *A History of Architecture*, Kimball's repeated reference to formalism may suggest that a building's aesthetic value, independent of other criteria, was his primary basis of evaluation. However, as the Harper's Fine Arts Series editor George Chase noted in his introduction to the volume, the authors sought to include factors associated with "spiritual influences and spontaneous creation in the formation of styles" to explain architectural development.[27] They also wanted to distinguish their interpretation of architecture from a dependence on "structural necessity," which had been the predisposition of many nineteenth-century writers. Chase asserted that the book's authors sought to debunk the biological analogy employed in earlier histories to explain the evolution of particular styles. With respect to periodization, the authors specifically noted their application of a more restrictive use of "Renaissance architecture," ending it ca. 1550–1600. Rather than apply "Baroque" to the period that followed, they chose the neutral "post-Renaissance."

Kimball and Edgell's *History of Architecture* was well received—most notably for the objectivity it brought to the topic. Above all, the reviewer praised the absence of "religious and patriotic prejudices, heretofore so frequent . . . [with] the subject discussed with scientific precision and freedom from emotional bias."[28] Chase's introduction indicated that the authors in the series sought to avoid biases found in earlier histories that defended a "particular system of aesthetics or glorify a phase of artistic development, often associated with a country." In contrast, Kimball and Edgell sought to achieve an objectivity in their presentation of information. Chase also noted that the chapter on American architecture was longer than had been typical of other surveys of architecture because the authors believed it merited fuller treatment than it usually received.

A *History of Architecture* in Context

Implicit in Chase's explanation of notable features of Kimball and Edgell's *History of Architecture* was a critique of the genre of the single-volume architectural survey. Foremost among the book's predecessors was Alfred Dwight Hamlin's

A Text-Book of the History of Architecture (1896, with numerous editions and re-prints), which was the leading American architectural textbook at the time their volume was published.[29] When Hamlin's volume was first published, and again when its final edition appeared, critics lauded his ability to condense a massive amount of material into a portable volume—one helpful to the college student or the world traveler.

Some of the shortcomings of Hamlin's volume were due to information limi-tations at the time specific editions were published. However, there are several weaknesses that can only be attributed to the author's predilections. In Hamlin's introduction, he explained the evolution of a civilization and its architecture by applying the biological theory of history still popular at the time. In his view, each undergoes "successive developments until it either reaches perfection or its possibilities are exhausted, after which a period of decline usually sets in. This is followed either by a reaction and the introduction of some radically new principle leading to the evolution of a new style, or by the final decay and extinc-tion of the civilization and its replacement by some younger and more virile ele-ment."[30] By comparison, Kimball and Edgell open with a chapter titled "Elements of Architecture," standard material still covered in the first year of an architec-ture program. This is then followed by historically based chapters, beginning with "Prehistoric Architecture," where known documentation is the basis for the analysis of architectural form.

Hamlin devotes a brief chapter to US architecture. In contrast with Kimball, who begins his chapter with a discussion of Mesoamerican civilizations, Hamlin suggests that the world the Europeans encountered was "virgin soil, destitute of cultivation, government, or civilized inhabitants."[31] The gap between their out-looks narrows as Hamlin prioritizes the architecture of the English colonists over any other developments during the colonial period. Likewise, classicism figures prominently in Hamlin's review of the early republican period. Among the works he discusses is Jefferson's design for the University of Virginia, and he includes a recent fire in the library. His discussion of the period lacks the vitality of Kimball's chapter, in which Kimball brings forth recent discoveries from his own research. By far the most interesting section in Hamlin is labeled "The Artistic Awaken-ing." As was true for Kimball, this concluding section focuses on architecture of his own time; for Hamlin, as a member of the generation preceding Kimball's, the clock started in the 1870s. A onetime student in Paris and an associate of Rob-ert Ware's when he introduced a Beaux-Arts curriculum at Columbia University, Hamlin brings a personal perspective to Richardson's work and to the impact of the École on American architectural education. The evolving architectural scene included the early skyscrapers of Chicago and New York through the turn of the twentieth century. Hamlin and Kimball shared many views: they both appreciated the impact of the École on American architecture and urbanism and admired the high-rises of Louis Sullivan (and they reserved judgment on his contemporaries' skyscrapers). No significant additions were made to the American architecture chapter in the 1909 edition of Hamlin's volume—the last one that the author updated. The volume was so lacking in its presentation of current architecture that Hamlin's son, Talbot F. Hamlin, who took charge of preparing the book's 1928 edition after his father was killed by an automobile in 1926, prepared a new chapter titled "Contemporary Architecture."

Talbot Hamlin's Emergent Scholarship, with a Debt to Kimball

Kimball's publications dating through the 1920s laid the foundation for subsequent research and writing on early American architecture by other historians and architects writing architectural histories. This was particularly true of Kimball's *Domestic Architecture of the American Colonies and the Early Republic* (1922), which was based on a lecture series he presented at the Metropolitan Museum of Art. Other notable contemporary works of the 1920s include Lewis Mumford's *Sticks and Stones* (1924) and Thomas Tallmadge's *Story of American Architecture* (1927). In the twenties, too, Talbot Hamlin began to focus his literary production in the area of historic American and contemporary architectural criticism. By the 1930s, he had become one of the leading exponents of architectural criticism, and he also added an expertise in architectural archives.

As noted above, Talbot Faulkner Hamlin was the son of A. D. F. Hamlin. He was educated as an architect (BArch Columbia, 1914). By the 1920s, he was a partner in the New York architecture firm Murphy, McGill and Hamlin, and he became an instructor in the Extension Program of the Columbia University School of Architecture in 1925. He was the author of two books—*The Enjoyment of Architecture* (1916) and *The American Spirit in Architecture* (1926).[32] Additionally, he had contributed the "Architecture" entry in *The New International Yearbook* since 1925, relevant preparation for the new chapter he added to *A Text-Book of the History of Architecture* (1928).

In 1924, Hamlin was engaged to write *The American Spirit in Architecture*, one in the fifteen-volume pictorial history series titled The Pageant of America published by Yale University Press and edited by Yale professor of history Ralph H. Gabriel.[33] Hamlin's volume presented the nation's architecture and urbanism, casting architecture as a phenomenon of America's cultural history. Gabriel's introduction and Hamlin's subsequent chapters placed more emphasis on the people and communities served by the buildings than was typical of other histories at the time, including Kimball's.

Yale University Press, perhaps more than any other entity, sought ways to accurately visualize America's architectural and cultural history. One of the most fascinating iterations of this effort was a project led by Yale's publisher, George Parmly Day, who engaged the Chronicles of America Picture Corporation around 1921 to produce "educational photoplays" based on material from Yale's Chronicles of America series. Members of Yale's history and education departments were responsible for the historical accuracy of the films. Kimball was an "advisor of the Colonial sets" in 1923–24. He reproduced a scene from "The Puritans" depicting a wigwam in his *American Architecture* (1928) volume. The series enjoyed popular success; one reviewer saw the venture as a means "to replace more or less obsolete myths and prejudices by modern and more genuine history in the minds of as general a public as possible—a Yalesian form of university extension."[34]

Hamlin's volume likewise offered history in a publicly accessible fashion. The subject matter was presented through graphic images contemporary (for the most part) with the historic architecture being presented. Each chapter opened with a brief introductory text followed by a rich selection of images, including engravings, architectural drawings of the works discussed, and photographs when the works were extant or of recent construction. Approximately half of the book was devoted to historic periods prior to 1900; these were organized by developments in northern and southern states and, to a lesser extent, those in the Midwest and West/Southwest. The second half of the book focused on buildings constructed since 1900, organized by type and urban patterns. A fundamental debt to Kimball's scholarship was expressed in Hamlin's inclusion of reproductions of original architectural drawings as primary documentation for historic architecture. Recent works were largely depicted through photographs.

Critical assessment of Hamlin's volume, and the series as a whole, was favorable. It was noted that its graphic format could "make the country's past more visually present, more actual to the mind by the help of the eye, than unimaginative reading can do."[35] This statement may reflect Yale's desire to create a readily accessible history of America appealing to a broad swath of Americans, including newly arrived immigrants from southern and eastern Europe, many unable to speak English. Additionally, the 1920s was a period of considerable unrest and fear of anarchy, factors that fueled more benign strategies like Yale's—or even the creation of the American Wing at the Metropolitan Museum (1924)—to visualize

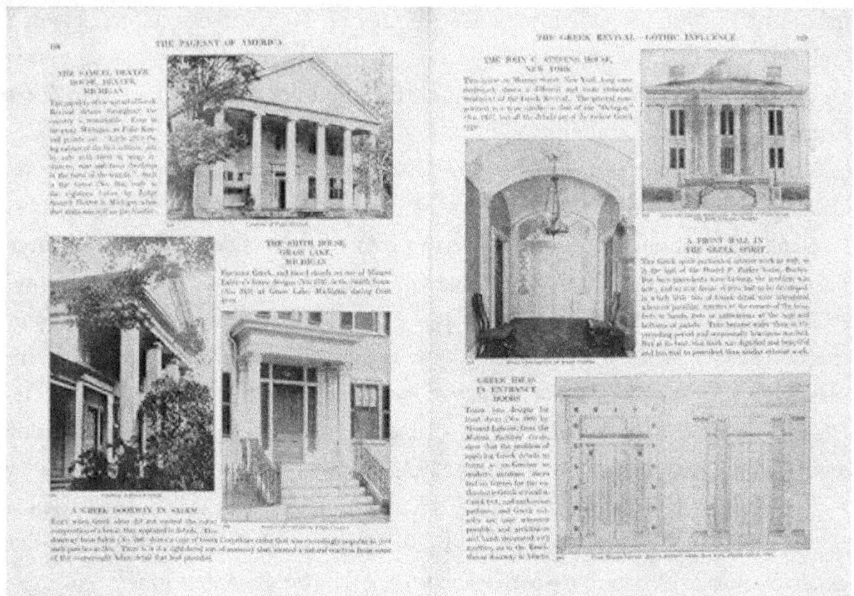

FIGURE 1. A spread from Talbot Hamlin's chapter "The Greek Revival—Gothic Influence" in *The American Spirit in Architecture* (1926, pp. 128–29) for The Pageant of America.

and affirm American values.[36] Hamlin's volume and other contemporary histories on American architecture had the capacity to stimulate new construction based on historic precedent. *The American Architect* (March 1920) reported on the construction of a seminary, for a largely "foreign priesthood," consisting of buildings based on "our early Colonial style and largely replicas of buildings that have empathetic historic interest . . . it will imbue a veneration for our historical traditions and result in the development of better ideas of citizenship."[37]

In the 1930s, Hamlin began to pursue in-depth research on historic American architecture. His primary areas of investigation were the Greek Revival and the architecture of Benjamin Henry Latrobe, resulting in major monographs, numerous scholarly articles, and invited lectures. In his preface to *Greek Revival Architecture in America: Being an Account of the Important Trends in American Architecture and American Life Prior to the War Between the States* (1944), Hamlin expressed his gratitude to Kimball's "brilliant pioneering in American architectural history [which] first aroused my interest in it and [on] whose works I have leaned heavily."[38] Hamlin built on Kimball's notion that America was best positioned to find its own architectural language from the societies that created democracy—Greece and Rome, rather than the monarchical governments of its seventeenth- and eighteenth-century colonizers. With the benefit of Kimball's and other pioneering studies, Hamlin expanded the topic into a national study, identifying key works and their architects or builders in every corner of the continental United States. Through the use of pattern books and periodicals, design concepts—especially during the primacy of the Greek Revival—were adapted to natural and cultural conditions found across the continental United States.

Hamlin's biography *Benjamin Henry Latrobe* was a natural outgrowth of his work on the Greek Revival.[39] As both a well-researched and highly readable biography, it was honored with the 1956 Pulitzer Prize for Biography. It shared with the author's volume on the Greek Revival a breadth of vision that expanded beyond the East Coast. In contrast with other major American architects' Eurocentric views, Hamlin considered the impact that the new nation had on the professionally trained European émigré who was Americanized by the architectural and engineering opportunities offered by the new nation.

As was true of the Greek Revival, Kimball pioneered the study of Latrobe's architecture with the discovery of drawings for the demolished Bank of Pennsylvania. Through careful analysis of the drawings housed in the Maryland Historical Society, Kimball identified the bank as the first Greek Revival work in America and as a model of a building typology—the American banking temple. Hamlin expanded on that history when he was given access to Latrobe's letter books, journals, sketchbooks, and drawings. While Kimball recognized Latrobe's technical ingenuity, it was left to Hamlin and later researchers to assess the range of Latrobe's talents as an architect and an engineer of waterworks of all types in Philadelphia and New Orleans.

Hamlin as Avery Librarian and Archivist of Architectural Drawings

The crushing economic impact of the Depression forced Hamlin to abandon his architectural practice and teach in Columbia University's architecture program, and in 1934 he was appointed Avery Librarian. In his new role, Hamlin made significant contributions that led the Avery to become America's preeminent architectural library.

Hamlin's role as librarian was pivotal to curricular changes instituted by Dean Joseph Hudnut. Hudnut believed that the architect of the future must be prepared for the "immediate and exigent desire to improve the environment and the human race . . . [and] to be able to take a much wider advantage of scientific progress, of technical invention and production."[40] Hudnut saw that history taught students about problem-solving processes and results achieved by great architects. With this goal in mind, as well as his knowledge that architectural drawings had played a fundamental role in Kimball's scholarship, Hamlin initiated what grew into one of the nation's most significant repositories of architectural drawings.

Hamlin was careful to distinguish his motivation to collect drawings from the precedent of Columbia's Beaux-Arts heritage: "Knowledge of work done by others both today and in the past is a necessity for the well-educated architect. Yet background knowledge, which helps the designer's critical sense, is very different from the parrot acquaintance with originals to be imitated. . . . [The librarian] must do everything to stimulate creative knowledge . . . [and] do much to discourage 'cribbing.'"[41] He began by collecting "early architectural drawings," which, he told a colleague, was one of his hobbies.[42] His initial acquisitions were works by late nineteenth- and early twentieth-century New York practitioners—Leopold Eidlitz (1823–1908), Cyrus Eidlitz (1853–1921), and perhaps of greatest national significance, Stanford White (1853–1906). By 1938, Hamlin had begun to collect works by twentieth-century practitioners, a focus he shared with the newly appointed Dean Leopold Arnaud. Among the luminaries whose work he collected were Raymond Hood, Lescaze and Howe, Cass Gilbert, Albert Kahn, and Bertram Grosvenor Goodhue.[43] Because his motivation was to demonstrate to students the development of a project, he requested that the donors include sketches, presentation drawings, and working drawings. We have no written record that Hamlin and Kimball discussed the nascent Avery Drawings Collection that Hamlin created. However, one can assume that Kimball approved of Hamlin's plan, since it had the capacity to preserve in perpetuity the drawings of important projects by major architects.

Kimball: An Obligatory Architectural Critic

One never loses sight of Kimball's historical lens when reading his architectural criticism. His passion was architectural history. His early historical writing—most notably *A History of Architecture*—demonstrated an ability to effectively assess works of his own time. Yet while writing that book, when seeking a definition for American architecture both historic and contemporary, Kimball looked to the classical roots established by Thomas Jefferson and his contemporaries. As he traced developments from the late eighteenth century to the work of McKim, Mead and White and other members of the latter's generation, his conception of formalism suggested a familiarity with the concept of form as "visual music," terminology used by art historian Roger Fry.[44]

By the 1920s, the world of art and art history became as much a part of Kimball's professional world as architecture. It was during this decade that he was appointed the Samuel F. B. Morse Professor of the Literature of the Arts of Design at New York University (1923), where Kimball developed a program encompassing studio art, art and architectural history, and interior design.[45] Art history and the exhibition and collection of great works of art became the central focus of Kimball's professional activities beginning in 1928, with his appointment as Director of the new Pennsylvania Museum (now Philadelphia Museum of Art).

Undoubtedly, these professional associations inspired Kimball to align America's "contemporary classic school" with the world of painting and sculpture. Rather than strictly focusing on the Jeffersonian origins of the movement, Kimball now explained the work of Charles Follen McKim, Stanford White, Charles Platt, and John Russell Pope as based on "an underlying affinity, real though not obvious, with the progressive work of modern painting and the other arts."[46]

Fry saw the paintings of Paul Cézanne and other Post-Impressionists as moving away from the emotional associations of romanticism. Instead, they record "a positive and disinterestedly passionate state of mind. [They communicate] a new and otherwise unattainable experience."[47] This he characterizes as a "classic spirit." In architectural terms, Kimball finds the "classic spirit" in "periods of renewed interest in unity and purity of form," creating "a universal language, of elementary geometrical simplicity. It is in this sense that we must interpret the new revival of the classic which has decidedly gained the upper hand in American architecture during the last generation."[48] Kimball concludes that "in their apparent classicism, the architects are really marching side by side with the modernists in sculpture and painting—alike votaries of a new worship of abstract beauty of form."[49]

Kimball had a personal affection and deep appreciation for the work of Frank Lloyd Wright; he was proud to have included works by Wright as early as 1918 in his *History of Architecture*. In the spring of 1932, the Pennsylvania Museum was the second venue for the exhibition *Modern Architecture: International Exhibition* (later referred to as the International Style) curated by the Museum of Modern Art in New York. Kimball wrote an article on the exhibition for the *Pennsylvania Museum Bulletin* (April 1932), which was largely about Frank Lloyd Wright, whose stature in the exhibition was relegated to an essential precursor to the international movement. Kimball considered Wright to be an "artist of individual creative genius" whom he saw as a "romantic individual, a poet, who knows that crude functional elements must be fused by imagination and emotion into vital and changing artistic forms; the 'Internationalists' still believing that a purely rational analysis may produce an abiding identity of style."[50] Despite the debt that two of the leaders of the international movement—Walter Gropius and Le Corbusier—acknowledged they owed to Wright, Kimball saw their architectural value as dependent on resolving functional needs and their adept use of machine-made products with little consideration of the resulting form.

While Kimball was critical of the Internationalists' design process, it is significant that the one section of the exhibition that he lauded was the presentation of design solutions to address housing conditions. He admired the "ingenuity and ability shown in dealing with the legacy of overcrowding and human waste." Though Kimball does not mention this in his article, the housing section of the catalogue accompanying the exhibition was the only section not written by co-curators Philip Johnson and Henry-Russell Hitchcock; its author was Lewis Mumford. When Johnson and Hitchcock repackaged the exhibition as *The International Style: Architecture Since 1922* (1932), they omitted Mumford's section on housing, and the social agenda of modernism was all but subsumed by the aesthetics of modernism.[51]

Hamlin as a Prominent Architectural Critic of the 1930s and 1940s

By the 1930s, Kimball had limited time to devote to architectural criticism; Hamlin was on the ascent to become one of the leading voices on contemporary design. Beginning in the mid-1920s, Talbot Hamlin devoted considerable time to writing contemporary criticism rather than analyses of historic American architecture. However, by the 1930s, much of his writing focused on contemporary architecture, and he became one of the nation's leading architectural critics; from 1938 to 1942, he was the in-house architectural critic for *Pencil Points / Progressive Architecture.* Much of Hamlin's writing addressed the federal government's unrivaled support for public works and housing. He took a broad view of American architecture, writing about subjects located throughout the country, some of which could rightly be labeled vernacular. His design standards included simplicity of form, inventive use of materials, and response to climate. When these qualities were present, Hamlin believed the resulting work was expressive of American democracy.[52]

Kimball and Hamlin were equally astute in their judgment of good design. However, there were several notable differences. The development of artistic form remained a deciding factor of good design for Kimball, while it was not always the prevailing criterion for Hamlin, as noted in the standards mentioned above. An early example of Hamlin's architectural criticism was a chapter he wrote for the final edition of his father's *A Text-Book of Architecture*. In Hamlin's "Contemporary Architecture" chapter, one senses a reticence to accept the dominance of European modernism, analogous to Kimball's assessment of the '32 exhibition. Hamlin was critical of the "theoretical, inevitable beauty of efficient machinery" that led to the "uncompromising cubical forms" of Le Corbusier, whose work he described as "largely design of the mind and not of the heart."[53] He noted that Le Corbusier's influence was evident in German housing estates, their planning based on both practical and aesthetic goals. On a positive note, he credited Germany with having the "most beautiful factories in the world," owing to its architects' ability to design industrial buildings expressive of their functional requirements.

In the early 1930s, Hamlin was philosophically opposed to expressing a single ideological view on contemporary European architecture. This put him at odds with a number of contemporary critics, some of whom had a fervent commitment to modernism and roundly voiced their disapproval. Hamlin's views about modern architecture evolved, and he became a stronger advocate for the movement as he recognized its potential to respond to human needs caused by the harsh realities of the Great Depression As the decade progressed, Hamlin found himself in the company of other advocates for modern architecture who recognized that its vocabulary had broadened to include materials native to specific regions as well as cultural references. When one compares Hamlin's architectural criticism with Kimball's, it is apparent they were not always in total accord. However, the two men were among the core group of authorities on American architecture whose depth of knowledge of its past greatly enriched their interpretation of contemporary works.

Conclusion

Looking back on the highly productive and successful careers of Fiske Kimball and Talbot Hamlin as well as their contemporaries Lewis Mumford and Thomas Tallmadge, one attribute they shared was their commitment to writing for the American public. While it may be difficult to assert that they were populists, they clearly sought to advance knowledge of the nation's architectural heritage.

Kimball balanced his scholarly pursuits with his applied research (we might call it public history today), his preservation efforts, and the creation of new educational and cultural institutions. Talbot Hamlin was inspired by Kimball's research; he also engaged in preservation efforts that included the foresight to collect historic and contemporary architectural drawings for posterity. Additionally, his instincts prompted him to broaden the study of specific styles, such as the Greek Revival, nationwide and also focus on topics such as public housing. For both Kimball and Hamlin, engagement with architecture mattered.

Notes

1. Fiske Kimball, "The History and Monuments of Our National Art," *Art & Archaeology* 4, no. 3 (1916): 163. The article grew out of a lecture he had delivered at the annual meeting of the Archaeological Institute of America in December 1915.

2. The committee members were William Sumner Appleton, Secretary of the Society for the Preservation of New England Antiquities; Glenn Brown, American Institute of Architects; George H. Chase, Harvard University; Allan Marquand, Princeton University; Charles Moore, President of the National Commission of Fine Arts; and F. W. Shipley, ex officio as President of the Archaeological Institute of America.

3. Kimball, "History and Monuments," 161.

4. Fiske Kimball, "Architecture at the Turn of the Century," revised from "An Architectural Guinea Pig" (unpublished manuscript), Fiske Kimball Papers, Philadelphia Museum of Art Library and Archives (hereafter FKP), box 159, folder 4.

5. Kimball, "Architecture at the Turn of the Century."

6. Herbert Langford Warren, *The Foundations of Classic Architecture*, ed. and intro. Fiske Kimball (New York: Macmillan, 1919).

7. See J. A. Chewning, "William Robert Ware at MIT and Columbia," *Journal of Architectural Education* 33, no. 2 (1979): 25–29.

8. See Marie Frank, *Denman Ross and American Design Theory* (Hanover, NH: University Press of New England, 2011).

9. I am indebted to David Brownlee for his reference to Fry's writing as influential on Kimball's criticism. See David B. Brownlee, *Building the City Beautiful: The Benjamin Franklin Parkway and the Philadelphia Museum of Art*, exh. cat. (Philadelphia: Philadelphia Museum of Art, 1989), 7.

10. Sidney Fiske Kimball, "A Great American Architect," *The Dial* 56, no. 669 (1914): 385.

11. Kimball, "Architecture at the Turn of the Century."

12. Charles-Victor Langlois and Charles Seignobos, *Introduction to the Study of History*, trans. G. G. Berry (London: Duckworth; New York: Henry Holt, 1898).

13. Fiske Kimball, "Harvard in Transition," FKP, box 159, folder 3.

14. Langlois and Seignobos, *Introduction to the Study of History*, 17.

15. Fiske Kimball and George Edgell, *A History of Architecture* (New York: Harper & Brothers, 1918).

16. See an extensive review of the history of architectural history texts in *Narrating the Globe: The Emergence of World Histories of Architecture*, ed. Petra Brower, Martin Bressani, and Christopher Armstrong (Cambridge, MA: MIT Press, 2023).

17. See my discussion of literature on Thomas Jefferson's architecture, "The Writings of Fiske Kimball: A Synthesis of Architectural History and Practice," in *The Architectural Historian in America: A Symposium in Celebration of the Fiftieth Anniversary of the Founding of the Society of Architectural Historians*, ed. Elisabeth Blair MacDougall, Studies in the History of Art 35 (Washington, DC: National Gallery of Art, 1990), 216.

18. Fiske Kimball, "Thomas Jefferson and the First Monument of the Classical Revival in America," *Journal of the American Institute of Architects* 3, nos. 9–11 (1915): 371–81, 421–33, 473–91.

19. "Memorandum of Manuscript Material for Research Toward a History of American Architecture Especially the Period 1776–1825," "Modified Plan of Work," and "General Proposal for Work on the Sachs Research Fellowship," FKP, box 2, folder 5, "Harvard University."

20. Fiske Kimball, "The Development of American Architecture," *Architectural Forum* 28, no. 1 (January 1918): 1–5; 28, no. 3 (March 1918): 81–86; and 29, no. 1 (July 1918): 21–25.

21. Fiske Kimball, "The Bank of Pennsylvania, 1799: An Unknown Masterpiece of American Classicism," *Architectural Record* 44, no. 8 (1918): 132–39; Fiske Kimball, "The Genesis of the White House," *The Century* 95, no. 4 (1918): 523–28; Fiske Kimball, "Latrobe's Designs for the Cathedral of Baltimore," *Architectural Record* 42, no. 6 (1917): 54–550, and 43, no. 1 (1918): 37–45; Fiske Kimball, *Mr. Samuel McIntire, Carver: The Architect of Salem* (Portland, ME: Southworth-Anthoensen Press, 1940).

22. Despite the difference of ten years between the first and second editions of *A History of Architecture*, the text for the "American Architecture" chapter remained unchanged. Revisions were limited to birth and death dates of twentieth-century architects and bibliographic additions from the 1920s, including Kimball's *Domestic Architecture of the American Colonies and of the Early Republic* (New York: Charles Scribner's Sons, 1922), which was based on lectures delivered by Kimball in 1920.

23. Kimball and Edgell, *History of Architecture*, 558–59.

24. Kimball and Edgell, *History of Architecture*, 560.

25. Kimball and Edgell, *History of Architecture*, 565.

26. Kimball and Edgell, *History of Architecture*, 565.

27. George Chase, "Editor's Introduction," in Kimball and Edgell, *History of Architecture*, xviii.

28. John Beverley Robinson, review of *A History of Architecture* by Fiske Kimball and George Harold Edgell, *American Historical Review* 23, no. 4 (1918): 839.

29. A. D. F. Hamlin, *A Text-Book of the History of Architecture* (New York: Longmans, Green, 1896). The book had three subsequent editions in 1909, 1922, and 1928, and twenty-two reprintings, the last occurring in 1954. For more extensive discussion of *A Text-Book of the History of Architecture*, see Lauren Weiss Bricker, "Generational Shifts: Talbot Hamlin's Revisions of A. D. F. Hamlin's *A Text-Book of the History of Architecture* (1896)," in Brower, Bressani, and Armstrong, *Narrating the Globe*, 433–52.

30. A. D. F. Hamlin, *Text-Book* (1896), xxii.

31. A. D. F. Hamlin, *Text-Book* (1896), 383.

32. For biographical information on Talbot Faulkner Hamlin, see my "The Contributions of Fiske Kimball and Talbot Faulkner Hamlin to the Study of American Architectural History" (PhD diss., University of California, Santa Barbara, 1992), and Peter S. Kaufman, "American Architectural Writing, Beaux Arts Style: The Lives and Works of Alfred Dwight Foster Hamlin and Talbot Faulkner Hamlin" (PhD diss., Cornell University, 1986).

33. Talbot Faulkner Hamlin, *The American Spirit in Architecture*, The Pageant of America 13 (New Haven, CT: Yale University Press, 1926).

34. Gay Walker, *The Works of Carl P. Rollins* (New Haven, CT: Yale University Press, 1982), 28.

35. "Book Reviews," edited by Harry J. Carman, *Historical Outlook* 17, no. 6 (1926): 297.

36. Jill Lepore, *These Truths: A History of the United States* (New York: W. W. Norton, 2018), 407.

37. "To Insure a Better Americanism," *American Architect* 117, no. 2308 (1920): 340.

38. Talbot Hamlin, *Greek Revival Architecture in America: Being an Account of the Important Trends in American Architecture and American Life Prior to the War Between the States* (New York: Oxford University Press, 1944; repr., New York: Dover, 1964), viii.

39. Talbot Hamlin, *Benjamin Henry Latrobe* (New York: Oxford University Press, 1955).

40. Joseph Hudnut, Address [before the] Annual Dinner of the Alumni Association of the School of Architecture of Columbia University, June 4, 1934.

Excerpted in "Columbia Reorganizes Teaching of Architecture," *Architectural Record* 76, no. 1 (1934), verso of frontispiece.

41. Talbot Hamlin, *Some European Architectural Libraries: Their Methods, Equipment and Administration* (New York: Columbia University Press, 1939), 2.

42. Talbot Faulkner Hamlin to [Mary Ellen Chase], ALS, December 3, 1935, Acquisition Files, Curator of Drawings, Avery Architectural and Fine Arts Library, Columbia University.

43. Acquisition Files, Curator of Drawings, Avery Architectural and Fine Arts Library, Columbia University.

44. See Kimball's review of the McKim volume referenced earlier in this article. Roger Fry, "The French Post-Impressionists," preface to the *Catalogue of the Second Post-Impressionists* (London[?]: Grafton Galleries, 1912), reprinted in *Vision and Design* (New York: Penguin Books, 1961), 196.

45. See Kimball(?), "Fine Arts" (23 April 1924), E. E. Brown Papers, New York University Archives, box 13, folder 6; Course Catalogues (1923–24) in Metropolitan Museum of Art Archives; Kimball's course records, "New York University, Department of Fine Arts, 1923–24," FKP.

46. Fiske Kimball, "What Is Modern Architecture?," *The Nation*, 119, no. 3082 (July 30, 1924): 128.

47. Fry, "French Post-Impressionists," 198.

48. Kimball, "What Is Modern Architecture?," 129.

49. Kimball, "What Is Modern Architecture?," 129.

50. Fiske Kimball, "Modern Architecture: An Exhibition in the Galleries of the Museum, March 30 to April 22," *Pennsylvania Museum Bulletin* 27, no. 148 (1932): 133.

51. *Modern Architecture: International Exhibition,* exh. cat. (New York: Museum of Modern Art, 1932); Henry-Russell Hitchcock and Philip Johnson, *The International Style: Architecture Since 1922* (New York: W. W. Norton, 1932).

52. Talbot Hamlin, "What Makes It American—Architecture in the Southwest and West," *Pencil Points* 20, no. 12 (1939): 762–76.

53. Talbot Hamlin, "Contemporary Architecture," in *A Text-Book of the History of Architecture,* by A. D. F. Hamlin, rev. ed. (New York: Longmans, Green, 1928), 452.

DOMESTIC ARCHITECTURE IN DIAGRAM

Fiske Kimball as Architect-Historian and the Case for Spatial Analysis

DANIELLE S. WILLKENS

Fiske Kimball's *Domestic Architecture of the American Colonies and of the Early Republic* (1922) introduced readers to a new way of seeing and understanding American architecture. His own original plan drawings, executed at the same scale and based on documentary evidence, presented clear, comparative studies that placed the analysis of early American architecture in conversation, graphically, with the published works of Palladio, James Gibbs, and the contemporary American Beaux-Arts. This essay will explore how Kimball composed text and image in *Domestic Architecture* to draw out the experiential qualities of edifices in terms of movement and circulation around a building and through its constructed spaces, orientation, light, and the tactility of materials, from elements of construction to refined decoration. Through these lenses, Kimball initiated an emerging construct that would shape theory and practice in the twentieth century and be one of the most prolific topics in twenty-first-century design education and research: spatial analysis. This concept specifically explores the intersections of architecture and narrative, since the term "space" may be used to assess several aspects of design on the printed page and within the built environment.[1] Kimball used the term "space" to refer to the absence of mass within a constructed interior or urban volume, the means of combining disparate parts, and the sequential order or hierarchy within a design. As evidenced in drawings and design proposals, this type of comparative analysis allowed Kimball to focus on form, arrangement, hierarchy, axes, and sequence instead of positing his arguments for the merit of early American architecture on elements such as style, biographical associations, materials, or decoration.

By combining the study of architectural drawings, extant architectural fabric, and contemporary publications, Kimball's work on the architecture of the Early Republic directly confronts persisting claims among certain circles of architectural historians that early American architects, like Jefferson, simply produced "a collection of visual quotations of the kind amateurs and professionals alike commonly mistake for design."[2] This chapter will evaluate *Domestic Architecture* as an exercise not just in scholarship but also in composition, placing a higher value on visual communication through the enhanced graphic quality of the layout. However, despite the rich graphic program of the book, including drawings, photographs, and period imagery, the publication consciously segregated "primitive" indigenous and vernacular examples from "academic" architectural forms and overlooked the architecture of the enslaved in the Early Republic.[3] With reference to studies of representation and equity in the built environment, this essay will also explore how Kimball selectively edited his drawings and descriptions to erase the designed spatial divisions between races within early American architectural landscapes. Interestingly, however, spatial analysis can also be applied to his restoration projects that aimed to present visitors with a more holistic view of the plantation landscape, as a brief examination of an overlooked and unbuilt project at Monticello at the end of this essay will suggest.

Writing and Drawing

In 1996, the University of Virginia hosted a symposium to celebrate the work of Fiske Kimball, highlighting the impact of Kimball's career at the university and within broader contexts. The exhibit accompanying the symposium showcased content from his scholarship, such as his first working notes on Jefferson's drawings, as well as Kimball's own architectural inventions, such as his drawings for his Charlottesville home, Shack Mountain (a personal ode to Monticello), and the university's Memorial Gymnasium. A vitrine in the exhibit highlighted the cacophony of an architect's desk: drawings and drawing instruments, photographs, notes, and even crumpled drafts completed the tableau. Contrary to the order and isolation of objects one might expect to see within an exhibit, this display placed the work of the architect-historian in motion and demonstrated that for Kimball, the processes of research and creativity were intertwined: the archive and the architect, inextricably linked. His scholarship was connected to his own work as an architect. In this way, even the composition of his research reflected the lens of a designer.

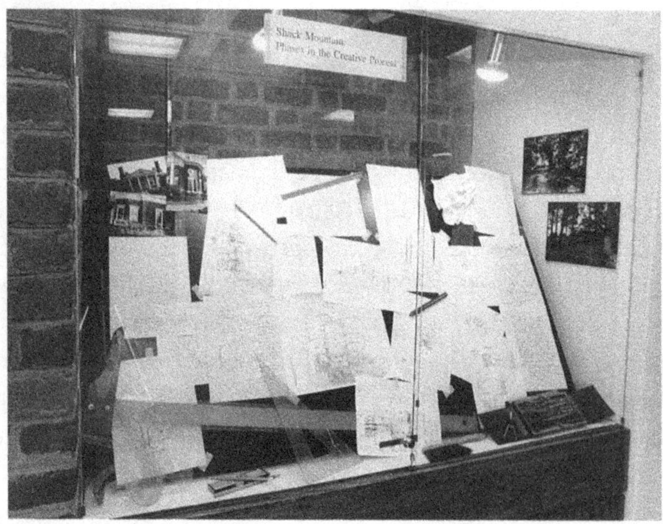

FIGURE 1. Exhibition vitrine for the 1996 symposium on Fiske Kimball, held at the University of Virginia, that featured the architect-historian as a "modern scholar." (Albert and Shirley Small Special Collections Library, University of Virginia, Fiske Kimball Symposium Photographs, 1995–1996, Accession #RG-12/13/3.071)

As evidenced by the symposium, Kimball's impact on American architectural scholarship and historical site interpretation was clearly recognized in the decades after his death. His restoration work and prolific publications introduced visitors to key sites of American history, ranging from Monticello and the State Capitol in Virginia to various sites in and around Washington, DC, and Philadelphia. He applied a scientific methodology to his research and underscored the significance of architectural drawings and architectural archives. And he notably crafted texts that were simultaneously accessible to general audiences and advantageous to architectural practitioners, educators, and historians.

It is important to establish, however, that Kimball did not start his career in a vacuum of architectural writing. Although he was one of the first Americans to complete a doctoral dissertation on a topic in American architectural history, his record of architectural publications in the first decades of the twentieth century was not unique. There were nearly 360 books on architecture published in the United States in the 1920s, largely focused on domestic architecture.[4] As noted in Richard Guy Wilson's essay in this volume, "The Arc of American Architectural History to Fiske Kimball," many of the authors had formal training in architectural design, and their texts propagated Beaux-Arts tenets and reinforced the stylistic divisions outlined in Banister Fletcher's *A History of Architecture on the Comparative Method.*

Unlike many other authors, however, Kimball used the architect's language within his analysis, and he heavily relied on images as visual evidence to support his text and not simply as complementary figures on a page. For example, within Kimball's published works, it is common to find terms such as "axes," "composition," "inelastic," "mass," and "lateral." He refers to the cardinal orientation of buildings rather than generic "front" or "back" façades, a practice that reminds the reader of the position of the sun and the influence of environmental factors. Other authors relied primarily on a formal analysis of procession and arrangement and only referenced the larger components of classical architecture (e.g., pediments, columns, entablature). Images might or might not evidence specific points made in the adjacent text. Kimball expected his readers to delve into the minutiae of classical design vocabulary (e.g., cyma, ovolo, necking), and he provided the images to aid that. Kimball's precise vocabulary and careful pairing of text and image made the content easier to decipher.

Other authors writing about early American architecture, such as Howard Eberlein and Frank Cousins, paid more attention to a building's associations—the architecture of famous founding families—than buildings with exceptional design or detailing. Consequently, their images were almost exclusively exterior photographs, typically captured from a three-quarter view that showed a front and side elevation. Details, materiality, and interior configurations were largely ignored, and some texts, such as Lewis Mumford's *Sticks and Stones* (1924), lacked illustrations altogether. Authors who did include drawings in addition to photographs, such as Joseph Jackson, reprinted line drawings from a variety of sources, often without attention to architectural projection (e.g., aligning the plans and elevations or sections), scale, or consistency across presentation methods.[5]

As we will see, Kimball also relied on photographs and line drawings by other people in *Domestic Architecture.* He sourced photographs from repositories such as the White Pine Bureau and Essex Institute while employing selected line drawings from earlier publications, such as Charles Shaw's *Description of Boston* (1817). He also used the tectonic isometrics and simplified orthogonal drawings, often arranged in a multiview composition, of Norman M. Isham and Albert F. Brown's *Early Connecticut Houses* (1900). But he supplemented these types of images in two important ways. First, as evidenced by his earlier research on Thomas Jefferson, he used original architectural drawings as primary documents to support conclusions in the text. Here Kimball followed the methodology of scientific history, which he encountered in the writings of Charles-Victor Langlois and

Charles Seignobos while a graduate student at Harvard.[6] Second, he created his own line drawings. These drawings—spare, minimal, and at the same scale—allowed him to establish a consistent graphic language within his texts.

There was a largely unprecedented use of graphic precision to Kimball's layouts and spreads (the term for two facing pages when a book is open). Elements were edited to feature one larger photograph or drawing within a simplified composition, or images were edited to be the same size on the page (for example, see pages 39, 42–43, and 152–53 of *Domestic Architecture*). When more than two images were used, they were placed within a clear series, such as stacked drawings or diagrams. For example, in his discussion of Bacon's Castle, he used a group of annotated drawings from Donald Millar's *Measured Drawings of Some Colonial and Georgian Houses* (1916), but unlike Millar, who showed the house in isolation, Kimball placed on the opposite page of the spread a sampled woodcut from *Frank Leslie's Illustrated Weekly*, which revealed the home in perspective. The combination of images allowed him to better illuminate the structure as a whole. This designed composition reflects Kimball's command of the material at hand, intentionality in using drawings and photographs, and use of graphics as visual evidence; through clear examples, he directed his readers. Although a seemingly logical arrangement for a spread, this was not a common compositional strategy for contemporary books on American architecture. Other authors' graphic compositions were more akin to a scrapbook, such as in Talbot Hamlin's *The American Spirit in Architecture* (1926), where images and headers crowd the spreads and text weaves around mismatched photographs and drawings, leaving the reader's eye without a clear focal point or path. (See, for example, figure 1 in Lauren Weiss Bricker's essay in this volume, "Fiske Kimball and His Contemporaries.")

Reviewers of *Domestic Architecture* were quick to acknowledge the volume's distinctions in terms of methodology, presentation, and audience. Accolades included the claim that the book was an "epoch-making occasion in the study of domestic architecture of the colonial and Early Federal Periods."[7] Covering works within the North American landscape from the seventeenth century to about 1857, a *New York Times* review asserted that *Domestic Architecture* was not only "an architect's handy reference book" but also a book where "care is wisely given to save space for the subjects with which the public is not familiar."[8] Rather than creating a book that solely catered to an architectural audience, Kimball made the visual language of architecture more accessible to those outside the profession by including architectural drawings alongside photographs. This also established an expectation for the audience of architectural scholarship: while reading a book about architecture, one should also expect to be able to read

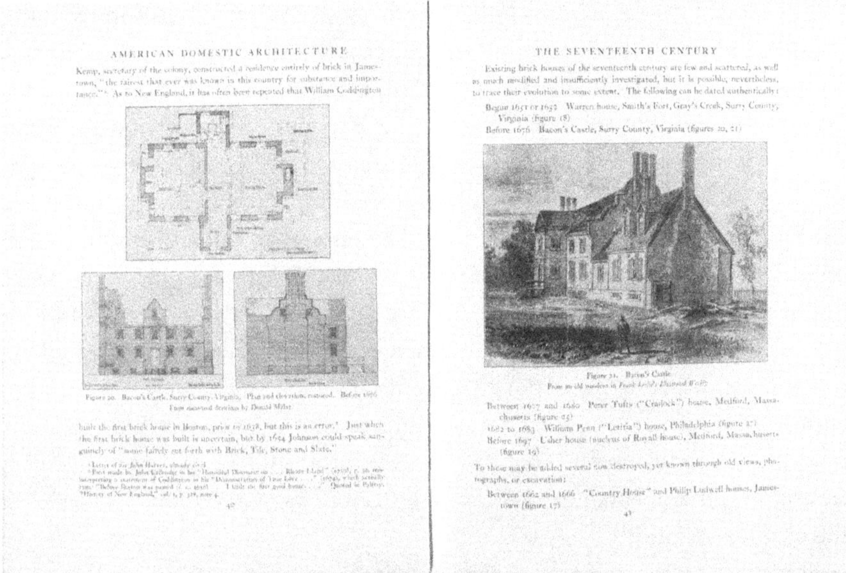

FIGURE 2. A spread from Kimball's *Domestic Architecture of the American Colonies and of the Early Republic* (1922, pp. 40–41) that includes a plan, elevations, and a perspectival drawing of Bacon's Castle in Surry County, Virginia.

architectural drawings. Kimball elevated expectations for his readers' comprehension, much as Jefferson was eager to elevate the architectural taste of his fellow citizens in the nation's early years.

The praise for *Domestic Architecture* persisted beyond Kimball's lifetime. In 1966, Dover published a reprint (which remains in print), and in 1979, the Atlanta historian and preservationist William R. Mitchell, born a decade and a half after the publication, said that the book was "the first to place any importance on post-Revolutionary buildings and to get away from the usual antiquarian and romantic idealization of the Colonial Period."[9] While the graphic layout made the subject easier to comprehend, it is also possible to discern another element in Kimball's choices: there is an implied focus on the spatial experiences of the inhabitant and visitor within and around these structures.

The Integration of Spatial Analysis

As Adrian Forty noted in *Words and Buildings*, the term "space" was first used in architectural vocabulary in the 1890s.[10] Discussions of "space" first began in Germany among philosophers as a description of a material enclosure (a room), and it would later be adopted by architects to distinguish discussions of mass, volume, and enclosure. Spatial analysis, for example, is distinct from spatial syntax. Developed in the 1970s at The Bartlett, University College London, spatial syntax is a scientific approach to analyzing use and behavior within a space, whether a contained interior or public space in a city.[11] The study of spatial syntax relies on an algorithmic approach to experience, interaction, and predictable use within architectural or urban forms. The phrase "spatial analysis," however, applies to the reduction of an edifice to its most elemental forms: open space and structure. Within *Domestic Architecture*, Kimball employs the term "space" in various capacities: to highlight the central area of architectural experience within a home (described as the "root space"), to discuss composition in contrast to surface or mass, and to contrast formal relationships with the abstract. Space was not used as a synonym for room; for Kimball, it was a term often associated with transition, experimentation, and invention. Space belonged within the realm of the creative architect.

It is also significant to recall the contemporary context of architectural education and practice when Kimball was working on *Domestic Architecture*. The Bauhaus and Russian Constructivist architects were exploring spatial analysis through abstraction in both drawing and modeling. Kimball engaged with the latter's work in *The Art of Soviet Russia*, an exhibition at the Philadelphia Museum of Art (December 15, 1934–January 21, 1935), but he was also aware of contemporary changes in architectural pedagogy while he was still a student at Harvard. In a reflective, unpublished manuscript, "Architecture at the Turn of the Century," he praised the courses taught by Herbert Langford Warren that provided "almost the only instruction that gave a broad view of the history of culture." Still, he noted that there was "no real analysis of spatial or plastic form" and claimed he only taught himself that later by reading the works of Heinrich Wölfflin.[12]

Within today's architectural publications as well as schools of architecture, spatial analysis is essential to architectural studies. From the qualitative to quantitative aspects of design, spatial analysis is used to reveal narratives and express tenets of evidence-based design. For example, post-occupancy studies focus on the lived experience of a building. Tectonics are not the only measure of a building's efficiency and success; architects also need to evaluate how a structure is used by its inhabitants, and this can often be different from what the architects envisioned within their design strategy. By analyzing the impression of and flow between spaces after a structure is in use, architects can shift certain programmatic elements or even change environmental conditions within a building, such as light or air circulation, to make spaces more comfortable and engaging for the occupants. Spatial analysis is also used in historic site interpretation strategies and for cultural landscape surveys. Here, forms of larger-scale, geospatial analysis are commonplace: GIS storymaps, for example, are abundant in educational and public history outreach initiatives that tie physical experience with specific spaces and locations.

The concept of spatial analysis, however, was not often found in the architectural texts of the early twentieth century. For example, the first five editions of Banister Fletcher's *A History of Architecture on the Comparative Method* used "space" to only denote meter, such as the measured distance between formal parts or objects in an architectural arrangement. Yet in an analysis of Kimball's early publications, it will become evident that he paired original texts and images to formulate an original discussion of "space." The scale and level of decoration of Kimball's American subjects were not comparable to the edifices examined in the survey tomes of European architecture or monographs on its significant architects of the late nineteenth and early twentieth centuries; therefore, Kimball turned his attention to a study of interior conditions of American buildings, examining both the plan and the experiential qualities of a structure. Not only did this method introduce a way of meaningfully studying the early American architectural landscape but it also enforced Kimball's working methodology, which paired documentary research with on-site exploration, combining the tools of the architectural researcher and the architectural practitioner.

Kimball as Architect-Historian

Modeling a case for the analysis of American architecture that strongly emphasized the relationship between text and image in the books' layout, Kimball's early publications were more like architectural treatises than extant architectural surveys. For example, *Thomas Jefferson, Architect* (1916) presented a unique image layout that has not been replicated in subsequent publications on Jefferson's architecture: the large folio allowed readers the opportunity to examine several related drawings on one spread, as if looking at a collection of documents on an archive's table. Additionally, by placing Jefferson's drawings, sometimes executed on small scraps or recto-verso, on the same page, Kimball presented an easy way to follow Jefferson's work in progress and understand the relationships between the drawings, even aligning elevations and plans in compositions to imply orthographic projection.[13]

Based upon a series of lectures delivered at the Metropolitan Museum of Art in February and March 1920, Kimball's *Domestic Architecture* presented 219 figures, with some that included multiple plans or diagrams within a single composition. Although this section will highlight the unique character of Kimball's visual composition, as already noted, he often relied on existing images (see figure 2, for example). Where satisfactory graphic information existed, Kimball did not duplicate efforts. However, this also allowed him to focus his attention on the creation of new comparative illustrations and the introduction of new photographic perspectives.

Rather than relying on sourced plan drawings, executed at different scales, on different media, and with different conventions, Kimball created a series of original plan diagrams that put significant American homes in conversation graphically. This was achieved by creating legible line drawings and distilling complex plan arrangements into straightforward spatial diagrams. The true innovation in Kimball's visual communication strategy is his use of comparative views.

Within *Domestic Architecture*, Kimball's original graphic layout presented various structures in parallel, rendered at the same scale and with the same drawing conventions, allowing the reader to make comparisons in functional arrangement and formal symmetry. The uniformity of presentation resulted in a volume that had graphic content as rich and synthesized as its textual elements, presenting historical analysis of architectural elements in a creative, curated way, akin

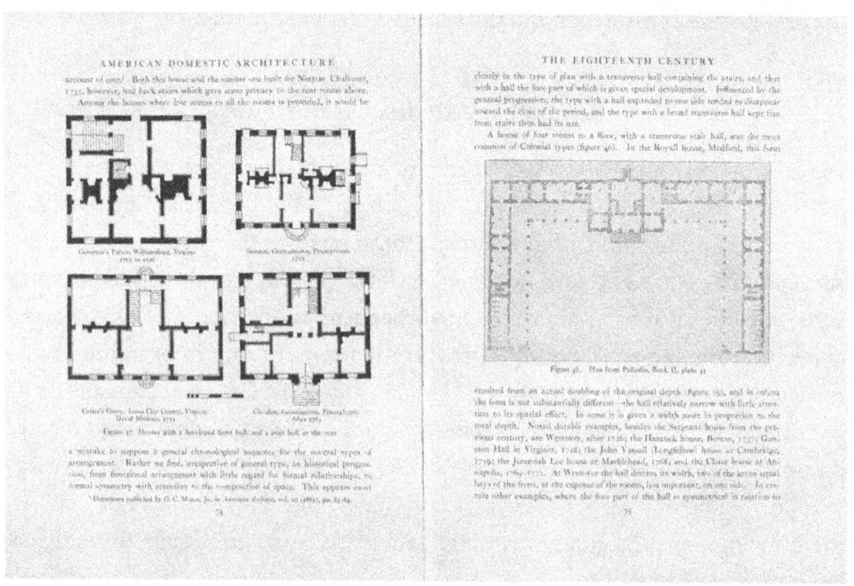

FIGURE 3. A spread from Kimball's *Domestic Architecture* (pp. 74–75) showing colonial plan configurations in comparison with Palladio's *Il quattro libri*, book 2, plate 41.

to the iconic architectural treatises that Kimball would have studied as a student, such as Palladio's *Quattro libri* (1570) or Gibbs's *Book of Architecture* (1739).

Much as in Palladio's treatise, the layout of Kimball's *Domestic Architecture* was a spatial exercise. Each page was created as a composition, with direct correlations between text and images. Kimball's approach is also interestingly similar to that of Le Corbusier's *Vers une architecture* (1923; *Toward an Architecture*), published around the same time, that also took a purposeful approach to graphic design to present an architectural and theoretical argument and made advantageous use of developments in photography. Kimball used photographs paired with orthogonal drawings, establishing simultaneous readings of interior and exterior and, consequentially, moved away from a form of architectural analysis that privileged the façade over considerations of form, circulation, or site. For example, within his analysis of the Swan House in Dorchester, Massachusetts, the page spread paired a plan with an oblique photograph of the exterior, captured at a lower elevational grade. This complementary composition illustrated how the curved projection of the Drawing Room was not simply a geometric or formal strategy but rather a responsive design strategy that navigated a steep and curving topographic change, resulting in what Kimball called a "variety of spatial effects" on the site.[14]

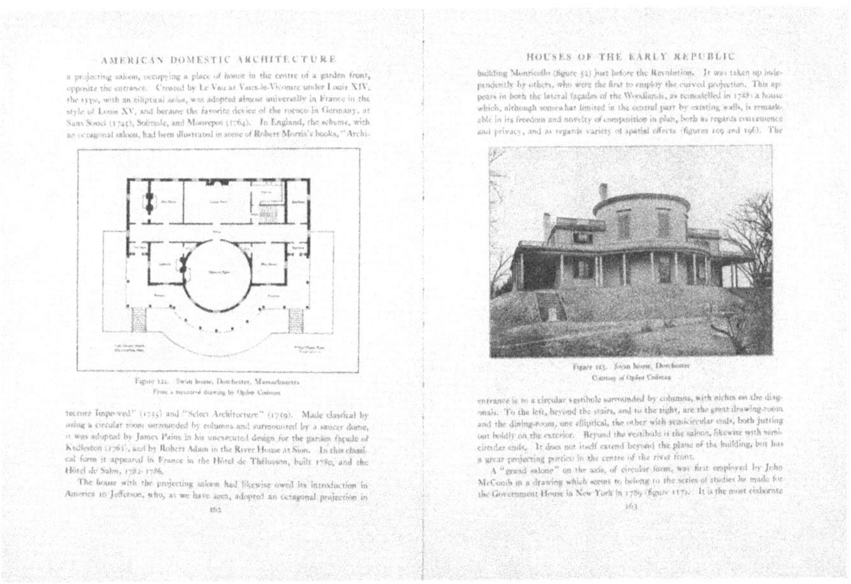

FIGURE 4. A spread from Kimball's *Domestic Architecture* (pp. 162–63) showing a plan and photograph of the Swan House, Dorchester, Massachusetts.

Kimball's exploration of interiors, particularly spatial sequences related to entrance transitions and vertical circulation, was facilitated by advancements in interior photography. During the early twentieth century, developments in lens apertures, light metering, and focal length as well as halftone reproduction techniques enriched the quality of published images.[15] This allowed Kimball to incorporate experiential photographs of interior spaces within his repertoire of visual evidence; no longer were these spaces too dark or compressed to be compelling subjects for a photographer's lens. Through the use of deep perspective and the avoidance of images that flattened interior elevations into singular planes by positioning the camera directly parallel to a wall, the interior photographs in Kimball's *Domestic Architecture* engage the viewer. Interior architectural elements, particularly stairs, are captured in a way that allows them to extend visually beyond the frame of the image. Significantly, these images support Kimball's claims that the architecture of the Early Republic revolted against the rectilinear arrangements and stair configurations of the colonial era to create "novel elements of space" and more picturesque experiences within a home's configuration.[16] The shift from utilitarian functionality to expression and craft within vertical circulation had not yet been assessed within published scholarship, but

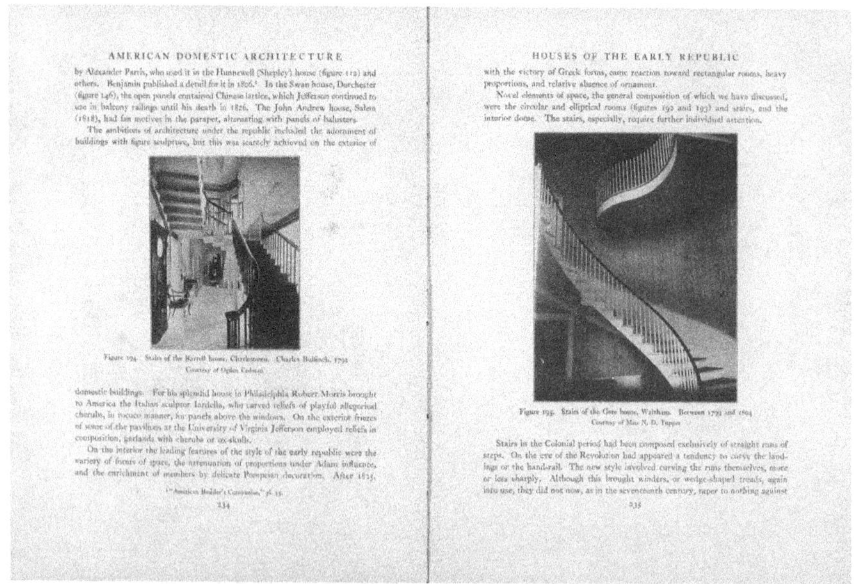

FIGURE 5. A spread from Kimball's *Domestic Architecture* (pp. 234–35) showing the interiors of the Barrell House, Charleston, South Carolina, and Gore House, Waltham, Massachusetts.

in Kimball's view it merited specific attention. American interior inventiveness fostered an exploration of form that shaped not only the decorative elements of a home but also its structural organization, creating a more dynamic experience for the inhabitant.[17]

Using orthogonal drawings, diagrams, and unconventionally framed photographs, Kimball introduced his readers to new ways of presenting visual evidence. He experimented with these methods a few years earlier, while a PhD candidate, in collaboration with Harvard professor George Harold Edgell (1887–1954). For example, a spread from their *A History of Architecture* (1918) exploring Gothic cathedrals puts ten buildings in conversation: five elevations align with five sections to illustrate "the development of the buttress and the development of the façade."[18] Edgell would use some of these illustrative techniques in his later publication *The American Architecture of To-day*, but from that volume's lack of diagrams, it seems clear that Kimball was the author with a more substantial interest in visual communication methods. The diagram of Mount Airy in Edgell's work is identical to Kimball's diagram in *Domestic Architecture*.[19]

In *Domestic Architecture*, the use of comparative analysis, rather than an in-depth study of only a select number of projects, allowed Kimball to develop themes that emphasized the manipulation of procession and volume during the transition from the colonial era to the Early Republic, identifying a spatial shift away from English precedents and toward experimentation that aligned with the nation's newly established independence. Some of this experimentation can be attributed to the availability of wood; frame houses were more common in America than in England, where the timber supply had drastically dwindled owing to the demands of shipbuilding and fuel. Colonial and Early Republic builders used wood to construct stairs with atypical forms (e.g., asymmetrical open frames or cantilevers) and they incorporated alcoves more regularly than in typical residences in England.[20] In addition, although many of the houses Kimball explored in *Domestic Architecture* were notable investments, such as Monticello or the works by Bulfinch or Latrobe, other examples presented more quotidian architecture. Examples of spatial experimentation went beyond the residences of the gentry class.

To illustrate the varied use of domes, double-height volumes, and galleries within domestic architecture, Kimball presented a spread that composed images of three buildings: sections of two Bulfinch projects, the Barrell and Swan Houses, on the left page, and on the opposite page, a photograph of the West Front of Monticello. This use of mixed graphics employed throughout the text may have reflected the evidence available to Kimball: when measured drawings

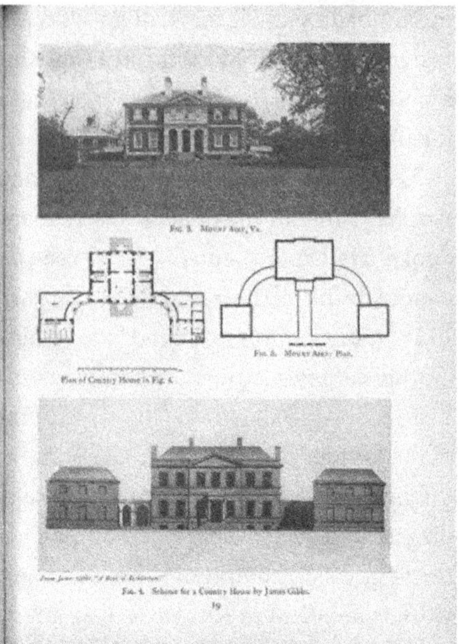
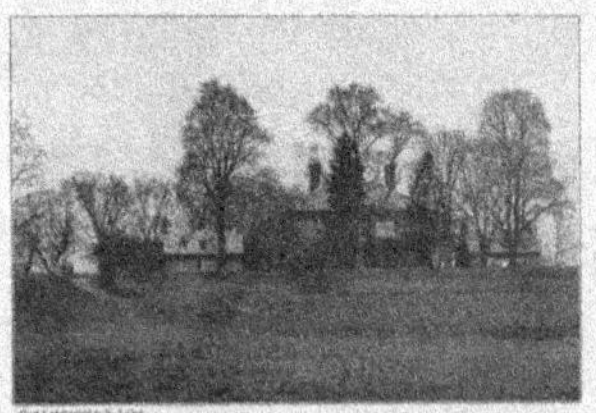

FIGURE 6. A spread from Edgell's *The American Architecture of To-day* (1928) showing Mount Airy in a plan diagram that repeats figure 53 in Kimball's *Domestic Architecture* (pp. 80–81). Kimball used the plan to highlight the relationship of the outbuildings to the main house in a group composition that allowed comparisons between the Governor's Palace in Williamsburg, Mount Pleasant, Stratford, Carter's Grove, and Mount Vernon.

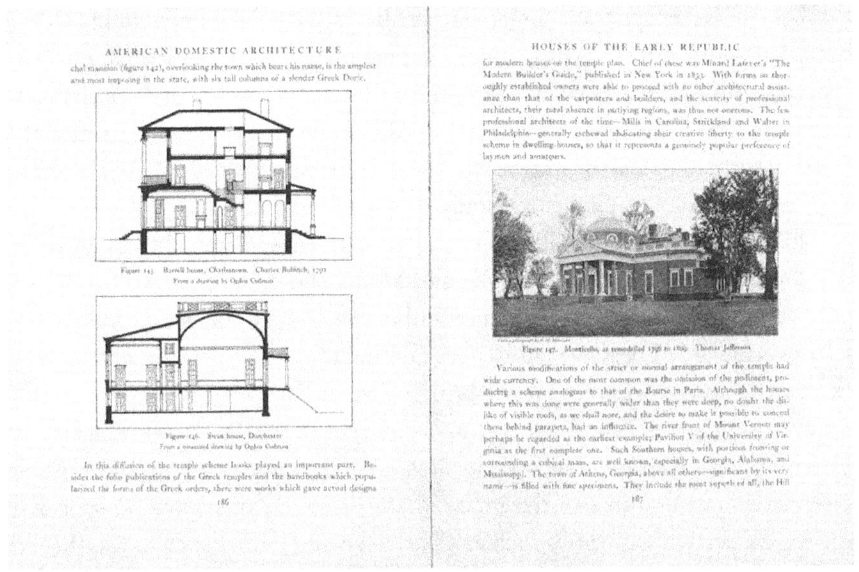

FIGURE 7. A spread from Kimball's *Domestic Architecture* (pp. 186–87) showing a section of Bulfinch's Barrell House in Charleston, South Carolina, and the Swan House, Dorchester, Massachusetts, alongside a photograph of Monticello, Charlottesville, Virginia.

were accessible, he presented orthogonal representations, but for projects like Monticello, Kimball featured the architect's primary drawings and sketches paired with photographs of interior and exterior conditions. This use of historic architectural drawings had limited precedent in American architectural history.[21] Identifying a gap in the documentary record of such an iconic site for American architectural invention, it was under Kimball's direction in the 1940s that the first full set of measured drawings for Monticello was executed.

Kimball, Monticello, and Spatial Analysis
Beyond the Published Page

For Kimball, Monticello was the ultimate example of American inventive architecture, and he consistently used the home as a reference point of exceptionalism in *Domestic Architecture,* citing it more than ten times in the text and using it in seven illustrations. Kimball often noted that early American architecture lacked the "academic character" of England, but he observed that Monticello and other selected sites, such as Graeme Park and Mount Pleasant, applied classical orders with rigor.[22] Monticello had, however, numerous examples of what Kimball highlighted as idiosyncratic American attributes: octagonal projections, alcove beds, flat roofs, terrace walks, concealing parapets, and other spatial and perspectival illusions that he called "deceptive additions."[23] The use of these elements reveals Jefferson's adaptive architectural skills as he changed and expanded the home, informed by his time in various cities in the nascent nation and abroad as well as his ceaseless architectural study through books.

Although unconventional in its graphic language, Kimball's composition with the Swan House, Barrell House, and Monticello is like most contemporary publications about early architecture within the United States that fundamentally overlooked oppressive landscapes and built forms associated with slavery. Within the spread, viewers see the principal volumetric elements of the homes, such as domes, processional stairs, and axial arrangements, but working spaces of the homes are either scantly delineated or, in the case of Monticello, entirely cropped from the frame of the image.[24] After decades of silence on spaces of slavery associated with cities such as Charleston and homes such as Monticello, there are now rich archeological, material, and cultural studies, but only once does *Domestic Architecture* mention architectural spaces for the enslaved.[25] This occurs in a passing reference to the "slave hospital" and quarters at The Hermitage in Savannah, Georgia, and these structures are used only to itemize the compositional elements, where the main house has a central lawn with flanking service buildings. Within Kimball's discussion of other homes, spaces for the enslaved are never directly addressed in the text. The plan diagrams emit no sense of control, established hierarchies, or even orientation, and their forms are distilled into compositions rather than architectural examples of social choreography. Within the book, basements appear in sections and outbuildings in diagrams; however, there is no explanatory text about these areas or their essential functions within the plantation landscape. This omission should not be overlooked, yet Kimball's work in preservation at Monticello illuminates his understanding of spatial segregation in ways his publications do not. Moreover, the unbuilt proposal for Monticello highlights how Kimball, as an architect-scholar, proposed alterations to the house-museum's landscape, outbuildings, and paths that could enhance interpretation at the plantation. Moving beyond the home's walls, Kimball explored how spatial sequences of the plantation's surrounding landscape and approaches from Charlottesville could be better incorporated into the visitor experience and overall conservation plan. His correspondence with Milton Grigg (1905–1982), architect and restoration architect of Monticello, and contractors R. E. Lee and Son, Inc., reveals a commitment to the formation of accurate spatial narratives for the historic interpretation of the site, including the enslaved.[26]

Kimball's abilities in research, design, and delegation were particularly useful in the discussions in the late 1940s regarding capital investments on the mountaintop. Amid the uncertainty of postwar austerity measures, Kimball and Grigg championed ambitious plans: changing the circulation pattern, restoring previously overlooked service spaces that would be essential to investigating and interpreting the lives of the enslaved, and constructing a new entrance building and entry sequence for visitors that would combine a ticket office with a shop. The removal of the extant shop from the south dependencies would restore those spaces to their original arrangements and enhance the historic interpretation about those enslaved on the mountaintop.

As part of a novel, holistic site plan, the new "Entrance Building" project proposal included a new circulation route for visitors using a combination of Jefferson's extant "roundabouts" and new paths. The route would serve two functions: it would create a smoother traffic flow with more parking spaces, and it would remove traffic from Mulberry Row. This road along the steeply sloped southern edge of the mountaintop once served as the industrial alley and site of several residences for Jefferson's enslaved workers.[27] At first, Kimball's proposal for an Entrance Building was on axis with the East Walk of the home, but the Foundation's president, William S. Hildreth, was "shocked by the proposed location of the buildings."[28] Kimball insisted that the structure was logical for three reasons: first, it maintained Jefferson's delineated axial relationships on the mountaintop; second, the proposed vernacular form would frame views of Monticello's east façade; and finally, it would leave Mulberry Row untouched in hopes that future excavations and restoration work could be completed.

But Kimball would lose this argument. In 1946, Monticello reached one hundred thousand visitors for the first time, and by 1951, that number doubled. This growth marked a significant change in the economics of the mountaintop: the admission fees, and not the gift shop profits, were now primarily responsible for the site's economic viability. To accommodate the more significant numbers, the location of the Entrance Building was changed to the site of Stewart's shop, and then again to Mulberry Row. This provided room for a more ambitious undertaking that combined a ticket office, gift shop, and administrative office that was authorized in 1950.

When the specifications were being prepared for the Mulberry Row building, Kimball wrote to Grigg that he regarded the revised design "with tolerance."[29]

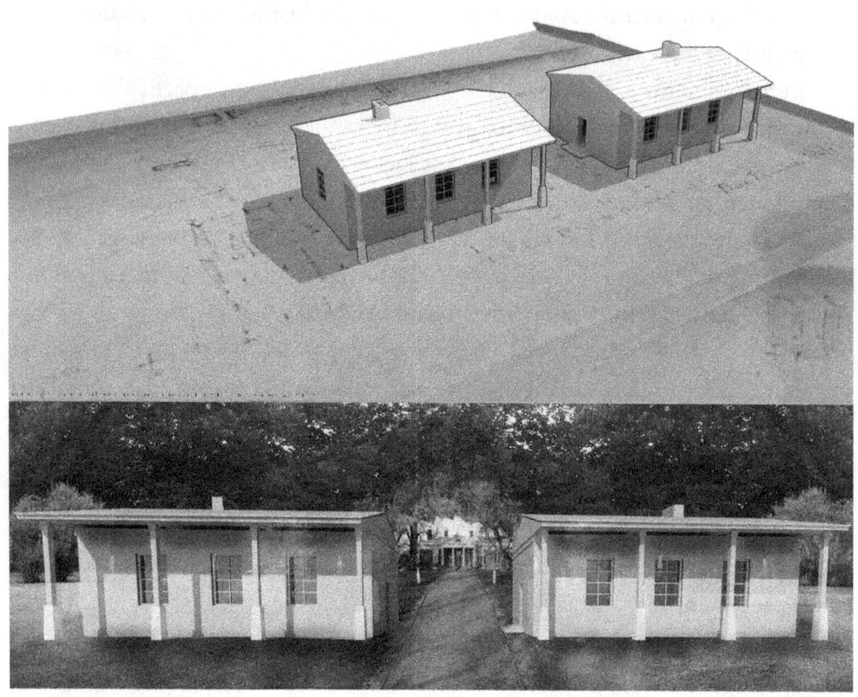

FIGURE 8. Kimball's annotated plan for a proposed entry building framing the East Walk of Monticello, with an overlay by the author of a rendering of the proposed building. Kimball's plan is located in Series 1 (1923–1984), 9820-c, Thomas Jefferson Memorial Foundation Archives, Jefferson Library, Thomas Jefferson Foundation, Inc., and appears courtesy of the Foundation.

He felt that its position adjacent to the "Weaver's Cottage" (ca. 1776) compromised historical accuracy and that it was too large: "I feel we are taking almost enough of a liberty in building this big new entrance building at all, on the sacred ground before the house at Monticello. That is why I would play it down in every possible way."[30] The desire for a profitable gift shop and increased visitor numbers, however, prevailed; Kimball yielded to the board's goal of keeping Monticello out of debt.

Through his correspondence and proposals for the Entrance Building, Kimball expressed a vision in the 1940s to return the experience of the mountaintop to one that addressed aspects of a working plantation rather than simply a "big house" placed on a sublime summit. These interpretive goals, relaying a spatial narrative of operations between several buildings, paths, cultivated fields, and picturesque lawns, have only been met in recent years at Monticello, with the Landscape of Slavery initiative along Mulberry Row and the Getting Word project.

For an architect-historian who deftly moved between the primary sources, construction sites, classrooms, and museums, it is unsurprising that a reading of Kimball's work requires one to move between sources, from the published page to archives and built works. Fully interpreting Kimball's work and its legacy requires that we leverage the varied forms of architectural documentation and experience.

Notes

1. Spatial analysis is extensively discussed in Sophia Psarra, *Architecture and Narrative: The Formation of Space and Cultural Meaning* (Abingdon: Routledge, 2009).

2. Dell Upton, *Architecture in the United States* (Oxford: Oxford University Press, 1998), 32.

3. Fiske Kimball, *Domestic Architecture of the American Colonies and of the Early Republic* (New York: Charles Scribner's Sons, 1922), 53.

4. Keith N. Morgan and Richard Cheek, "History in the Service of Design: American Architect-Historians, 1870–1940," in *The Architectural Historian in America: A Symposium in Celebration of the Fiftieth Anniversary of the Founding of the Society of Architectural Historians,* ed. Elisabeth Blair MacDougall, Studies in the History of Art 35 (Washington, DC: National Gallery of Art, 1990), 61.

5. See Joseph Jackson, *American Colonial Architecture* (Philadelphia: D. McKay, 1924); Joseph Jackson, *Development of American Architecture, 1783–1830* (Philadelphia: D. McKay, 1926).

6. Lauren Weiss Bricker, "The Writings of Fiske Kimball: A Synthesis of Architectural History and Practice," in MacDougall, *Architectural Historian,* 218.

7. C. O. C., review of *Domestic Architecture* in *American Magazine of Art* 14, no. 7 (1923): 16.

8. Welles Bosworth, "Book Review: Domestic Architecture of Early America," *New York Times,* February 4, 1923.

9. William R. Mitchell, "A Look at Historic Preservation and American Architecture, Emphasizing Georgia," *Georgia Historical Quarterly* 63, no. 1 (1979): 40.

10. Adrian Forty, *Words and Buildings: A Vocabulary of Modern Architecture* (London: Thames & Hudson, 2000), 256.

11. See Bill Hillier and Julienne Hanson, *The Social Logic of Space* (Cambridge: Cambridge University Press, 1984); Bill Hillier, "Space and Spatiality: What the Built Environment Needs from Social Theory," *Building Research and Information* 36, no. 3 (2008), https://doi.org/10.1080/09613210801928073; Akkelies

van Nes and Claudia Yamu, *Introduction to Space Syntax in Urban Studies* (Cham: Springer, 2021); John Peponis, *Architecture and Spatial Culture* (London: Routledge, 2024).

12. Bricker, "Writings of Fiske Kimball," 216.

13. Absent from this discussion of early publications is *A History of Architecture* (1918). It presented readers with more analysis on contemporary architectural developments than the comparative texts of Fletcher, yet Kimball's *History* did not contain original drawings for the chapters on American architecture, perhaps underscoring the book's rapid production between two projects that he found more captivating: Jeffersonian research and a survey text on the architecture of the Early Republic.

14. Kimball, *Domestic Architecture*, 163.

15. Robert Elwall, *Building with Light: The International History of Architectural Photography* (London: Merrell Publishers in association with the Royal Institute of British Architects, 2004).

16. Elwall, *Building with Light*, 235.

17. Elwall, *Building with Light*, 235.

18. In 1913, Edgell was the first recipient of a PhD in the fine arts from Harvard. Fiske Kimball and George Harold Edgell, *A History of Architecture* (New York: Harper & Brothers, 1918), 290.

19. George Harold Edgell, *The American Architecture of To-day* (New York: Charles Scribner's Sons, 1928), 354. The only other diagram in Edgell's text was a section study of New York City's urban setback rules for skyscrapers.

20. Kimball, *Domestic Architecture*, 155.

21. Bricker, "Writings of Fiske Kimball," 218.

22. Kimball, *Domestic Architecture*, 102.

23. Kimball, *Domestic Architecture*, 114.

24. As a Scottish immigrant and financier active in the American Revolution, Swan was outspoken about the slave trade, but the home clearly reflects the divisions in section between the servant and the served.

25. Kimball, *Domestic Architecture*, 190.

26. Papers of Milton L. Grigg 1930–1981, Accession #6478-b, University of Virginia Special Collections, University of Virginia, Charlottesville, VA; Papers of R. E. Lee and Son, Inc., 1935–1962, Accession #7615, University of Virginia Special Collections, University of Virginia, Charlottesville, VA.

27. Crucial archaeological data were compromised in 1934, when Mulberry Row was paved as part of a Works Progress Administration project intended to increase vehicular access to the presidential shrine. The paving between the "Weaver's Cottage" (now Textile Workshop) and joinery was not removed until 1977–78.

28. Milton Grigg to Fiske Kimball, October 24, 1945, series 1 (1922–1984), 9820-c, box 20, Thomas Jefferson Foundation Archives, Jefferson Library, Thomas Jefferson Foundation, Inc.

29. Fiske Kimball to Milton Grigg, May 22, 1950, series 1 (1923–1984), 9820-c, box 20, Thomas Jefferson Foundation Archives, Jefferson Library, Thomas Jefferson Foundation, Inc.

30. Kimball to Grigg, May 22, 1950.

MARIE KIMBALL,
SCHOLAR AND HISTORIAN

SUSAN KERN

In the 1940s, as the first three volumes of Marie Kimball's biography of Thomas Jefferson went into print, her peers considered her an important scholar and historian. She brought new documents, rigor, and fresh perspective to Jefferson biography in *Jefferson: The Road to Glory, 1743–1776* (1943); *Jefferson: War and Peace, 1776–1784* (1947); and *Jefferson: The Scene of Europe, 1784–1789* (1950), all published by Coward-McCann in New York. Her books met the demands of peer review, and she maintained an active and recognized place in the growing field of Jefferson studies and commemoration, which focused new scholarly attention on Jefferson through historical and biographical work, the editing and publication of his papers, the Jefferson Memorial in Washington, DC, and the preservation and furnishing of his home at Monticello. There is no argument that Kimball's historical work started strong but was completely eclipsed by Dumas Malone's six-volume, Pulitzer Prize–winning *Jefferson and His Time* (1948–81). Kimball's biography of Jefferson comprises three volumes of likely five or more that she planned. The first three volumes followed Jefferson to 1789, and she had another manuscript in preparation when she died in 1955.[1] Yet Kimball's biographical work is little used today. How are we to think of her published work, and how has it held up after eighty years of further research on Jefferson?[2]

Three recent essays on Kimball begin to measure her contributions. Anna Berkes considers Kimball's career in "Marie Kimball: Pioneering Scholar and First Curator of Monticello" for the 2016 collection *Virginia Women: Their Lives and Times.* Berkes looks at how Kimball's efforts fit into the professional work of curators, preservationists, and historians during the years of Monticello's restoration, concluding that her contributions were sizeable but had gone mostly unrecognized. Berkes offers a solid overview of Kimball's career and considers the role of women in preservation as men professionalized the field during the mid-twentieth century. Kimball stood somewhat precariously as a respected woman professional on the cusp of this change. Berkes outlines the role of the Kimballs together in the research and publication of *Thomas Jefferson, Architect,* for which Fiske was listed as author, though he recognized Marie's contributions: "She plowed through the manuscripts of all, turning up ever so many which had a bearing, identifying, dating, and illuminating various designs" as well as tying them to references in other Jefferson documents. Berkes follows Kimball's career at Monticello and her notable contributions to understanding furniture, kitchens, and the style and substance of cooking. Kimball maintained standing among scholars, published in decorative arts publications, and understood the appeal of writing about design and curatorial decisions in popular magazines, all of which made her an ideal curator at Monticello. Berkes also includes a thorough summary of the archives and libraries that house Kimball's papers and recognizes the scale of her impact on Monticello.[3]

Megan Stubbendeck's 2010 essay, "A Woman's Touch: Gender at Monticello, 1945–1960," examines how Marie Kimball's curatorial roles fit conveniently into assumptions by male academic historians that research on domestic furnishings and activities was appropriate for women. Stubbendeck proposes that Kimball recognized how her work on topics traditionally assigned to women diminished her professional status. Kimball held her place within the changing field of museums and preservation as men claimed professional authority during the twentieth century, but historic shrines that presented the domestic lives of founders reflected Cold War gender roles. At Monticello, white women became hostesses, replacing Black men who worked as guides. Kimball challenged what had become gender norms at Monticello; the academically trained scholar became a curator. Despite the depth of the expertise she brought to Monticello, she had to defend her work and distance herself from women's magazines, even as she understood the popular press as part of Monticello's outreach to middle-class women who often made decisions about family vacations. In Stubbendeck's analysis, Kimball's course is a useful measure of mid-twentieth-century norms for women and men as museum work changed.[4]

Herbert Sloan offers a measure of how Kimball's work was reviewed and accepted among other academics in "The Cosmopolitan and the Curator: Gilbert Chinard, Marie Kimball, and Jefferson Biography in the Mid-Twentieth Century" (2019). Sloan places Kimball and Chinard firmly in the early age of Jefferson studies. Both biographers wrote hagiographic defenses of Jefferson, and both were overshadowed by Malone. Berkes and Sloan both acknowledge that Kimball has a place among historians, even as most midcentury historians were men. Kimball seemed to understand that, too.[5]

What do we learn when we ask questions about the importance of earlier scholars? Are we including Kimball because we want to include women, or was her work important? (As a feminist, I would like nothing more than to claim that her work stands the test of time.) If it was significant in her time, is it necessarily so in ours? I ask this, struck by Herb Sloan's essay on Gilbert Chinard and Marie Kimball. Sloan's sleight of hand is that we can dispatch with really considering her importance if we merely lump her with other historians of the early age of Jefferson studies. I mean no slight here to Sloan, whose work I admire. In fact, both Chinard and Kimball are elevated by Sloan's paper as he evaluates their contributions in their respective times. But the conference for his paper was about biographers of Jefferson, so asking how and why historians stare at their collective reflection is fair game.

Kimball's place in the chain of Monticello's preservation and curation seems secure. But her history writing will likely always be positioned versus that of other historians. Sloan decided that she was most like Chinard, a relic of the age before Malone. She is also, in some ways, like Malone in having a vision for the big study based in solid documentary research. It says something about historians and about Kimball's work that it is not immediately lumped with work by other women.

Kimball's reputation as a historian rests on her attention to manuscript material in archives. Other historians recognized her use of primary source material to inform her research and also her labor in cataloging drawings and papers. Fiske gives her plenty of credit for the cataloguing projects, as the Kimballs collectively worked at a moment that was important to building various Jefferson archives. Malone, then editor of the *Dictionary of American Biography*, asked her to contribute to the *DAB* on William Short, Jefferson's secretary and a US diplomat. Berkes and other biographers ask a legitimate question: Did Kimball's work recede because she worked on domestic topics, furnishings, art, and food? Kimball herself referred to cookery as "mundane matters," which may be her way of acknowledging the pressure she felt to handle domestic topics carefully if she wanted to remain respected within the male-dominated side of the profession. Her biographies include domestic and social details at a time when books about Great Men highlighted their careers and their political, economic, and military benchmarks.[6] Of necessity, Jefferson studies would later become part of changing that approach.

Fiske seemed genuinely respectful of Marie's biographical work. In a letter to her editor Tom Coward, he wrote: "I have always written all Marie's blurbs as she is much too modest to do it herself. . . . I really believe that the material is so novel and extensive, and the whole conception of Jefferson which emerges is so new and interesting."[7] The "new and interesting" is based in large part on the documentary resources that the Kimballs helped bring to light. In the foreword to *Jefferson: The Road to Glory*, Kimball recounts the letters, account books, and public and private papers that had become available at repositories since Jefferson's nineteenth-century biographers wrote their works. She wanted the world to know about the man and the archive.[8] Some of her reviewers, such as historian Caroline Sparrow, noticed: "[Mrs. Kimball's] method is interesting. She takes her readers gently but firmly by the hand and leads them to her sources."[9]

In another letter to Coward, Fiske discusses the writing deadline for Marie's first volume and the reality of a 1942 or 1943 publication date. He lays out the likely competition for the Pulitzer Prizes in biography and history for books published in 1942. He mentions Saul Padover's *Jefferson* and Esther Forbes's *Paul Revere and the World He Lived In* as Marie's challengers. Fiske clearly thought Marie's work would enter the canon with a major national award, and he kept a strategic eye on the publishing industry. Marie received Guggenheim Fellowships in 1945 and 1946 in support of her work on the biography.[10]

All of Kimball's Jefferson volumes were peer-reviewed in the *American Historical Review*, the journal of record of the American Historical Association. Prominent Cornell historian Carl Becker enthusiastically reviewed the first volume and called it "a work of art." He also referred to the author as "Mrs. Kimball" throughout the review and nowhere mentioned her credentials. Christopher Crittenden, a longtime director of the North Carolina Department of Archives and History, reviewed volumes 2 and 3 as each was released. He was generally appreciative of her work but thought that she defended and celebrated Jefferson. He refers to her as "the scholarly and distinguished curator of the Thomas Jefferson Memorial Foundation" and also as "Mrs. Kimball," who "is to be congratulated for the standard of excellence she is maintaining in her biography of this great American."[11] In the professional apparatus of historians, Kimball seems to have been given fair treatment, even though her gender and her work in a museum were not generally accepted as part of the academy.

This brings us back to Marie Kimball and the question of how her work as a historian stands the test of time. Has her method, use of evidence, and moment of interpretation created a durable contribution to the Jefferson canon? Her writing style is dated and can be annoying. She writes to defend Jefferson from the calumny of James Calendar's publication of stories about Jefferson and Hemings and what she calls "the scurrilous charge of miscegenation"; she makes excuses for mistakes during his governorship. As we might expect, Kimball utterly fails on the subject of slavery. She does well to use various account books (not yet collected and edited) to reconstruct Jefferson's purchases in Williamsburg in the 1770s. But she does not see that the enslaved man Jupiter [Evans?] performed many of the commercial exchanges on Jefferson's behalf. This is where her work reveals that her eyes are only on Jefferson and what the documents tell her about him. In her discussion of *Notes on the State of Virginia,* she describes slavery as "odious to Jefferson" but says that he does nothing about it because his "convictions were nothing short of treasonable—treason to his heritage and treason to his class." She takes Jefferson at his word in ways that seem quite like naïve boosterism. In her books and articles, she calls Jefferson "a prophet" for saying that "nothing is more certainly written in the book of fate than that these people are to be free." In her words, she and Jefferson condemn slaveholding and are absolved from further action. In this, her work sits squarely on the wrong side of history.[12]

Yet Kimball brought to Jefferson studies the complexity of a man who imagined both systems of government and the buildings to house them. She claimed that his designs were ahead of their time and advanced in style.[13] His kitchens reflected his attention to botany, landscape design, and what he considered fine dining. She had the capacity to comprehend how tangible aspects of Jefferson's tastes related to how he imagined human civilization—at least her mid-twentieth-century version that equated civilization with white Eurocentrism. For Kimball, the matter was not just curiosity or decoration; it was essential to explaining Jefferson and his vision for an enlightened nation.

Kimball is a rigorous and empathetic biographer. In my work on Shadwell, Jefferson's birthplace, I traced the sources of major myths about Jefferson and found that many originated in writing by midcentury historians. If Malone asserted something about Jane Jefferson (Jefferson's mother), other historians were unlikely to question it and would repeat it wholesale. Kimball was one of the few historians writing about the time of Jefferson's bicentennial whose voice differed. She was willing to assess evidence on its own merit and she showed resistance to trendy authority. She offered the first scholarly revision that Jefferson was born into wealth on both sides of his family, a thesis supported by the archaeological excavations that I led at Shadwell (and that Fiske could not reconcile with his understanding of mid-eighteenth-century domestic architecture).[14]

Where Marie Kimball's work stands up is on topics of culture and the arts. It is, in fact, those topics where her work stands apart from Malone's. When Becker reviewed *Jefferson: The Road to Glory* in *American Historical Review*, he observed that "Mrs. Fiske Kimball has wisely chosen that part of [Jefferson's life] about which his biographers have known the least."[15] Kimball's research refocused Jefferson studies and Monticello's interpretation not only because newly available documents supported research into architecture, art, gardening, and dining, but also because she could see how it defined Jefferson's worldview. Other historians—including Malone—noted this evidence, but either it was beyond their skills or they did not consider it important enough to ask how it reframed their understanding of Jefferson.

Despite the fact that material evidence lay before her as a source, Kimball used it in limited ways. She included it as part of the important cultural landscape that Jefferson inhabited; in this, it is much more than mere illustration to her. But she does not parse the physical reality of buildings for what they might reveal about Jefferson. Kimball's analysis of buildings is surprisingly documents-based, not objects-based. She is an archives sleuth. For instance, she notes every detail of the only manuscript copy of *Notes on Virginia* at the Massachusetts Historical Society and Jefferson's annotations in his copy at the University of Virginia. She can see how minutiae might reveal a new chronology or change in Jefferson's thinking.[16] Kimball is working while archives are building the apparatus that will fuel the next half century of Jefferson studies—and while key sites related to the history she is writing are being researched, restored, or rebuilt.

Kimball had almost unparalleled access to the major restorations going on around her at Monticello, Williamsburg, and Philadelphia, but building investigation did not become a source for her biography. Neither old nor "new" buildings affected her analysis—she looked at written records and not buildings to make her assessments. For instance, what she writes about the Raleigh Tavern in Williamsburg is boilerplate from published early twentieth-century sources, not from details exposed during the Rockefeller restoration for which Fiske served as an advisor.[17]

Kimball's notes indicate that as part of her scholarly research, she traveled to see many of the places that Jefferson saw. William G. Perry's journal, which he kept while working on the restoration of Williamsburg, tells us that Mrs. Kimball—as Perry called her—was often in attendance when Perry sought the counsel of Fiske Kimball, whether at Lemon Hill, Williamsburg, or elsewhere. The closest her notes get to fieldwork—recording observations and making inferences based on the sites that she visits—is calculating distances between places where Jefferson traveled. Occasionally, she tallied the distances. Describing travels in the spring of 1768, she observes, "All this involved riding about five hundred miles in a little less than two months."[18] Other than the length of travel, her notes do not suggest that her interactions with buildings and objects played a role in her thinking about how Jefferson may have encountered them. She reconstructs Jefferson's experience from what Jefferson and others wrote.

She travels to Natural Bridge, for example, but her notes and brief commentary in *Jefferson: The Road to Glory* reflect only contemporary published and manuscript sources about Jefferson and Natural Bridge. What Kimball brings to this moment in Jefferson's life, however, is important. She considers Natural Bridge within the travels that challenged young Jefferson to consider his place in the world, where he marveled at the cultural and natural riches of America from Virginia to New York. She uses the archival record as evidence of Jefferson's fascination with Natural Bridge, telling readers he was so smitten "that the first page of his extant pocket account and memorandum books should be devoted to a diagram and description of this natural wonder." Then she quotes Jefferson's description in *Notes on Virginia,* this time letting his own words express his delight in "'the most sublime of nature's wonders. . . . It is impossible for the emotions arising from the sublime to be felt beyond what they are here; so beautiful an arch, so elevated, so light, and springing as it were up to heaven. The rapture of the spectator is really indescribable.'" She tempers Jefferson's enthusiasm with comments by "neighboring countrymen" who noted that the "bridge was only a 'commodious passage.'"[19] This brief excerpt on Natural Bridge reveals Kimball's method. She first gathers and mines Jefferson documents and other contemporary sources for their content. She then asks how that content makes Jefferson like or unlike his contemporaries, then how the material facts of Jefferson's record reveal the moment's importance to him. As a scholar deeply invested in Jefferson's papers, she can see that Natural Bridge excited him and enlivened his notes on it in a way that made them different from his notes on other topics. In contrast, Malone's remarks about Jefferson and Natural Bridge seem passing: "[H]e afterwards described [it] as the most sublime of the works of nature."[20]

Like other Jefferson biographers, Kimball gives a chapter to the design and construction of Monticello. While Fiske may have guided the content of this section, Marie decided how it would fit into the larger project of interpreting Jefferson. Berkes observes the editorial role that Fiske and Marie had in each other's work, noting that Fiske wrote much of Marie's chapter on the construction of Monticello but that she substantially rewrote the chapter. Their proofreading marks and notes line each other's papers.[21] In other words, Marie's opinions, scholarship, and prose are her own. She and Fiske were a partnership; she was

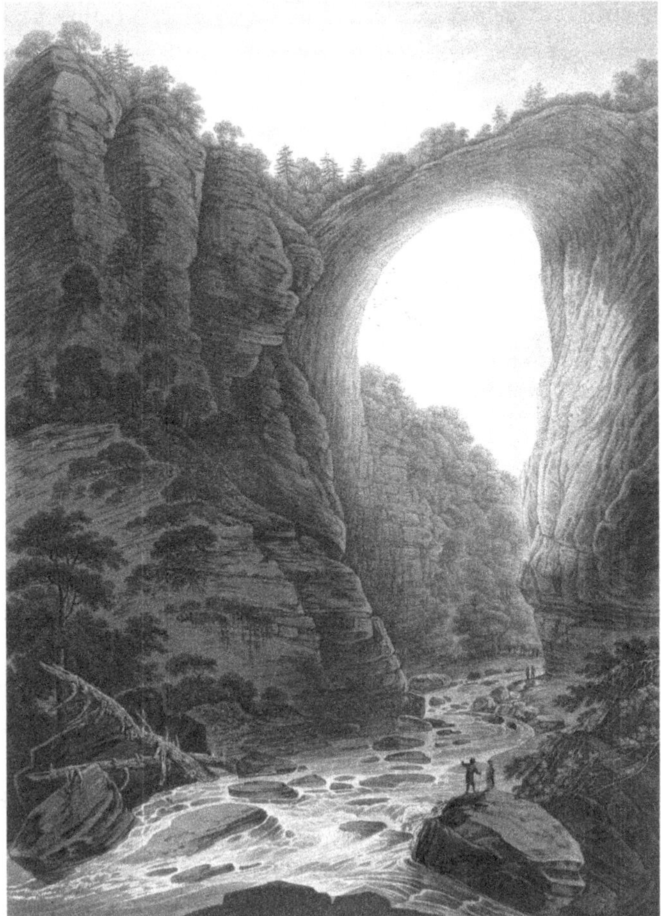

FIGURE 1. *The Natural Bridge,* engraving by J. C. Stadler, after William Roberts, 1808. Jefferson wrote about the Natural Bridge in *Notes on the State of Virginia* and hung William Roberts's painting of it in Monticello's dining room. Marie Kimball observed Jefferson's delight at documenting and describing the natural wonder. (© Thomas Jefferson Foundation at Monticello)

not his amanuensis, and he was not her director. They knew and relied on each other's strengths.

Little of the analysis of Monticello comes from field observation. Only a few measurements suggest that observations on site informed the writing. Despite unlimited access to the house and grounds, Kimball's analysis relies on documents, which, she says, "now permit a much more precise dating of the plantation and construction of Monticello than has hitherto been possible."[22] Her citations are often to Fiske's *Thomas Jefferson, Architect,* as we might expect. Marie's work cataloguing the drawings guided the chronology that informs the chapter. Thus, the documents lead both the biographical project and the restoration project. Asking what evidence the building offers is not part of Kimball's explanation of Jefferson.

Kimball's worldview does not separate culture from political and public life, as she and Jefferson both knew that art often acts as statecraft and state building. One profoundly clear example is in her third book, *Jefferson and the Scene of Europe, 1784–1789,* in the chapter titled "The World of Art." In this chapter, she focuses on Jefferson's interest in the arts: designing the Virginia State Capitol, commissioning medals for Congress to award to military leaders, and overseeing Jean-Antoine Houdon's statue of Washington and busts of Lafayette and of himself. Kimball investigates Jefferson's every move with Houdon. On the standing Washington statue for the Virginia Capitol, she develops a meaningful chronology that explains details of the design and exactly who influenced which decisions. Her sources are letters, the state papers of Virginia, bills of lading—the full trace of correspondence from the statue's conception to its installation.

Jefferson advised Governor Benjamin Harrison about the need for the statue. They then sought Charles Willson Peale's expert advice on an appropriate artist. Jefferson and Franklin subsequently convinced Washington to sit for Houdon and persuaded Houdon to take the commission. They also arranged Houdon's pay and insurance requirements, his travels, and the shipment of casts and materials. The result was the perfectly sited sculpture of Washington as Cincinnatus, retiring his sword for a plow to serve as a citizen-farmer in a new Virginia and new United States. Kimball's narrative unfolds over almost ten pages. In contrast, Malone gives about a page to Jefferson's work with Houdon and the statue of Washington. Malone does not see this as much more than a decoration. In Kimball's treatment, connections, power, taste, and knowledge are essential elements in Jefferson's demonstration of the competence of government.[23]

Kimball clearly works through mostly unpublished and published primary sources to articulate Jefferson's role in bringing Houdon's statue of Washington into being. On the Capitol building, however, she cites Fiske Kimball on the building, as Malone does. Clearly both Marie and Malone cede the floor to Fiske on the Virginia State Capitol. Her reliance on Fiske on the Capitol serves to emphasize her own work on the statue.[24]

On Jefferson's design for the Virginia State Capitol, just as the statue, Malone gives little more than a page, offering instead a robust footnote: "Exhaustively

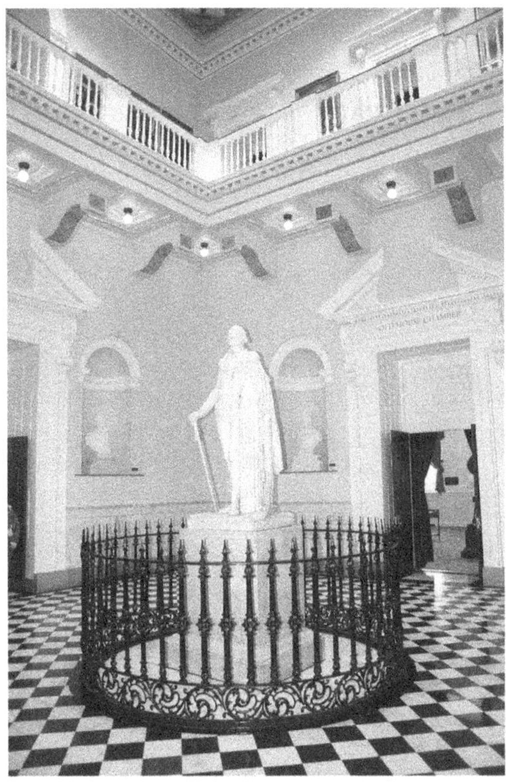

FIGURE 2. *George Washington,* Jean-Antoine Houdon, 1785–92, Virginia State Capitol. Marie Kimball's exploration of the commissioning of Houdon's statue for the Virginia State Capitol is a tour de force of her research, which takes us from the governor's desk to the artist's studio to the work of convincing Washington to sit for this iconic portrait. (Photo by Richard Guy Wilson, courtesy of Richard Guy Wilson)

and authoritatively discussed by Fiske Kimball in *Thomas Jefferson and the First Monument of the Classical Revival in America* (1915), where the documents are given *in extenso;* and in *Thomas Jefferson, Architect . . .* where conclusions are summarized, and . . . where the drawings are analyzed."[25] Malone's reliance on the Kimballs' authority on cultural artifacts amplifies their roles in adding those documents to the canon and also demonstrates how Malone's training as a historian did not include the skills to work with such material. He can see that cultural properties are important to Jefferson's story but must defer to others on how to manage them. Other historians saw the value in Kimball's approach. Richard Beale Davis, then the leading historian of southern intellectual history, reviewed Kimball's third book, *Jefferson: The Scene of Europe.* He noted, "Here one learns how a forty-one year old country Virginian became a collector of statuary and copies of classical paintings, an architect who could adapt Roman and Renaissance models to his own building needs, and an imaginative designer of gardens who could fit the features of European landscaping to the New World estate."[26]

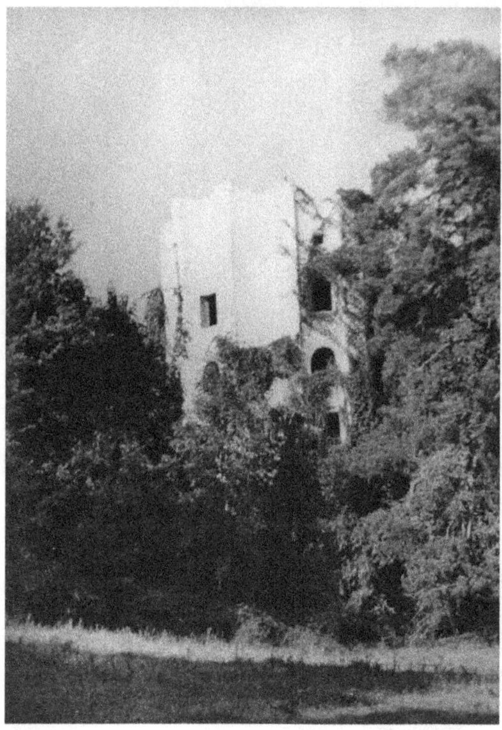

FIGURE 3. "Vue perspective de la Colonne." Interestingly, Marie Kimball chose to include this contemporary photograph of Désert de Retz in *Jefferson: The Scene of Europe, 1784–1789*, rather than an illustration of the monument dated closer to Jefferson's visit. (Photo by Lionel Friedman, 1947. From the Howard C. Rice Collection, Jefferson Library, © Thomas Jefferson Foundation at Monticello)

The biographies written by Kimball and by Malone are rife with examples that contrast their skills and styles as writers who seek to convey Jefferson's vast knowledge and understanding of the world. Kimball's style defers to Jefferson, quoting his exuberant comments when possible. Malone tends to explain. Their treatments of Jefferson's visit with Maria Cosway to the Désert de Retz outside of Paris stand in almost perfect contrast to each other. Kimball describes the garden built by Monsieur de Monville and its *style anglo-chinois,* noting that contemporary guidebooks published images of its twenty-six follies. "Small wonder Jefferson exclaimed, in recalling the scene to Mrs. Cosway, 'How grand the idea excited by the remains of such a column!'"[27] Malone offers not more than a nod to the day, remarking that the gardens had a "house built rather fantastically . . . in the form of a ruined column . . . which Jefferson much admired."[28] Kimball includes an image of the column; Malone does not. Beyond how she describes the experience of Jefferson and Cosway at Désert de Retz, Kimball offers commentary of her own, noting overgrown vines and ruined structures: "Even now in its sad decay we still sense its ancient grandeur." She summarizes, too, the damage it suffered during World War II. She takes on the role of emissary between the reader and the past.

Another historian who asked questions about Jefferson's personal life in addition to the world of statecraft, government, and the arts also found Kimball's work valuable. Kimball's close reading of spatial and material attributes that give way to sensory experience shows up in Fawn Brodie's 1974 *Thomas Jefferson: An Intimate History.* Brodie writes that "Maria [*sic*] Kimball, in *Jefferson: The Scene of Europe,* reconstructed with loving detective work descriptions of what all these gardens, grottoes, intimate restaurants, and inns were like in 1786, and one can see in reading her pages that Jefferson sought out some of the most idyllic spots in all the environs of Paris." In her effort to write about "Thomas Jefferson, The Sensual Man," Brodie finds Kimball a perfect model for exploring the ways that Jefferson interacted with the buildings, arts, and people around him.[29]

Both Malone and Kimball wrote at a time of expanding source material for Jefferson studies. The Kimballs were instrumental in the repair of an artificial archival separation in the ways Jefferson could be studied. Heirs and executors spent the nineteenth century trying to divide Jefferson and his papers into tidy categories, dispersing his presidential papers, his family letters, his architectural drawings, and documents like his farm and garden books among assorted libraries and archives. The mid-twentieth century found scholars trying to bring the disparate collections back together. The Kimballs did this quite literally, in finding and publishing collections, but Marie also did it through her historical writings.

Kimball constructed her histories during a watershed moment in Jefferson studies. The watershed, of course, was the coordinated and well-funded effort to create scholarly editions of Jefferson's papers. It was part of what Merrill Peterson regarded as the academy's escalating attempts to assume custody of Jefferson's reputation since his bicentennial.[30]

Kimball understood the critical failures in the published papers available to date. In response, she sought original documents in archives whenever possible, including drawings, inventories, books, and Jefferson's memoranda, which structured the chronology of his activities. Her work shows careful study of the range of Jefferson documents and close reading of how Jefferson wrote, recorded, sketched, and collected. It is important to note that the first volume of Julian Boyd's *Papers of Thomas Jefferson* came out in 1950, the same year as Kimball's third (and last) volume. Kimball worked without the apparatus that has defined Jefferson studies since 1950.[31]

Kimball's books are a lesson in how biography works for someone as well known and complex as Jefferson. Historians construct biographies and make strategic choices in how to move a story from one point to the next. Specialists bring their particular eye and can add substantive interventions that elevate details of place, buildings, dress, or other historical events. Scholarship requires us to ask whether the specialists' work—in decorative arts, gardening, wine, or music, for example—bears greater fruit when it is mainstreamed into history or when it remains in its own particular domain. The Jefferson Industrial Complex simultaneously supports the specialized work and the broad studies, offering us useful measures of the state of the field of history and of its subfields at a given time. Kimball's work as a historian had reach during her own time, even if we now tend to notice her contributions more in the specialist category. What she inserted into general biography has legs. Kimball's work is tactile, specific to place and time, and considers how people experience the world. It reflects her engagement with Jefferson as he engaged with the world.

Kimball also wrote without the benefit of two scholarly developments that would have supported her work were she doing it now. The first is the field of material culture, which did not exist when she was writing. In his book *The Jefferson Image in the American Mind* (1960), Merrill Peterson compared Kimball and Malone. He asserted that "Malone avoided [Kimball's] extravagances. He wrote in the firm conviction that Jefferson did not need an advocate."[32] (Peterson forgot that Malone was not in need of an advocate either.) Peterson says that Kimball's work "evinced an essentially antiquarian interest in the paraphernalia of Jefferson's life," suggesting that her history was old hat a decade after her last volume.[33] Serious scholarship on "paraphernalia" came into its own when, in the decade that Peterson wrote, material culture studies turned decorative arts into social history.

An example of what Peterson called "antiquarian" appears in *Jefferson: War and Peace*, where Kimball presents two paragraphs that list furnishings at the Governor's Palace in Williamsburg but almost no context for how to consider them. Thus, they remain in the realm of gratuitous detail: "We can picture him living among no less than scores of mahogany chairs with hair or leather bottoms (the twelve 'best,' along with six elbow chairs were covered with crimson damask); some fifteen mahogany tables, described as dining, Pembroke, and card tables."[34] What Kimball does not do here is use her skills to separate what furnishings might be essential to the work of administering a war and what might serve Jefferson's particular tastes in domestic activities. She does not read the objects to tell us anything more than "here is a document that lists furnishings" and does not offer the nonspecialist any tools for how to make sense of this list. On the other hand, her two-part article "The Furnishings of Monticello" in *Magazine Antiques* shows her polished ability to write for its particular readership of antique collectors and dealers—a public that academic historians mostly scorned.[35]

The 1960s brought scholarly study to material culture, with a multipronged charge by professionally trained museum staff, decorative arts historians, anthropologists, and, finally, historians. Method in archives and academic discipline from people like Elizabeth Wood, E. McClung Fleming, and Jules Prown partnered with the growing field of historical archaeology to make material culture far more than the female-centered domestic topic derided as "pots and pans history." Kimball had few colleagues with whom to build typologies, trade articles, or debate theories of human behavior.[36] I suspect she would have enjoyed this discipline.

The second development centered on the problem of region. Despite the best efforts to make Jefferson a national figure, Monticello remains in the geographic and cultural US South. The Kimballs understood what this meant. One need only be reminded of the gloriously ignorant comment by Metropolitan Museum of Art Curator Joseph Downs at the 1949 Colonial Williamsburg Antiques Forum that "little of artistic merit was made south of Baltimore."[37] In the three-quarters of a century since Kimball began her biographical project on Jefferson, the geographic focus of early American history has shifted multiple times. The professionalization of the museum field forced the establishment of academic research departments at many house museums and historic sites—especially those of the Founders. The growth and influence of Chesapeake studies produced expansive architectural histories, archaeological projects, studies of nomenclature, probate inventories, social and economic metrics, and a wholesale reconsideration of all of these topics in light of an imperative to understand material commodities within global economies of European and African immigration, racial slavery, and slave society.

Reading Kimball now, I marvel at her potential had she gotten to lay more than the foundation courses. She was rigorous in her review of historical sources from published collections to archives; she investigated every lead. She also performed a scholar's due diligence: she read and responded as needed to other scholars and their work, trying to engage critically with the moment of Jefferson studies as she found it. She knew that Jefferson was important and that her access to sources placed her work at a key moment in the field. However, the Jefferson she saw sat squarely on a pedestal, even as she combed through the mundane corners of his house and papers.

In her papers at the University of Virginia is a manuscript for an unpublished fourth and final volume in the Jefferson biography. She had planned five books in the series, but she clearly adjusted her sights because of failing health. Fiske wrote the foreword; Marie finished the last chapter as she died. I include the foreword here in toto because it encapsulates Kimball's work as a historian in the words of one of her greatest advocates:

> Marie Kimball, who had only begun in 1940 to write her life of Jefferson, knew that her own frail life might not suffice her to treat all on the comprehensive scale of the earlier volumes. She would not have been content to have discussed his Presidency for instance, without mastering all the material and making her independent and notable contribution, as she had done in each earlier volume. She hesitated whether to continue following the course of his career, or to round up all in a final volume. Her conclusion was that the Presidency and its preliminaries had been treated endlessly, indeed *ad nauseam*; that this phase of his life—a phase of expediency, in the application of principles long urged and already fully discussed—was the one best left aside. As she finished the final chapter on March 2d, 1955, it was indeed, for her also "a ripeness of time for death."
> —Fiske Kimball[38]

As this foreword suggests, for Marie Kimball the exciting part of working on Jefferson lay in unearthing and interpreting new documents, not retreading the most studied scenes in Jefferson's long career. Jefferson's presidential papers became available in the nineteenth century as descendants sorted and culled the public papers from domestic and family records. The papers relating to Jefferson's national offices—his public duties—constitute the lion's share of the Jefferson collection at the Library of Congress and informed the political biographies.[39] Kimball dutifully revisited the well-known episodes tied to Jefferson's public offices, but she brought to them the expanded perspective that the newly catalogued records brought to his other activities, as we see with her chapter on Jefferson and the arts and the remodeling of Monticello in the fourth volume. Her place in the canon was in highlighting how new document collections would inform the field and magnify Jefferson's contributions to the nation.

The fourth volume moved quickly through national politics to explore in detail the remodeling of Monticello and its gardens, service spaces, and furnishings—spaces that Kimball shaped and interpreted—and to Poplar Forest and the University of Virginia. The surviving illustration list for the book includes "The Kitchen at Monticello" and "The Wine Cellar at Monticello," but it does not indicate whether the images would be photographs of Kimball's work furnishing those rooms or Jefferson's drawings from the Massachusetts Historical

Society, which would also represent her work. Her contribution, as in other volumes, was to reunite his public and private chronology, showing how Jefferson's retirement from the presidency created opportunities for him to work on his homes and the university.

The twists of history have ensured that Kimball's contributions to published Jefferson history are not as significant as her contributions to the Thomas Jefferson Memorial Foundation's (TJMF) project of furnishing Monticello to interpret Jefferson's life there. Had Malone not claimed center stage with his biography, Kimball's might have become our standard reference for the wider view of Jefferson's life. Fiske Kimball charged Malone with plagiarizing Marie's work and inveighed bitterly against Malone's ascension. After Fiske's death in August 1955, the TJMF needed to name his successor as their Jefferson expert on the advisory board. Board member Thomas J. Michie wrote to Julian Boyd, asking his advice on whether inviting Malone to take up the role would be a betrayal of the Kimballs. Michie knew that Fiske did not trust Malone, "accusing him of plagiarism from Mrs. Kimball's work and various other sins," but Boyd nonetheless endorsed Malone.[40] It is clear in comparing either of the Kimballs' work with Malone's that Malone was never capable of wholly integrating buildings, design, or other arts into his evaluation of Jefferson. He relied on the Kimballs, and their influence remains embedded in his work, regardless of whether Fiske was right about the plagiarism.

Marie Kimball made sophisticated use of evidence, posed interventions in the accepted narrative, and supported her argument with quotations and examples, but the limitations of the field curtailed the enduring value of her biographical project on Jefferson. Much of her work does not meet today's standards. After Annette Gordon-Reed's important lessons for how historians use evidence and Dr. Eugene Foster's DNA tests, Jefferson scholars revisited Fawn Brodie's book and brought it into the canon, but there is nothing in Kimball that will produce a similar response.[41] The value in revisiting her lies in recognizing her role in constructing the archive and apparatus of Jefferson studies, her navigation of the male-dominated history profession, and her anticipation of questions about the interpretation and furnishing of Monticello in the early- to mid-twentieth century and, by extension, other house museums.

In most instances, Kimball shows her passion to understand place through all the ways that humans designed buildings, landscapes, sculpture, or furnishings to convey the weighty importance of civic architecture or the pleasures of private estates. She brought to the surface the documents that used Jefferson's words to describe the places that mattered to him. She certainly understood

Jefferson's capacity to observe the material world and wield design to impress and influence people.

Kimball's scholarship suggests that she worked much like we do. In the three pages where she follows Jefferson out of Virginia to Annapolis, Philadelphia, and New York in 1766, we get the sense that she has a deep research capacity to dive into the facts, trace them on the ground, think critically about what is missing from the tableau, imagine the presence of competent people in that picture— except for enslaved people—and know there is potential to learn something by going through the exercise.[42] This is her contribution. Some historians might still need to be convinced that the arts and culture matter to imagining society; Kimball's assemblage of documents would not let them off the hook. When material culture scholars start a new project in Jefferson studies prior to 1789, Marie Kimball is a useful reference and partner. She will have asked many of the same questions, with many fewer sources at hand. Sometimes she will have been right; sometimes not. But usually, the exercise will have been essential to the larger project. In this she is our colleague.

Notes

1. Marie Goebel Kimball Papers, ca. 1920–1955, Accession #5232, Special Collections, University of Virginia Library, Charlottesville, VA (hereafter MGKP). In a somewhat ironic coda to Marie's life as an archives scholar, there is no finding aid for the twenty-five boxes of her papers at the University of Virginia. The files represent a mind consumed with research and include notes scrawled on every size and type of paper, including hotel stationery from Charlottesville, Washington, DC, Paris, Versailles, and Munich; the back of her checks from the Girard Trust Company in Philadelphia; the back of correspondence with a therapist and with the Office of the Secretary of the Interior; and notes cut, pinned, and otherwise interleaved with typescripts for her books.

2. In this essay, "Kimball" refers to Marie Kimball. When I reference both Kimballs, I use their first names.

3. Fiske Kimball, Memoirs, Fiske Kimball Papers, Philadelphia Museum of Art Archives, box 159, folder 5, pp. 4, 6, quoted in Anna Berkes, "Marie Kimball: Pioneering Scholar and First Curator of Monticello," in *Virginia Women: Their Lives and Times*, vol. 2, ed. Cynthia A. Kierner and Sandra Gioia Treadway (Athens: University of Georgia Press, 2016), 210.

4. Megan Stubbendeck, "A Woman's Touch: Gender at Monticello, 1945–1960," in *Entering the Fray: Gender, Politics, and Culture in the New South*, ed. Jonathan

Daniel Wells and Sheila R. Phipps (Columbia: University of Missouri Press, 2010), 118–35.

5. Herbert Sloan, "The Cosmopolitan and the Curator: Gilbert Chinard, Marie Kimball, and Jefferson Biography in the Mid-Twentieth Century," in *Thomas Jefferson's Lives: Biographers and the Battle for History*, ed. Robert M. S. McDonald (Charlottesville: University of Virginia Press, 2019), 200–218.

6. Berkes, "Marie Kimball," 210, 211, 217.

7. Berkes, "Marie Kimball," 213.

8. Marie Kimball, *Jefferson: The Road to Glory, 1743–1776* (New York: Coward-McCann, 1943), 5.

9. Caroline L. Sparrow, "*Jefferson, The Road to Glory, 1743–1776*, by Marie Fiske Kimball. Coward-McCann, 1943," in *Virginia Magazine of History and Biography* 51, no. 4 (1943): 405.

10. Fiske Kimball to Thomas R. Coward, n.d. (1942), MGKP, box 2, folder "Introduction." Esther Forbes's *Paul Revere and the World He Lived In* won the Pulitzer Prize for history in 1942, and Samuel Eliot Morison took the prize for biography for his two-volume work on Christopher Columbus. The 1944 awards went to Merle Curti, *The Growth of American Thought*, for history, and Carleton Mabee, *The American Leonardo: The Life of Samuel F. B. Morse*, for biography. See also the John Simon Guggenheim Memorial Foundation, "Marie Kimball," https://www.gf.org/fellows/marie-kimball/.

11. Carl Becker, "*Jefferson: The Road to Glory, 1743–1776* by Marie Kimball," *American Historical Review* 49, no. 1 (1943): 111. Christopher Crittenden, "*Jefferson: War and Peace, 1776–1784* by Marie Kimball," *American Historical Review* 53, no. 3 (1948): 556–57. Christopher Crittenden, "*Jefferson: The Scene of Europe, 1784–1789* by Marie Kimball," *American Historical Review* 56, no. 1 (1950): 122, 123.

12. Kimball, *Road to Glory*, 146, on Calendar; Kimball, *Jefferson: War and Peace, 1776–1784* (New York: Coward-McCann, 1947), esp. 251–58, for vindication of governorship; 295, on slavery; 294, on treason. Marie Kimball, "Jefferson's Four Freedoms," *Virginia Quarterly Review* 19, no. 2 (1943): 217.

13. Kimball, *Road to Glory*, 147, on advanced style.

14. Susan Kern, *The Jeffersons at Shadwell* (New Haven, CT: Yale University Press, 2010), esp. 3–4, 69.

15. Becker on Kimball's *Road to Glory*, 109.

16. Kimball, *War and Peace*, 382–83n30, 383n42.

17. Kimball, *Road to Glory*, 61. See Carl Lounsbury's essay in this volume, "Fiske Kimball and the Williamsburg Decalogue," for Fiske Kimball's role in the Williamsburg restoration.

18. Kimball, *Road to Glory*, 135.

19. [Packet on Natural Bridge], MGKP, box 1. Kimball, *Road to Glory*, 139–40.

20. Dumas Malone, *Jefferson, the Virginian* (Boston: Little, Brown, 1948), 162.

21. Berkes, "Marie Kimball," 214.

22. Kimball, *Road to Glory*, 149.

23. Marie Kimball, *Jefferson: The Scene of Europe, 1784–1789* (New York: Coward-McCann, 1950), 55–63. Dumas Malone, *Jefferson and the Rights of Man* (Boston: Little, Brown, 1951), 88.

24. Kimball, *Scene of Europe*, 71–77; Malone, *Rights*, 89.

25. Malone, *Rights*, 89n22.

26. Richard Beale Davis, "*Jefferson: The Scene of Europe, 1784–1789* by Marie Kimball; *Jefferson and Madison: The Great Collaboration* by Adrienne Koch," *Virginia Magazine of History and Biography* 58, no. 3 (1950): 409.

27. Kimball, *Scene of Europe*, 167.

28. Malone, *Rights*, 72–73, for which Malone cites L. H. Butterfield and H. C. Rice, "Jefferson's Earliest Note to Maria Cosway with Some New Facts and Conjectures on His Broken Wrist," *William and Mary Quarterly*, 3rd ser., 5 (January 1948): 31–32.

29. Fawn M. Brodie, *Thomas Jefferson: An Intimate History* (New York: Norton, 1974), 260. "Thomas Jefferson, The Sensual Man," from cover copy for the book's fourth edition (New York: Bantam, 1975).

30. Merrill D. Peterson, *The Jefferson Image in the American Mind* (New York: Oxford University Press, 1960), 418.

31. The chronology of Kimball's writing alongside Malone's volumes and the *Papers of Thomas Jefferson* is instructive.

1943	Kimball, *Road to Glory*
1947	Kimball, *War and Peace*
1948	Malone, *Virginian*
1950	Kimball, *Scene of Europe*
	Volume I Papers
	Volume II Papers* (The Papers project proceeds at about two volumes each year and is not yet complete.)
1951	Malone, *Rights of Man*
1962	Malone, *Ordeal of Liberty*
1970	Malone, *President I*
1974	Malone, *President II*
1977	Malone, *Sage of Monticello*

Malone was awarded the Pulitzer Prize in history in 1975 for the first five volumes.

32. Peterson, *Jefferson Image*, 454.

33. Peterson, *Jefferson Image*, 417.

34. Kimball, *War and Peace*, 58.

35. Marie Kimball, "The Furnishing of Monticello, Part I," *Magazine Antiques* 12, no. 5 (1927): 380–85; "The Furnishing of Monticello, Part II," *Magazine Antiques* 12, no. 6 (1927): 482–86.

36. Elizabeth B. Wood, "Pots and Pans History: Relating Manuscripts and Printed Sources to the Study of Domestic Art Objects," *American Archivist* 30, no. 3 (1967): 431–42. E. McClung Fleming, "Artifact Study: A Proposed Model," *Winterthur Portfolio* 9 (1974): 153–73. Jules David Prown, "Mind in Matter: An Introduction to Material Culture Theory and Method," *Winterthur Portfolio* 17, no. 1 (1982): 1–19.

37. Luke Beckerdite, introduction to *American Furniture*, ed. Luke Beckerdite (Milwaukee, WI: Chipstone Foundation, 1997), xii.

38. "Fiske Kimball, (Foreword)?," MGKP, box 4a, folder "Jeff. Vol IV Front matter, Jacket etc."

39. Peterson, *Jefferson Image*, and Francis D. Cogliano, *Thomas Jefferson: Reputation and Legacy* (Charlottesville: University of Virginia Press, 2006), explore the contours of Jefferson's changing popularity and interest to historians and to the public.

40. Thomas J. Michie to Julian Boyd, October 21, 1955; Julian Boyd to Thomas J. Michie, October 25, 1955, box 3, Thomas Jefferson Memorial Foundation: Early History, 1935–1973, folder 31, Thomas Jefferson Memorial Foundation: Correspondence, 1935–1956, Thomas Jefferson Foundation Archives, Jefferson Library, Thomas Jefferson Foundation, Inc. Michie and Boyd served on the TJMF Board of Directors. Boyd was editor of the first twenty volumes of the *Papers of Thomas Jefferson*, published between 1950 and 1982. I have not found specific passages that support Kimball's charges against Malone. It is likely that the flurry to publish from newly uncovered archival sources put the Kimballs and Malone in constant competition.

41. Historians who had defended Jefferson's "character" fell all over themselves apologizing to Brodie for how systematically they had silenced her when her *Thomas Jefferson: An Intimate History* considered whether the Sally Hemings story might be true. See Peter S. Onuf and Jan Ellen Lewis, eds., *Sally Hemings and Thomas Jefferson: History, Memory, and Civic Culture* (Charlottesville: University of Virginia Press, 1999). Annette Gordon-Reed, "'That Woman': Fawn Brodie and Thomas Jefferson's Intimate History," in McDonald, *Thomas Jefferson's Lives*, 265–80.

42. Kimball, *Road to Glory*, 136–39.

FISKE KIMBALL AND THE WILLIAMSBURG DECALOGUE

CARL R. LOUNSBURY

Nearly half a century before the Secretary of the Interior's Standards for the Rehabilitation of Old Buildings became the guidelines for restoration projects in America, the Boston firm of Perry, Shaw and Hepburn adopted a set of principles in 1928 that would govern its approach to the restoration of the colonial capital of Williamsburg. Designated the "decalogue," these restoration policies did not appear *sui generis* but were shaped by members of a national advisory panel composed of many of the country's foremost architects and scholars of early American architecture, who were called upon in the early days of the Williamsburg restoration to vet the designs and methods used to restore and re-create the colonial capital of Virginia. William Graves Perry, the principal architect of the firm charged with this monumental undertaking, admitted a few years later that "there was no precedent in this country for a reconstruction or restoration of such scope and magnitude; there was no precedent for the reconstruction of a large group of buildings which were to represent the appearance of a complete town at a given period."[1]

Acknowledging that they were basically starting from scratch, the Boston architectural firm needed informed professional guidance as it embarked upon the task of fulfilling the Reverend W. A. R. Goodwin's dream of conjuring out of fragmentary remains an entire city at its golden moment in the 1770s, when it played an instrumental part in the founding of the nation. The audacity to conceive and execute such a vision was made possible by the philanthropic largesse of John D. Rockefeller Jr., who brought to the endeavor a scale of investment and organization that would transform a heretofore piecemeal and haphazard approach to historic preservation. A naturally cautious man with his money, Rockefeller had always sought out the expertise of outside scholars and specialists to keep his many projects (such as the restoration of Versailles and the construction of the Cloisters at the northern tip of Manhattan) from turning into fairy-tale castles, shining baubles with little grounding in the reality of the past. Restoring Williamsburg would be no different. Not long after Rockefeller approved the project, he instructed Perry and his partners, Thomas Mott Shaw and Andrew H. Hepburn, to ask the "leading colonial architects and art critics" in the country to serve on an advisory board that would meet annually in Williamsburg to review the restoration work. He told Perry that his firm should refer all serious issues that might arise to this independent body.[2] Rockefeller wanted "their opinions simply to be able to say that the points raised by critics have been considered by ourselves and submitted to others."[3] With the approval of nationally prominent architects, Rockefeller believed that "no one could ever say we got it wrong."[4]

The Advisory Committee of Architects

In the fall of 1928, the Boston firm assembled a team of professional colleagues well respected in the field. They invited stalwarts such as Thomas Tallmadge of Chicago, an architect whose design work was influenced by the Prairie School and who had earlier turned down Goodwin's offer to oversee the restoration. Tallmadge served on the American Institute of Architects Committee on the Preservation of Historic Monuments and Scenic Beauties, as had Robert Bellows, president of the Boston Society of Architects, and Lawrence Kocher of New York, editor of the *Architectural Record*. Kocher's interests and work straddled the emerging artistic divide between traditional Beaux-Arts aesthetics and European modernism. Adding prestige to the committee were Everett Waid of New York and Milton Medary of Philadelphia, the two immediate past presidents of the AIA. Other architects who agreed to serve were Robert E. Lee Taylor, of Baltimore, a native of Norfolk who was a graduate of the University of Virginia and MIT, where he had been one of Andrew Hepburn's classmates. Taylor and Hepburn worked together for a few years in Norfolk before Hepburn departed. Taylor remained and became partners with Finlay Ferguson Sr. from 1910 to 1915. When invited to become a member of the advisory committee, Ferguson was serving as the president of the Virginia AIA. His son and namesake would soon join the ranks of young draftsmen in Perry, Shaw and Hepburn's Williamsburg office.

Also joining the board were Richmond architects Marcellus Wright Sr., a skilled designer who worked in a variety of styles and building types, and Duncan Lee, who specialized in the design of Colonial Revival dwellings in the

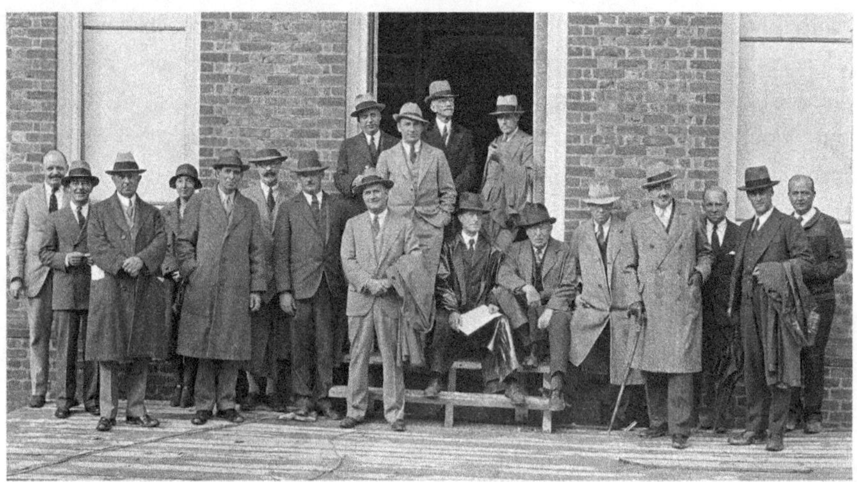

FIGURE 1. Advisory Committee of Architects in front of the Governor's Palace, October 27, 1932. Fiske Kimball is standing fourth from the right. (Courtesy of Visual Resources, John D. Rockefeller Jr. Library, The Colonial Williamsburg Foundation)

growing suburbs of the state capital. At the moment of the formation of the advisory board, Lee had just been hired by Archibald and Mollie McCrae, the new owners of Carter's Grove, to restore the two-story brick mansion built by Carter Burwell in the early 1750s on a bluff overlooking the James River a few miles south of Williamsburg.[5] Appointed from Charlottesville was Edmund S. Campbell, professor of architecture at the University of Virginia. Campbell would wear two hats in the early years of the restoration, since he was also selected as a member of the state art commission, a committee of Virginia architects, scholars, and artists appointed by Governor Harry F. Byrd to oversee design issues for major public works—which immediately led to a contentious debate with Perry, Shaw and Hepburn about the restoration of the "Wren Building," the main colonial building on the campus of William and Mary.[6]

Perry also received advice about other possible advisory members from Goodwin and from Rockefeller himself, whose wishes were conveyed through Colonel Arthur Woods, a former New York City police commissioner and the philanthropist's first president of the new Williamsburg Holding Corporation, which was formed to oversee the restoration project. Goodwin favored adding Charles A. Platt of New York, who had an extensive practice among those individuals and institutions who favored buildings designed in the Renaissance Revival and Colonial Revival styles. Months before Rockefeller agreed to pay for the restoration of William and Mary's colonial buildings, the minister believed that Platt's approval of the early designs for the college would help his fundraising efforts among the architect's wealthy clientele.[7] Colonel Woods wished to add Boston architect William Aldrich to the committee. Aldrich had been a partner with Robert Bellows for a dozen years before they had gone their separate ways in 1924. Perhaps even more important than Aldrich's bona fides as a designer trained at MIT and the École des Beaux-Arts was the fact that he was Abby Aldrich Rockefeller's younger brother.[8] To provide additional luster to the committee, Woods suggested appointing two older but extremely distinguished Boston architects: Ralph Adams Cram, who was the foremost authority in Gothic ecclesiastic design, and Charles A. Coolidge of Shepley, Rutan and Coolidge, all three principals who had trained in the office of the influential Henry Hobson Richardson in the early 1880s.[9] As was true with so many of these architects, there was a personal connection as well. Earlier in his career, Perry had served two stints as a draughtsman in Coolidge's firm.

The youngest but by far the most instrumental of these outside advisors was Fiske Kimball of the Philadelphia Museum of Art. A few weeks shy of his fortieth birthday when the committee first met in late November 1928, Kimball was perhaps the best qualified of all the members selected to advise Perry, Shaw and Hepburn, because he was as well versed as anyone in the country about the history of early American architecture. Kimball had published two monographs on the subject, including the canonical *Domestic Architecture of the American Colonies and of the Early Republic* in 1922 (still in print one hundred years later) and *American Architecture* in 1928. In 1916, Kimball had rehabilitated Thomas Jefferson's architectural design reputation in his monograph *Thomas Jefferson, Architect,* in which he made sense of the mass of drawings by the third president that had been given by the Coolidge family to the Massachusetts Historical Society. Having someone who understood Jefferson's design ideas proved especially useful to Perry, Shaw and Hepburn, since their first job in Williamsburg was to restore the college building—for which Jefferson had designed an uncompleted wing in the early 1770s—followed by the reconstruction of the Governor's Palace a few years later, a building that Jefferson had inhabited and sketched when he was its last resident, before it burned in 1781.

As the chair and outspoken advocate for committees of two of the nation's leading professional societies concerned with the preservation of historic monuments, a museum administrator and restoration architect responsible for the renovation of several early houses in Fairmont Park in Philadelphia, and the chairman for the rehabilitation of Monticello, Kimball understood the philosophy and methodologies of the restoration process thoroughly.[10] He valued the importance of field-based evidence and interdisciplinary research, not only documentary but archaeological. He argued that excavations could do more than locate foundations. Unlike most architects, who thought little about what was buried in the soil, Kimball recognized that such artifacts offered clues to a site's history. He observed that from "the great pains and care taken to collect and record objects and fragments discovered by excavation of old foundations" it was possible to determine their "provenance and in many cases the known dates of their burial." These artifacts were "an incalculable resource, not only indispensably necessary for a correct restoration of the buildings themselves, but immensely valuable for the study of Colonial life."[11] Few other architects of the time had such an appreciation of evidence drawn from these diverse sources. He came to the discussions with the Williamsburg architects prepared to advocate for an integrated philosophy and new practices needed to restore and reconstruct buildings.

Kimball not only possessed the experience that would prove so valuable in shaping restoration philosophy at Colonial Williamsburg but also had a commanding physical presence, combined with the personality of a preacher willing to exhort those who labored in the field to strive for higher standards. He was seldom reluctant to offer his advice. He had already formed strong opinions about restoration practices, believing that a close analysis of a building's fabric could reveal evidence of its original form and finishes. After he became chair of the AIA preservation committee in 1922–23, he argued that it should initiate "a campaign of education both of architects and of the public as to the proper methods of treatment of old buildings."[12] He lamented the fact that too many historic buildings suffered from "inexperienced and unsympathetic hands" and called for the committee to take on the responsibility of correcting the ill-informed errors that amateurs and architects made in the restoration of old buildings.[13]

A Clash of Restoration Philosophies: The College Building

A year before the first meeting of the advisory committee, William Perry decided to sound out Kimball and others on design issues that the firm encountered in its first major restoration project, the rehabilitation of the much-altered college building at William and Mary, whose cost Rockefeller had agreed to underwrite in the fall of 1927. As it was a state-owned building, Perry, Shaw and Hepburn had to win the approval of the state art commission, on which Edmund Campbell played a leading role as its secretary. Because an early eighteenth-century professor at William and Mary, the Reverend Hugh Jones, had mentioned Sir Christopher Wren's name as the inspiration for the general form of the design, early twentieth-century architects and historians had assumed that the great architect had actually designed the building. All those involved in this new restoration of the building firmly believed in the Wren attribution but had discovered that the thrice-burned building displayed little evidence of the sophistication associated with the designer of St. Paul's Cathedral.[14] Though direct documentary evidence to support this supposition could not be found in the colonial records, most were nonetheless convinced that Wren may have supplied preliminary sketches even if he had not been fully engaged in the final design for the building.[15]

A fundamental disagreement arose between the art commission and restoration architects over the period to which the building would be restored. The commissioners favored the first incarnation of the building, between 1695, when construction began, and 1705, when the building suffered the first of its many destructive fires. Although the documentary evidence concerning this first building was slim, they placed great stock in a very rough sketch of its front elevation made in 1702 by a Swiss visitor to the city. The sketch showed a much taller structure than the one that was rebuilt in the 1710s and survived until

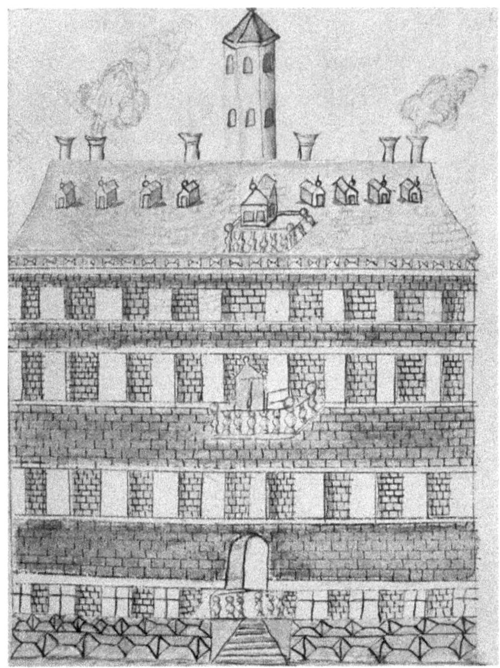

FIGURE 2. Sketch of the College Building, Francis Michel, 1702. (Courtesy of the Burgerbibliothek Bern, Switzerland, Mss.h.h.X.152 f. 63r)

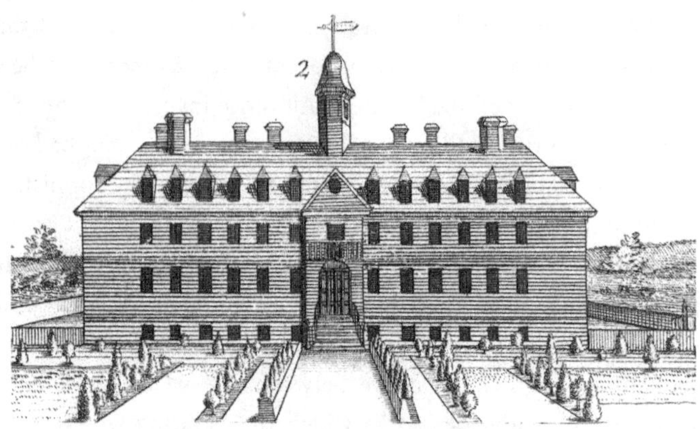

FIGURE 3. Detail, East Elevation of the College Building, College of William & Mary, from the Bodleian Plate (modern restrike). (Courtesy of The Colonial Williamsburg Foundation)

it burned again in 1859. Campbell and his associates on the commission felt that the first building would have reflected Wren's design ideas more faithfully than the later reconstruction, when it was rebuilt by local craftsmen. During the century and a half that followed the second reconstruction, the documentary record was far more thorough, with period images (including a detailed copperplate engraving of the front façade and a rear view showing the two side wings that contained the great hall and the later chapel), early photographs, and descriptions. This was the era that the restoration architects advocated, since it also reflected the college as it had expanded with the addition of the south chapel wing, completed in 1732.

The commissioners balked at this approach mainly because they observed a degree of awkwardness in the details of the building, which was hard to ascribe to the masterful hand of Wren. They disliked the slightly projecting center bay of the east front, with its acutely sloped pediment and ungainly front door and balcony, as it existed between the 1710s and 1859. Campbell found the features undignified and dismissed them as post-fire alterations since there was no projecting central bay shown in the 1702 elevational sketch. A misreading of an early document that listed materials shipped from London for the building led him to speculate that the modillions of the cornice might have been enriched (that is, carved) like the "ones such as Wren used on Middle Temple, Merton College [chapel], or Christ Hospital [London]. Also, perhaps for doors on the balcony or both."[16] He pushed the restoration architects for a more imaginative resolution that reflected Wren's artistry, including a larger cupola than the one that appeared in the later documentary evidence.[17]

In order to resolve outstanding design issues, in September 1927 Perry showed preliminary drawings for the restored building to several leading architects, including Cram and Coolidge in Boston and Platt and Kocher in New York, to elicit their views. Perry observed that the first three individuals encouraged him to choose one of a number of design features that Wren had used in his many works to serve as a precedent for the college building. Coolidge, for example, suggested a revision of the east front door by lowering its height and adding an iron balcony over it, a common feature in English architectural design in the late seventeenth century.[18] Perry noted that Kocher begged to differ with the advice given by the Boston architects, arguing instead that the design should adhere to the physical evidence of the building. He stressed "the importance of chimneys, the unique Williamsburg character of existing work, and the likelihood that much that now exists was copied from the old [original] College Building." He advocated that the architects should "work backwards" from the standing structure to fill in the details that were now missing. Kocher favored "a true restoration" and encouraged him to seek out the advice of Kimball in Philadelphia.[19]

Meeting Perry at his home at Lemon Hill in Fairmount Park, Kimball agreed entirely with Kocher's views and insisted that no "element should be used which

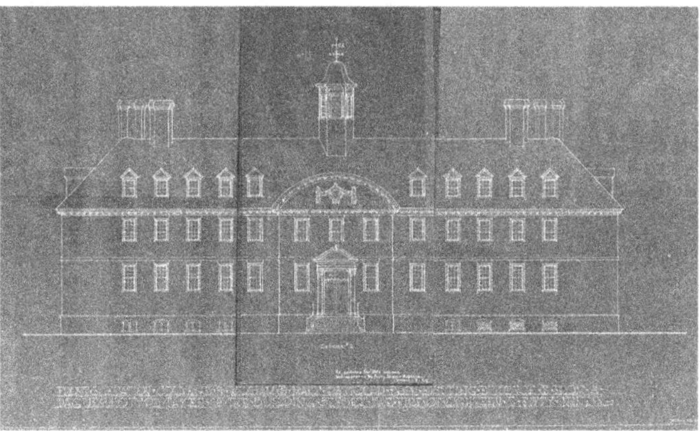

FIGURE 4. Scheme #2, Front Elevation, College of William & Mary. Perry, Shaw & Hepburn, Architects, May 13, 1929. William G. Perry, design drawing of the front façade of the college building, 1927. (Courtesy of Special Collections, John D. Rockefeller Jr. Library, The Colonial Williamsburg Foundation)

did not have an authentic Virginia precedent." He maintained that the restoration drawings for the college building should be "as simple as possible, no matter what the 'Wren tradition'" dictated.[20] A few weeks later, Perry met with Kocher and Kimball again, this time in New York at the *Architectural Record* office, where they reviewed revised drawings of the building. Kimball criticized the doorway design that had been based on the English stone frontispiece that had been installed at Westover, William Byrd III's home built in Charles City County, after it was constructed in 1750.[21] He also observed that the original balcony over the doorway would have been wooden rather than iron, as Coolidge had recommended, and would have had twisted balusters and a ramped handrail.[22] The conflicting advice Perry was given accentuated the fact that there was no coherent acceptable restoration philosophy among his peers. Some had encouraged adapting designs in the Wren idiom, while others urged that the architects should stick to the historical evidence. The philosophy of "Cram, Platt, and Coolidge encouraged design that was artistically and architecturally pleasing," and its advocates were "less troubled if the work strayed from more accurate" details. Campbell and his fellow commissioners shared this attitude. On the other hand, Kimball and Kocher "favored strict adherence to documentary and archaeological evidence" based on common regional practices of the colonial period.[23] As Kimball emphasized, the restoration architects needed to become "passionate historical students, happy to subordinate their creative abilities to a loyal interpretation of the ample evidence" discovered in the physical and documentary sources.[24] This latter perspective won the approval of Perry and his colleagues, who began to revise their designs based on the recommendations of Kocher and Kimball. They also believed that they needed an endorsement from Rockefeller's national advisory board to win final approval for the college restoration from the state art commissioners.

Establishing the Ground Rules of the Williamsburg Restoration

With such divergent philosophical perspectives on how to proceed with the restoration of the colonial town of Williamsburg and the college building at William and Mary in particular, the convening of the first meeting of the Advisory Committee of Architects in Williamsburg on November 25–26, 1928, took on added urgency. Perry considered one the most pressing tasks facing the advisory group to be the formulation of a code of principles that would govern restoration policies. He opened the meeting by explaining that the purpose of the committee was to provide advice on "the scope of the restoration" to those in charge of it.

In their earlier discussions with the Williamsburg architects, the advisors may have heard some of the ideas that Goodwin and Rockefeller had for the restoration, but many were undoubtedly taken aback by the magnitude of the project as it slowly revealed itself in the first day of deliberations. Kimball had definitive philosophies about restoration practices for individual structures, but the idea of transforming the entire town brought up many new questions about roads, gardens, and spaces between buildings, issues concerning the removal of anachronistic features, and the methods and materials that might be used in the reconstruction of long-lost structures as well as the integration of modern amenities and services. Kimball launched the wide-ranging discussion by asking the restoration architects and Goodwin to explain more precisely their vision of the restoration—whether it was "primarily to preserve what is left or to rebuild in such a way as to show the whole colonial economy in its complete relation to great events and as an inspiration to visitors." Goodwin replied that the goal was "to present a picture which, while not absolutely a reproduction, will be representative of the past" and asked the committee's help in deciding "how many buildings should be preserved or removed." Prodded further, Goodwin envisioned the restoration of the entire town.[25]

Besides developing specific restoration guidelines, the Williamsburg Holding Corporation was eager for the advisory board to help define the geographic and temporal limits of the project.[26] The restoration architects used the Frenchman's Map, a plan of Williamsburg drawn by a French engineer for billeting troops following the battle of Yorktown in 1781, to define the boundary of the historic area that was to be preserved; the number and location of the buildings depicted on the map would serve as a guide in developing plans for the restoration of those that had survived and those that needed to be reconstructed. They would oversee the demolition of all unwanted houses within this area as a first step before undertaking the reconstruction of historic ones on their original foundations.[27] In establishing a rule for what was to be retained and what was to be demolished within the historic area, the committee came to a consensus: buildings that postdated the Revolution but still retained classical design features should be preserved, and those modern structures dating to after 1840 should be removed. Kimball and Taylor recognized that this criterion was not as clear as it could have been if they had recommended a specific date around the time of the Revolution. They also admitted that there were a few borderline cases, such as the Armistead House (1858), which they agreed was a fine house but one "which is missing much of the colonial tradition." Kimball suggested that "a time may come when [buildings of] the antebellum period would be looked back upon" with admiration, "just as we look back upon the pre-revolutionary period."[28]

Kimball raised the issue of the number of reconstructions that might be necessary in order to recover the historical scale and density of the city in the era of the Revolution. He argued strongly for the retention of old foundations and building fragments to preserve the patina of age, contrasting with the regularity and newness of modern reconstructions. When devising designs for the reconstruction of important buildings such as the Governor's Palace, Raleigh Tavern, the Capitol, and others, he strongly urged the restoration architects to forgo the temptation to incorporate specific details from standing structures. He felt that no architectural motif "should be a copy of any other however admirable, that might exist in any other part of the Town or be well known to exist elsewhere," since, he argued, "by copying an example the value of the original might be lowered."[29] He had argued against such a practice the previous year, when, reviewing the early design drawings for the college building, he cautioned against using the stone frontispiece at Westover as the model for its west front doorway.[30] Besides his doubts about using a feature that would have been historically inappropriate, he knew it would also be a distraction in Williamsburg because of its association with the well-known James River plantation, which had become a popular design motif that contemporaries such as Duncan Lee and William Lawrence Bottomley had used in many of their designs of Colonial Revival houses in Richmond and elsewhere.[31]

Lawrence Kocher urged the preservation architects not to be too heavy-handed with the surviving colonial buildings. He stressed that "the historic integrity of a building should be preserved. Preservation," he noted, "is one thing. Restoration quite another. Restoration means the bringing back of a thing to its conjectured former condition. Preservation means the retention of a thing as it is. Where many buildings have changed, preservation would mean preservation of the changes, also without substitution of old material or old detail for the more modern existing material." He argued that "any new addition might be built or any new work done—as it is done in England, under similar circumstances, in modern material and manner and even with the use of concrete, to indicate that no attempt at Restoration is being made. This method preserves the historic integrity of the building."[32] This "anti-scrape" philosophy, derived from William Morris and his English followers, received little endorsement from the other advisors and later was ignored by the restoration architects. Kimball did not support this stricter approach to preserving old fabric, favoring compromises when necessary, but later opined that "the desire for reasonable permanence in the restored buildings has led" the preservation architects at Colonial Williamsburg "to more far-reaching structural renewal than might otherwise have been desirable."[33]

Goodwin envisioned that only a handful of public buildings and dwellings would be open to the public and that those used for offices, private residences, and other modern functions did not necessarily need to follow their original plan on the inside. The principals of Perry, Shaw and Hepburn all agreed that there would have to be compromises made for modern necessities, such as adding back porches, bathrooms, and kitchens and installing modern heating, lighting, and plumbing systems. In some cases new materials and construction practices would be used where needed. Perry pointed out the necessity of concrete and steel framing to reinforce or replace the old internal brick walls of the college building and concrete asbestos shingles to make the building structurally sound, fireproof, and usable for modern educational purposes. He noted that the architects would have to take into account such features but observed that from an outward appearance, "nothing must be done" to detract from the "educational value of the restoration." Hepburn added that the "preservation of the town is essential. Exact restoration need not apply to everything. What is desired is a town unspoiled architecturally."[34] In other words, the footprint and form of buildings in the historic area should mimic colonial design, but the work would be executed with modern materials and methods that would imitate but not replicate traditional craftsmanship.

The discussion then turned to the use of old materials. Unlike Kimball, Campbell did not consider the preservation of old foundations necessary and would be happy to see them removed once they were recorded. Tallmadge and Goodwin were amenable to reusing what was described as "antique material" in the restorations and reconstructions. They fully endorsed the idea of buying materials from old houses in the area that were already doomed to destruction. Although he spoke earlier in favor of using new materials rather than old, Kocher thought that if old mantels, flooring, and paneling were to be used, then they should come from Virginia rather than farther afield to avoid mixing regional variations. Robert Bellows objected to what he called the "promiscuous looting of old buildings," feeling that once it became known that Colonial Williamsburg was willing to purchase "antique" fabric, there would be unscrupulous dealers offering up illgotten materials.[35] Rather than buying old bricks, which would also encourage the destruction of historic buildings, the committee recommended that they be "hand made as near like the old as possible."[36]

Establishing the Resolutions Behind the Decalogue

At the end of two days of wide-ranging discussions, Kimball, with the assistance of Campbell and Kocher, proposed a series of resolutions that reflected "the sense of the committee after their consideration of the evidence and problems" presented by the restoration architects. In twenty pithy paragraphs consisting of one or two sentences, Kimball and his colleagues laid out a series of general principles that they felt would serve as guidelines for addressing many of the issues raised in the meeting.

The resolutions recommended that all buildings that reflected "the colonial tradition" should be preserved, regardless of date; structures that retained classical design features ought to be removed only after careful consideration. More modern buildings, dating from after 1840, should be pulled down. Large-scale buildings in the Greek Revival style, such as the Baptist Church on Market Square, were clearly seen to be outside that tradition.[37] Old foundations should be kept where possible. Historic buildings should remain in their original locations and none should be moved from outside into the historic area. Great care should be taken in preserving original fabric, even if it might be more costly to do so. A distinction should be made between the preservation of a building by ordinary repair compared to the restoration of one through wholesale reconstruction. All work in the historic area required a slower pace of repair and reconstruction compared to the rapidity associated with modern construction methods in order to achieve superior results. Old material could be used in restorations and reconstructions where it could be secured without destroying other buildings; no effort should be made to artificially age new fabric. The advisory board concluded by acknowledging the debt they owed to Goodwin for devising "the program for the preservation of the historic character of Williamsburg" and to Rockefeller's "decision to undertake and finance the preservation and restoration on a comprehensive scale." They also conveyed their appreciation of the early work of the restoration architects, engineers, and others involved and expressed their "confidence in their judgment and discretion in applying these principles in specific cases" as they arose.[38]

The twenty resolutions were unanimously approved by the advisory board. The restoration architects, Goodwin, and Rockefeller had what they needed from these professionals: a set of rules that laid out principles considered by these experts to be best practices in the field of historic preservation. The scope of the project had been defined, which recognized a commitment to restore or reconstruct all the historic structures that stood within the colonial boundaries of Williamsburg, not just a selective sampling of the most important public buildings and dwellings. Finally, as Rockefeller had wished, the Williamsburg restoration received the blessing of nationally recognized leaders in the field of architectural restoration, who committed themselves to return to Williamsburg on a yearly basis to carefully review all new projects undertaken by the restoration architects.

The Decalogue and Its Impact in the Early Years

The adoption of these restoration rules immediately broke the impasse that had emerged over the restoration of the college building at William and Mary. As Perry noted, the art commission had "been unwilling to approve a restoration of the building" as it appeared in its second incarnation, when it was rebuilt following the first fire of 1705. In May 1929, Kimball led a special executive subcommittee of the advisory board, which made short shrift of arguments that favored a more pleasing aesthetic design of the east front entrance, an iron balcony, and the taller cupola that Edmund Campbell and others had preferred. Kimball, Bellows, and Medary used the physical evidence of the building that showed that the central front projection had not been added after the fire but had been integral to it from the very beginning; it needed to be accepted, since the physical and documentary evidence of the post-1705 rebuilding made these original forms undisputable, though they were more prosaic.[39] Any variation from the evidence was not warranted, as they argued, "if the purpose of the present undertaking is to restore the building to its appearance as an historic building of outstanding interest in the history of Virginia and America." As they noted, if this evidence were "to be set aside and the work regarded as an example of the work of Sir Christopher Wren, a conjectural estimate of what might or might not have been his work might be plausible," but they doubted it. Any designs that were not anchored to the physical or documentary evidence but based on aesthetic preferences found in Wren's English works were deemed untenable.[40]

Here, in its first test, the principles of the resolutions were reaffirmed.[41] They set the parameters for weighing the merits of future discussions. For example, three years later, when a landscape designer called for an elaborate symmetrical plan for the gardens and outbuildings of the Governor's Palace despite archaeological and documentary evidence that directly contradicted the design, the Advisory Committee of Architects cut short the discussion, noting that there was no precedent for such an ahistorical scheme. They observed that "the records indicate a succession of designers and frequent changes in the intentions of the plan. The evidence of records and foundations are the only reliable documents to follow."[42]

By the mid-1930s, the restoration had reached a crescendo with the design, reconstruction, and opening of the Governor's Palace, Capitol, Raleigh Tavern, and many other public and domestic buildings. During this time, Perry, Shaw and Hepburn revised the resolutions passed by the Advisory Committee of Architects in 1928, paring them down to ten points by eliminating a few specific issues and the encomiums paid to the founder and patron of the Williamsburg project. The "decalogue," as it became known, received national attention when it was published in *Architectural Record* in December 1935:

The Williamsburg Decalogue by Perry, Shaw and Hepburn

That all buildings or parts of buildings in which the Colonial tradition persists, should be retained irrespective of their actual date.

That where the Classical Tradition persists in buildings or parts of buildings, great discretion should be exercised before destroying them.

That within the "Restoration Area" all work which no longer represents Colonial or Classical tradition should be demolished or removed.

That old buildings in Williamsburg outside the "Restoration Area" wherever possible should be left, and if possible preserved on their original sites and restored there rather than moved within the "Area."

That no surviving old work should be rebuilt for structural reasons if any reasonable additional trouble and expense would suffice to preserve it.

That there should be held in the mind of the architects and in the marking of buildings—The distinction between *preservation*, where the object is scrupulous retention of the surviving work by ordinary repair, and *restoration*, where the object is the recovery of the old form by new work; and that the largest practicable number of buildings should be preserved rather than restored.

That such preservation and restoration work requires a slower pace than ordinary modern construction work and that in our opinion a superior result should be preferred to more rapid progress.

That in restoration the use of old materials and details of the period and character, properly marked, is commendable when they can be secured.

That in the securing of old materials there should be no demolition or removal of buildings where there seems a reasonable prospect that they will persist intact on their original sites.

That where new materials must be used, they should be of a character approximating the old as closely as possible, but that no attempt should be made to "antique" them by theatrical means.

Perry's richly illustrated essay, with an introduction by Kimball, highlighted the accomplishments of the first years of the restoration and included the ten restoration principles that had guided their decisions. They were a verbatim reiteration of the first half of the Kimball/Campbell/Kocher proposals of November 1928.[43] However, there were some noticeable departures from the earlier document. Perry dropped Kimball's concern that wholesale reconstructions would predominate over the restoration of surviving structures in the historic area, which Kimball believed would weaken the veracity of the entire enterprise. By 1935, with the reconstruction of the Raleigh Tavern, Capitol, and Governor's Palace, that appeared to be the case.[44] They also ignored the distinction between reconstructions and restorations. In the case of the latter, they rarely retained later additions, as Kocher had advocated. Kimball's admonition about copying conspicuous features from well-known buildings in the new restorations had also been set aside. As the project progressed at full tilt in the early 1930s, the architects drew upon a storehouse of examples, ranging from English precedents to features found in many of the larger plantation houses in Tidewater Virginia. Astute students strolling through the historic area can easily spot the knockoffs. An elaborate iron balcony based on one of Wren's designs (as recommended earlier by Charles A. Coolidge for the college restoration) showed up on the Capitol where none should have been, so now there is a little bit of Wren at both ends of the Duke of Gloucester Street.[45] The unique set of chimney stacks linked by arches erected by William Walker at Stratford in the late 1730s reappeared in the reconstruction of Shields Tavern. The arched shouldered panels found in the doors at Four Mile Tree in Surry County feature prominently in Singleton Moorehead's design of the pulpit at Bruton Parish Church. Lawrence Kocher's restoration reports of Williamsburg buildings written twenty years after they were restored contain a litany of such wholesale borrowings.

Kimball's laws were not inviolable. Management and the restoration architects deliberately disregarded some of the principles enshrined in the decalogue. A small number of eighteenth-century buildings in the historic area were dismantled by Colonial Williamsburg, an infringement of the very first "commandment." Perhaps threatened by the widening of the intersection of Lafayette and Francis Streets in the southeast corner of town, the one-story framed Mayo House was taken down and never reerected. Easily the most shameful act of removing a historic building occurred with the dismantling of Tazewell Hall, the elegant residence built by the colony's last attorney general, John Randolph, in 1762, which had once formed a dramatic vista at the terminus of South England Street. Unfortunately, the house suffered three strikes against its preservation. First, it was the home of the most prominent Tory in Williamsburg, whose political preferences did not fit Goodwin and Rockefeller's patriotic storyline. Second, the building had been altered in the 1830s by the Tazewell family and moved in 1908 when the street was lengthened to accommodate new housing. And finally, the owner of the house, Peyton Randolph Nelson—who sold it with life rights to Goodwin in the late 1920s—was an irascible man who refused to pay his lighting bills after it had been restored. When the Williamsburg Lodge was built next to it in the late 1930s, its fate was sealed. After Nelson's death, Colonial Williamsburg decided to take it down in the early 1950s to make room for the hotel's expansion. Systematically dismantled with its fine collection of paneled rooms, the house was sold to a purchaser who reconstructed it in Newport News.[46]

The Travis House was moved off its original site on Francis Street, near Eastern State Hospital, to the bottom of Palace Green, where it was restored and opened as a restaurant in the early days. It was moved back to its original location a few years later. The Digges House, a small frame dwelling on the northwest edge of town, was moved a block west of its original site on the southwest corner of Prince George and Boundary Streets to make way for a new college dormitory in 1930. The building was not in the hands of Colonial Williamsburg at the time, minimizing the organization's culpability, but its management had turned down an offer to purchase the building before it was moved, despite the structure's eighteenth-century origins and location within the boundaries of the colonial city. In recent years, the house has been identified as the home of the Bray School, which was established in 1760 to teach enslaved and free Black children, and it now claims a cultural and social significance it would not have had ninety years ago. In 2023, Colonial Williamsburg moved it to a new site in the historic area, where it was restored but disconnected from its original historical context.[47]

During the first years of the restoration, the use of antique material for restorations and reconstructions had flourished, much to the detriment of early houses in the region (as Robert Bellows had predicted in the first meeting of the advisory committee). In the late 1920s and early 1930s, vandals stripped old houses of their doors, paneling, staircases, floorboards, mantels, and other woodwork and sold their plunder to middlemen who asked few questions about their origins; rather, they jacked up the prices of the material and sold it to the restoration team. The paneling that was installed in the Ludwell-Paradise House, which was converted into a museum for Abby Rockefeller's folk art collection, came from an old house in southside Virginia, a particularly vulnerable region filled with abandoned farmhouses brought low by the crisis of the Great Depression. Less pernicious was the stocking of the elaborate gardens created by landscape architect Arthur Shurcliff, who went on a purchasing spree through North and South Carolina in the early 1930s, buying up old boxwood by the boxcar load. Within ten years, Colonial Williamsburg put an end to this trade and renounced the use of antique materials in its restorations after seeing many buildings and gardens stripped of their historical assets.

Despite ignoring the spirit of the decalogue in these few instances, having it in place and endorsed by Goodwin and Rockefeller gave cover to the architects and subsequent generations of Colonial Williamsburg historians to use against those within the organization and outside critics who, as Rockefeller anticipated, would question the direction or validity of the enterprise.[48] The pledge to base design and restoration decisions on diligent research and to undertake new work at a pace that, as Goodwin put it, placed "fidelity to an ideal rather than fidelity to a time schedule" kept new buildings from being erected anywhere but on historic foundations and helped blunt fanciful designs or ahistorical building programs.[49]

The advisory committee of architects who devised the protocols that became the Williamsburg decalogue steered future restoration philosophy in America toward a more cautious, evidentiary approach to design. The current Secretary of the Interior restoration standards can trace their lineage to the Williamsburg decalogue. As the advisory committee returned to Williamsburg every year, they saw those ideals implemented in the massive amount of work that constituted the earliest phase of the restoration.[50] Perry paid public tribute to them for their guidance in formulating the "ground rules in the early days of 1928 before the architects could go far astray. This decalogue is figuratively engraved in each building, roadway, garden, furnishing or decoration, however slight its relative importance."[51] Its impact would be lasting, thanks in no small part to the scale and successful reception of the Colonial Williamsburg project and the leadership of Fiske Kimball. Over the twenty years the committee gathered to review the work of the Colonial Williamsburg architects, Kimball never missed a meeting. He continued to emphasize the decalogue's essential principles and firmly believed that design should be governed by evidence found in the fabric of buildings, in the ground, in documents, and in regional precedents. So valuable was his advice that Thomas Mott Shaw later recalled that all meetings were convened to fit Kimball's busy schedule.[52] It was a timetable worth honoring.

Notes

1. William Graves Perry, "Notes on the Architecture," *Architectural Record* 78, no. 6 (1935): 369.
2. Charles B. Hosmer Jr., *Preservation Comes of Age: From Williamsburg to the National Trust, 1926–1949* (Charlottesville: University of Virginia Press, 1981), 898, 900.
3. Colonel Arthur Woods to William G. Perry, "The Williamsburg Journals of William G. Perry, 1927–1942 in Five Volumes," transcriptions, Rockefeller Library, Colonial Williamsburg Foundation, 2:11, April 8, 1929; hereafter cited as Perry Journals.
4. Travis McDonald, "The Fundamental Practice of Fieldwork at Colonial Williamsburg," *Perspectives in Vernacular Architecture* 13, no. 2 (2006/2007): 36.
5. Mark R. Wenger, *Carter's Grove: The Story of a Virginia Plantation* (Williamsburg, VA: Colonial Williamsburg, 1994), 12–14.
6. The much-altered main building of the College of William and Mary was designated simply as the "college building" from its construction until 1931, after its restoration by Perry, Shaw and Hepburn, when it was officially renamed the "Wren Building" under the assumption that architect Sir Christopher Wren had actually supplied the designs for the structure, although no direct evidence was ever discovered to prove the assertion.
7. Perry Journals, 1:5, June 29, 1927.
8. Perry Journals, 1:24, November 9, 1928.
9. Perry Journals, 1:26, November 21, 1928.
10. Early in his career, Kimball was keen to promote the study and preservation of early American architecture among professional organizations. While a member of the faculty at the University of Michigan in 1916, Kimball organized a Committee on Colonial and National Art in North America for the Archaeological Institute of America to promote the historical study and preservation of the nation's early monuments and works of art. His committee included architect Glenn Brown of Washington, DC, William Sumner Appleton of the Society for the Preservation of New England Antiquities in Boston, and R. T. Halsey, the chairman of the committee on American art at the Metropolitan Museum in New York. Kimball believed that the preeminent archaeological society in the country should promote the "accurate historical study of our early monuments and works of art" through a series of publications, "stimulate museums to develop their collections of early American art and handicraft," and "encourage public authorities to undertake an inventory" of important monuments, following the lead of other countries. *Bulletin of the Archaeological Institute of America: Annual Reports* 7 (December 1916): 65–66. In a similar vein, Kimball chaired the Committee on the Preservation of Historic Monuments and Scenic Beauties for the American Institute of Architects from 1922 to 1925. *Proceedings of the*

Fifty-Eighth Annual Convention of the American Institute of Architects (Washington, DC: American Institute of Architects, 1925), 44–45.

11. "Minutes of the Meetings of the Advisory Committee of Architects, 1928–1948," transcriptions, Rockefeller Library, Colonial Williamsburg Foundation, December 2, 1930, 5; hereafter cited as "Minutes."

12. Charles B. Hosmer Jr., *Presence of the Past: A History of the Preservation Movement in the United States Before Williamsburg* (New York: G. P. Putnam's Sons, 1965), 207.

13. Hosmer, *Presence of the Past*, 207; McDonald, "Fundamental Practice of Fieldwork," 37.

14. For a detailed discussion of changing opinions on the validity of Wren's association with the design of the college building, see James D. Kornwolf, *"So Good a Design": The Colonial Campus of the College of William and Mary; Its History, Background, and Legacy* (Williamsburg, VA: College of William and Mary, 1989), 163–71.

15. Both the restoration architects and the art commissioners agreed that the restoration should be based as far as possible on the evidence of the surviving early walls of the building, but they parted ways when no such evidence existed. Campbell and his fellow commissioners maintained that lost features should replicate designs found in Wren's work to recapture the manner and spirit of the original designer. Memo from the Advisory Committee of Architects to the Art Commission, January 4, 1929, J. A. C. Chandler Papers, President's Office, 1930–31, Restoration of the Wren Building, Special Collections, Swem Library, College of William and Mary; hereafter cited as Chandler Papers.

16. Campbell memo to art commissioners, December 28, 1928, Chandler Papers.

17. Hosmer, *Preservation Comes of Age*, 966.

18. Perry Journals, 1:5, September 6, 1927.

19. Perry Journals, 1:6, September 13, 1927.

20. Perry Journals, 1:6, October 1, 1927; George Yetter and Carl Lounsbury, *Restoring Williamsburg* (Williamsburg, VA: Colonial Williamsburg, 2019), 66.

21. Perry Journals, 1:7, November 19, 1927. In the 1920s, most historians and architects believed that Westover was built by William Byrd II in the late 1720s or early 1730s. In 2002, dendrochronological investigation of the framing timbers of the house revealed that it was constructed in 1750–51 by his son, William Byrd III. Cary Carson and Carl Lounsbury, eds., *The Chesapeake House: Architectural Investigation by Colonial Williamsburg* (Chapel Hill: University of North Carolina Press, 2013), 408.

22. Perry Journals, 1:7, November 19, 1927.

23. Yetter and Lounsbury, *Restoring Williamsburg*, 66.

24. Fiske Kimball, "The Restoration of Colonial Williamsburg in Virginia," *Architectural Record* 78, no. 6 (1935): 359.

25. "Minutes," November 25, 1928, 2–4.

26. Perry Journals, 1:26, November 21, 1928; "Minutes," November 25, 1928, 2.

27. "Minutes," November 26, 1928, 9–10.

28. "Minutes," November 25, 1928, 6.

29. "Minutes," November 26, 1928, 9.

30. Perry Journals, 1:7, November 19, 1927.

31. Charles E. Brownell, Calder Loth, William M. S. Rasmussen, and Richard Guy Wilson, *The Making of Virginia Architecture* (Richmond: Virginia Museum of Fine Arts, 1992); Sarah Shields Driggs, Richard Guy Wilson, and Robert P. Winthrop, *Richmond's Monument Avenue* (Chapel Hill: University of North Carolina Press, 2001).

32. "Minutes," November 25, 1928, 3.

33. "Minutes," November 25, 1928, 5; Fiske Kimball, "The Preservation Movement in America," *Journal of the Society of Architectural Historians* 1, nos. 3–4 (1941): 16.

34. "Minutes," November 25, 1928, 5.

35. "Minutes," November 25, 1928, 7.

36. "Minutes," November 25, 1928, 8.

37. Built in 1856, the First Baptist Church, a stuccoed tetrastyle temple elevated on a raised basement, was demolished in 1934. It stood too close to—and dwarfed—the 1715 octagonal brick magazine.

38. "Minutes," November 26, 1928, 11–12.

39. Perry Journals, 2:18, May 29, 1929.

40. "Minutes," May 29, 1929, 7–8.

41. Edmund Campbell, writing on behalf of the art commissioners to William and Mary President J. A. C. Chandler, did not take the opinions of Kimball and others concerning the validity of their evidence as gospel and was sorry that the college architect Charles M. Robinson and the president had accepted the recommendations of Perry, Shaw and Hepburn over that of the commissioners. He observed that "undoubtedly the Governor will write us we better forget it and let the building [be] a joke as a restoration." Although he maintained that Kimball, Kocher, Bellows, and Taylor were his friends, he remained steadfast in believing that he was "near right in my views and discoveries regarding the building." Campbell to Chandler, August 8, 1929, Chandler Papers.

42. "Minutes," October 27, 1932, 4.

43. Perry, "Notes on the Architecture," 370.

44. Hosmer, *Preservation Comes of Age*, 964–65.

45. On the impact of this practice on the design of the Williamsburg capitol, see Carl Lounsbury, "Beaux-Arts Ideals and Colonial Reality: The Reconstruction of Williamsburg's Capitol, 1928–1934," *Journal of the Society of Architectural Historians* 49 (December 1990): 373–89.

46. Yetter and Lounsbury, *Restoring Williamsburg*, 87–88.

47. Carl Lounsbury and students, William and Mary Architectural Field School, Spring 2021, "Dudley Digges House: Room-by-Room Inventory of the Building Fabric," unpublished report, May 2021. An agreement between William and Mary and Colonial Williamsburg in 2021 enabled the house to be moved from its location on college property in 2023 to a new site on the north side of Francis Street in the historic area, where it was restored to its 1760 appearance. Although the move violated one of the principles of the decalogue, it was impossible to return the Digges House to its original site, since a college dormitory had been built on it in 1930.

48. With the rise of modernism in American design after World War II, the restoration of Williamsburg began to be criticized for a variety of reasons, including the notion that the work was inauthentic—a pale if not false image of the past that glossed over the harsher realities of colonial life and the racial and social injustices that permeated early American culture. *New York Times* architecture critic Ada Louise Huxtable maintained for many decades that there was an inherent futility in the belief that past landscapes could be re-created through careful research. See, for example, Huxtable's "The Way It Never Was" in *The Unreal America: Architecture and Illusion* (New York: New Press, 1997), 15–36.

49. Hosmer, *Preservation Comes of Age*, 961.

50. America's entry into World War II brought an end to the first phase of work in the historic area. Between 1928 and 1942, 590 modern buildings were demolished; 18 more had been moved out of the historic area. The Williamsburg architects had overseen the restoration of 84 colonial buildings, and 231 new buildings had been reconstructed on colonial foundations. Yetter and Lounsbury, *Restoring Williamsburg*, 86.

51. Perry, "Notes on the Architecture," 363.

52. Hosmer, *Preservation Comes of Age*, 961.

"BETTER TO PRESERVE THAN TO REPAIR"

Fiske Kimball and the Preservation Movement

JOHN H. SPRINKLE JR.

Fiske Kimball had a profound and lasting impact on American historic preservation practice as it matured on either side of World War II. Coining the phrase "preservation movement" in a 1941 article, he helped establish the concept that American architecture was inherently worthy of national recognition and stewardship, even in the absence of other historical associations. This assured the inclusion of superlative American architecture within an emerging panorama of official recognition that evolved with the National Park Service's (NPS) implementation of the Historic Sites Act of 1935.[1] Recognizing threats to a surplus of architecturally significant federal buildings in urban settings, he was an early and strong advocate for the adaptive use of historic buildings beyond their traditional associative, educational, and interpretive values. Perhaps his most lasting contribution was a three-part preservation mantra that served as the foundation for American stewardship practices for decades: "Better to preserve than to repair; better to repair than to restore; better to restore than to construct or reconstruct."[2]

To paraphrase Kimball's famous quip that it was easier to get a PhD than explain why you hadn't, it would be simpler to describe the few aspects of American historic preservation that were untouched by his authoritative, scholarly, and larger-than-life character during the first half of the twentieth century.[3] Nonetheless, this essay will indicate specific examples of his contributions.

Dr. Kimball's List

One vehicle for Kimball's broad influence within the preservation movement was his fifteen years of service (1936–51) on the National Park System Advisory Board.[4] The Advisory Board was established by the Historic Sites Act of 1935 to provide the Department of the Interior with access to professional, academic, and pragmatic advice and to protect it from the undue influence of patrons and politicians. Its main duty was to grade the historical significance of buildings and sites proposed for addition to a growing list of National Parks. Because the NPS was bound by limits set by Congress and sought to slow the tide of a potentially unwieldy list of new acquisitions, the Advisory Board deliberated, deferred, and deterred consideration on a wide range of issues. Through its operation it established many of the criteria and conventions for the identification, evaluation, and recognition of historic places that continue to serve in the National Register of Historic Places.[5] Noted for his "sincerity, ability, and historic devotion,"[6] Kimball was appointed to the Advisory Board as a result of his acknowledged expertise in the history of American architecture, his breadth of experience with the restoration of numerous historic properties throughout the eastern United States, and his prior service on the advisory board at Colonial Williamsburg.[7]

Authorized by the Historic Sites Act, the NPS embarked on creating a national inventory of historic places using a catalogue of historical themes, such as "English Colonization," the logic being that a comprehensive and comparative context was required for the impartial evaluation of the significance of any one historic site.[8] At the first meeting of the Advisory Board in 1936, NPS Chief Historian Verne Chatelain elaborated on those "certain matchless or unique qualities" possessed by nationally significant places associated with either great Americans or dramatic events in history.[9]

But could examples of American architecture be seen as nationally significant on their own? Chatelain suggested that it might be "desirable . . . to preserve outstanding examples of historical architecture even in some cases where important historical events have not occurred," but only "if such examples are the best to be found and if other contemporary examples, with perhaps more historic merit, have disappeared."[10] From his perspective, places associated with historic events, regardless of their physical integrity, were inherently more important for stewardship by the NPS than examples of great architecture. Kimball happily pounced on this opening, noting that places "in which no outstanding historical events took place, but which are typical examples of architecture," were also worthy of consideration.[11]

Based on his own experience and expertise, Kimball then "undertook a list of surviving buildings which could be regarded as of national significance—not only for events which took place there but equally for their artistic merit."[12] First presented to the Advisory Board in 1938 and formally adopted in 1941, Kimball's catalogue was a unique expression of what one nationally recognized authority thought were the most important examples of American architecture.[13] While this list included a cornucopia of expected properties, such as the seventeenth-century Bacon's Castle in Surry County, Virginia, it also included the Allegheny County Courthouse (H. H. Richardson, 1888); the Wainwright Building (Adler & Sullivan, 1892); and the Larkin Administration Building (Frank Lloyd Wright, 1906). Each of these three buildings was quite a bit more recent than the initial 1860 cut-off date for consideration established by the Park Service staff. Often pigeonholed as the champion of traditional design, from the 1910s on Kimball had recognized the impact of modern design within American architectural practice.[14]

Through his scholarship, Kimball helped craft a context for American architectural history. As late as the beginning of the 1930s, he claimed, even the best colonial American designs were not regarded as "masterpieces of architecture" on the same level as European examples, although they provided "convincing evidence of the cultural life and the appreciation of the beautiful in eighteenth-century America which until recent years has had little recognition."[15] In order for the early preservation movement to justify its goals, American architecture had to be surveyed, documented, and interpreted so that its importance could be established within a wider architectural and historical context. Kimball's authority within the field led the NPS leadership to accept—albeit reluctantly—the concept of architectural significance as separate from historical or archaeological associations. His work with the Advisory Board helped ensure that American architecture was "equal in importance" to the study of European designs.[16] Soon after Kimball's list of nationally significant examples of American architecture was adopted by the Advisory Board, the Park Service was confronted by the unanticipated gift of one such property to the American people.

Hampton

On the morning of December 11, 1945, Fiske Kimball arrived about thirty minutes after the start of a postwar "interim" meeting of the Advisory Board. Immediately bringing up a topic that was not on the official meeting agenda, Kimball interjected with his usual bluster: "Has anyone said anything about Hampton?"[17]

Located outside Baltimore, Hampton was the late eighteenth-century home of the Ridgely family. Today, among other accolades, Hampton is notable as the first property federally designated as nationally significant *only* for its architectural qualities. Hampton's federal recognition and acquisition was a threshold in the story of creating official memory. It served as the administrative foundation for

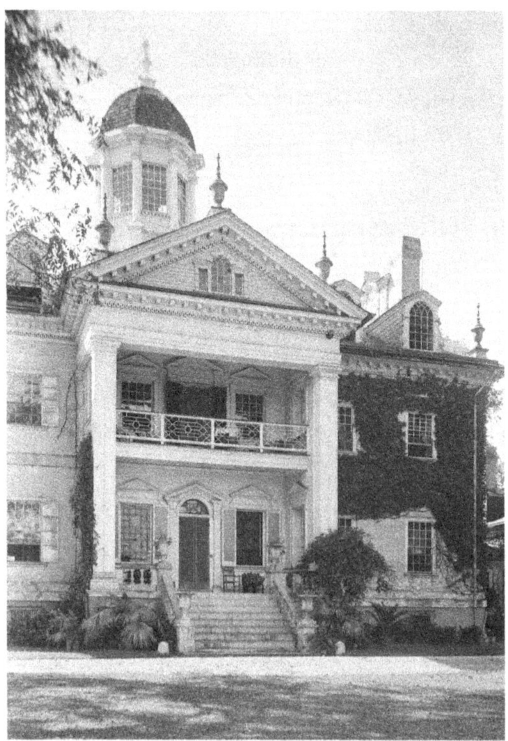

FIGURE 1. North portico of Hampton, home of the Ridgely family, Towson, Maryland, 1936. Construction began in 1783. (Charles Ridgely et al., Historic American Buildings Survey, HABS MD, 3-TOW.V, 1A, Library of Congress Prints and Photographs Division, Washington, DC)

the National Register of Historic Places Criterion C, the most common category used to demonstrate a property's significance over the last six decades.[18]

In this effort Kimball partnered with David Finley, the head of the National Gallery of Art, who had discussed the plight of Hampton over dinner in New York City with Ailsa Mellon Bruce, the recently divorced daughter of the National Gallery of Art's recently deceased patron, Andrew Mellon.[19] Using a drawing from the 1933 book *Great Georgian Houses of America* (another Kimball project) to illustrate the architectural qualities of the building, Finley persuaded her to rescue the core of the colonial estate and donate it to the federal government.[20]

After convincing the donor, the next step was to persuade the NPS. Kimball was extremely confident in his estimation of Hampton's qualities and distinctiveness. "As one of the leading mansions of one of the 13 colonies," he observed, "it deserves permanent preservation, and is of a significance to justify that its maintenance should be at the expense of the nation."[21] But regardless of the estate's architectural assets (and projected endowment), Congress remained reluctant to adequately fund the preservation and interpretation of new historical parks.

Even homes associated with former presidents were not automatically considered for federal stewardship.[22] In the end, the acceptance of Hampton within the collection of National Park properties was directly tied to the creation of the National Trust for Historic Preservation in 1948.[23]

Separation of Church and State

In Kimball's overlapping worlds as an academic, architect, museum curator, and preservationist, it was impossible to avoid the considerable impact that influential and privileged persons and politicians had on determining what kinds of places would be considered worthy of conservation. Recalling Kimball's courting of art collectors Louise and Walter Arensberg, Beatrice Wood described him as a "first-rate, charming rascal. The kind of man who should be the head of a museum because he knew exactly how to handle rich people."[24] Clearly, Kimball had significant skills in negotiating among the diverse interests of his patrons, a talent that helped solidify the recognition of American architecture as yet another form of art worth curating. In the recognition of historic American church architecture, he aptly demonstrated his skills in navigating the interests of influential people while constructing a regulatory shortcut that avoided a potential constitutional dilemma found in the separation of church and state.

Located in Mount Vernon, New York, the present St. Paul's Church was begun during the mid-1760s and completed in 1805. St. Paul's claim to fame rested on its association with the Great Election of 1733, which was held somewhere on the village green. The acquittal of John Peter Zenger in 1735 for his allegedly seditious and libelous newspaper coverage of the election is one of the foundations of the principle of freedom of the press, as set forth in the First Amendment of the Constitution. Over the years, the site vanished from the landscape, but the church, even though it was built decades after the Great Election, had become a monument to the earlier event.

Given the constitutionally mandated separation of church and state, the Park Service was justifiably wary of granting federal recognition to a historic site associated with an actively used religious property. Just as the provisions of the Historic Sites Act were being established, a cluster of influential persons, led by President Franklin Delano Roosevelt's mother, Sara Delano Roosevelt, began efforts to restore St. Paul's with an eye toward making it a national shrine for freedom of the press.[25] In 1938, Congressman James Fitzpatrick requested that the Advisory Board weigh in on the site's national significance. While NPS historians were extremely reluctant to legitimize the building's tenuous association

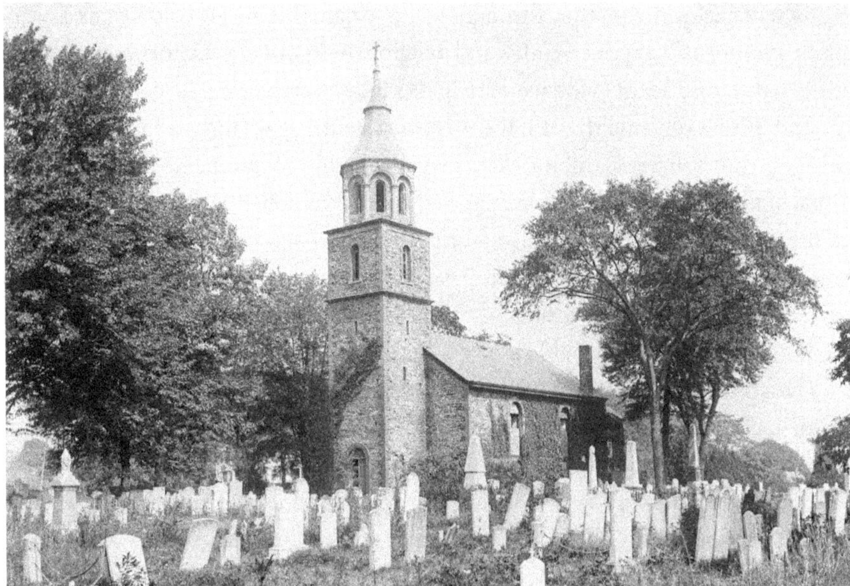

FIGURE 2. St. Paul's Church, Mount Vernon, New York, ca. 1903. (Detroit Publishing Co., LC-D418–9188, Library of Congress Prints and Photographs Division, Washington, DC)

with any historic events, Kimball offered his frank opinion: "On the strength of its architectural merit (not of its history), we might be able to declare the church to be of national significance," but only if an ensemble of churches of "equal or greater merit" were first recognized by the NPS.[26] Based on this assessment, the Advisory Board bravely rejected the church's national significance. Not to be deterred, three years later Congressman Fitzpatrick used the occasion of a Park Service budget hearing to revisit the historical status of St. Paul's Church. The timing of Fitzpatrick's question was not lost on the agency's leadership, and it quickly complied with Kimball's request. Kimball may not have thought St. Paul's was nationally significant, but given its patrons, he used the opportunity to secure the designation for churches he thought were nationally significant. Having achieved his goal of establishing a precedent for the recognition of a cohort of more architecturally significant churches, Kimball declared, "Let the President and Mrs. Roosevelt have what they want."[27]

While the qualities of historic architecture proved a viable means to circumvent any constitutional issues with the designation of religious properties, the symbolic use of such places often proved difficult. In early 1944, Arthur Sulzberger, publisher of the *New York Times,* asked the Park Service to identify important historic churches throughout the original thirteen colonies as a wartime "symbol of American unity and religious tolerance."[28] Unfortunately, NPS historians found scant evidence of religious toleration among the colonies. To get around this inconvenient truth, the Advisory Board again turned to Kimball's list of significant religious architecture. Kimball highly recommend the fine Touro Synagogue in Newport, Rhode Island, designed by Peter Harrison, "the prince of the colonial amateurs," whose work "set a new standard of classical dignity and correctness."[29] Fortunately, the site also had important historical associations with both George Washington and the Sulzberger family, which helped support its designation as a National Historic Site in 1946.

The administrative and constitutional conflict over the federal recognition of historic church properties was matched by the tension between the emerging field of historic preservation professionals and the other heritage enthusiasts. From his perspective, Kimball observed the "great contrast between the inconsequent opportunism of the lay members and the long-range view of the professionals" on the Advisory Board.[30] The NPS leadership used thematic studies, like Kimball's list of important architecture, as a tool in managing expectations about potential federal recognition and stewardship. This pragmatic and reportedly objective approach reflected the maturation of the historic preservation movement, and from the Park Service's perspective, it significantly reduced the potential for controversy. Kimball's creativity in developing a means by which churches could be recognized while avoiding constitutional entanglements laid the foundation for yet another convention adopted by the National Register of Historic Places after 1966.

Better to Preserve Than to Repair . . .

During the 1930s, as more than sixty historic sites were added to its portfolio and Depression-era work programs included substantial historic preservation projects, the NPS endeavored to rapidly develop its internal expertise in the identification, evaluation, and treatment of historic properties.[31] Bound to the management of the sublimely tall, deep, and vast landscapes of the American West, the NPS was administratively ill-prepared for the challenges of stewardship that came with old buildings and their settings.[32] Fiske Kimball provided the expertise, experience, and authority that set lasting standards for the conservation of historic properties.

"Thoroughly versed in the history of restoration policy and practice" dating back to the works of John Ruskin and Eugène Viollet-le-Duc, Kimball, according to NPS historian Charles Porter, was the only member of the Advisory Board "competent . . . to speak on the subject" of historic preservation.[33] Describing the state of historic preservation in the 1920s, Kimball's longtime collaborator Erling Pedersen noted that most contemporary architects had "very little regard for . . . colonial buildings or restorations. . . . They wanted to tear them down; they saw no charm whatsoever in them. . . . But he [Kimball] was the only real restoration man that I ever ran into."[34] As Charles Hosmer concluded, he "was as dedicated to historical truth as any architect of his time."[35]

Just as the agency was eager to establish criteria and procedures for its survey of historic sites, it was also interested in creating policy and conventions for the treatment of historic buildings and other resources within the park system. As noted above, Kimball laid the foundation for the NPS's restoration and rehabilitation practices in a three-part preservation philosophy: "Better to preserve than to repair; better to repair than to restore; better to restore than to construct or reconstruct." This preservationist's Hippocratic Oath had its origins in nineteenth-century European practices and in the decalogue adopted by the Colonial Williamsburg restoration (to which Kimball contributed). Indeed, it owes a direct debt to the French archaeologist Adolphe-Napoléon Didron's 1839 slogan. Kimball's transatlantic adoption of it illustrated a continuing thread in American historic preservation—that of looking toward western Europe for preservation philosophy and practice.[36] It reflected the philosophical contrast between those who believe, as noted by Henry James, "what is left is more precious than what is added; the one is history, the other is fiction," and those who sought a more activist restoration of historic properties.[37] Kimball addressed the issue forthrightly in his 1941 article "The Preservation Movement" for the *Journal of the Society of Architectural Historians:* "With the advantage of European experience," American preservationists were increasingly focused on documentary and archaeological research and "on preservation and repair, rather than on reconstruction or 'purification.'"[38] Respecting the work of past builders and designers, according to Kimball, required "different qualities in an architect—not imagination, but historical knowledge; not originality, but self-abnegation."[39] Indeed, he concluded, "More harm has perhaps been done to historic buildings by ill-judged 'restoration' than by neglect, and such damage is really irreparable."[40]

The antithesis of Kimball's stated philosophy was the reconstruction of vanished historic buildings. Asked by NPS Chief Historian Ronald Lee about the fanciful and controversial reconstruction at Wakefield, Virginia, Kimball suggested that "it might be good to pull down the memorial mansion" once certain patrons had passed away.[41] In the late 1930s his harsh criticism of the poorly conceived reconstruction of Pennsbury Manor in Bucks County, Pennsylvania, resulted in the NPS closely reviewing all subsequent Public Works Authority (PWA) restoration projects.[42] After years of deterring efforts to reconstruct buildings at Jamestown Island, Kimball wrote to David Finley to ensure that he would be "on the side of the angels" and not support "any plausible unwise scheme" for creative reconstruction as part of the upcoming 350th commemorations at the site.[43]

Hosmer credited Kimball with setting "preservation's philosophical course" with his often-repeated (and often-ignored) prescription for the treatment of historic buildings.[44] Forty years later, the National Trust for Historic Preservation adaptively used the axiom to explain and justify the diverse and special (and more costly) professional knowledge, skills, and abilities associated with preservation and restoration work.[45] At the twentieth anniversary of the National Historic Preservation Act in 1986, Robert Stipe referenced the phrase as "our basic guideline" passed down from the nineteenth century, which NPS Chief Historian Robert Utley called an "old saw."[46] The philosophy of "minimum intervention" found its way into the core of the NPS's 1998 textbook for the management of cultural resources nationwide—the well-thumbed policy known to wonks everywhere as "Director's Order 28."[47]

Great White Elephants

While Kimball's own execution of this preservation mantra may not have been perfect, its widespread adoption by the preservation community helped address perhaps one of the most pressing issues in American historic preservation on either side of World War II: what to do with an increasing number of "Great White Elephant" federal buildings. Here, too, Kimball was at the forefront of promoting the adaptive use of historic properties.

In January 1938, Kimball sent a hurried telegram to Secretary of the Interior Harold Ickes warning of an imminent "artistic calamity" represented by the impending sale of the Old Philadelphia Custom House to private developers.[48] Designed by William Strickland and built from 1819 to 1824 in the Greek Revival style, the Custom House had served as the home of the Second Bank of the United States and symbolized the national banking controversy that was a theme of Andrew Jackson's second presidential campaign in 1832. Thus, the building was an architectural masterpiece with nationally significant historical associations. As Kimball later recalled, "The time to strike for its preservation was when it was still in federal hands and could be transferred to the Park Service merely

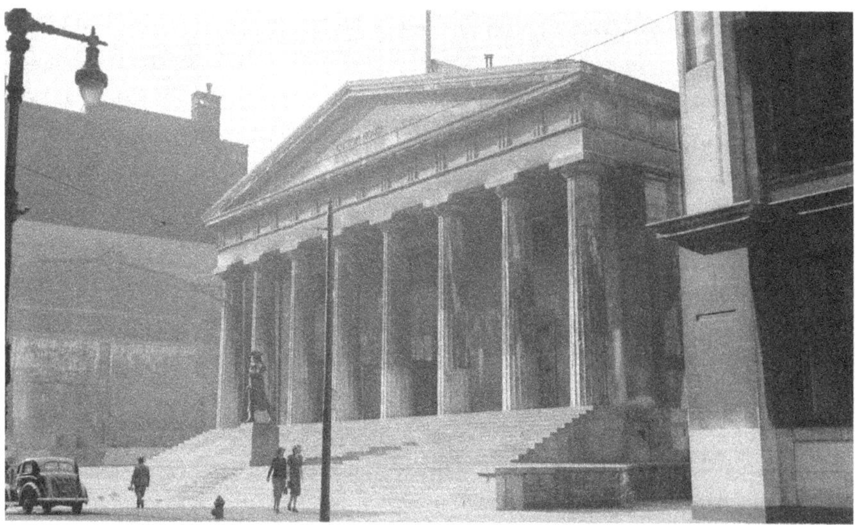

FIGURE 3. Second Bank of the United States, Philadelphia, Pennsylvania, designed by William Strickland, 1818. North façade photographed in 1939. (William Strickland et al., Historic American Buildings Survey, HABS PA, 51-PHILA, 223, Library of Congress Prints and Photographs Division, Washington, DC)

by executive action."[49] Bypassing the usual Advisory Board approval process, Kimball convinced Secretary Ickes to designate the property as a National Historic Site in May 1939.

The next task was to find an organization to occupy and use the building. Marie Kimball suggested that the Philadelphia-based Carl Schurz Memorial Foundation, a well-funded cultural and artistic exchange group (established in 1930 and named after a former Secretary of the Interior), could successfully adapt the bank as a headquarters and library while retaining the property's memorial atmosphere. Unfortunately, in 1940, just as the building was to reopen after a $28,000 restoration, the Foundation was accused of being too close to the Nazi regime—publicity that soured the project's potential impact on the historic preservation movement.[50]

The Second Bank was the first example of the preservation of a major historical building by means of a cooperative agreement between a federal agency and a nonprofit organization. Handled correctly, this approach was seen as an important tool for the continued use of surplus federal buildings. Thus its implementation garnered "special attention as a new departure in American historic preservation methods."[51] As a project of urban renewal, it was also, reflected Charles Peterson, "the entry of the National Park Service into the Philadelphia scene."[52]

In the 1930s there were at least four hundred house museums located across the United States, places that fulfilled a new and growing use for instruction and inspiration. But as Fiske Kimball predicted, despite the success of Colonial Williamsburg, there would soon come a time when tourist traffic alone could not sustain the plethora of house museums. To survive, old houses and other types of historic buildings needed to be adapted to new uses while retaining the physical qualities that demonstrated their connections with the past. At the Second Bank, Kimball set forth many of the principles still applied to adaptively used historic properties, including unfettered access to the principal public spaces, restoration of the most significant interior offices "so that their original character was not erased by their adaptation to modern use," and limited physical changes throughout a building without harming the original building fabric.[53]

Kimball would not live to see the overt commercialization of historic properties through adaptive use that some criticized as subverting the dignity of the building or place (for example, the encroachment of what some folks referred to as drive-in culture or honky-tonk design). After his death in 1955, the concept of adaptive use was frequently linked to the economic advantages of heritage tourism. Knowing how he was an early proponent for the adaptive use of historic properties as a vital part of the preservation movement, one wonders how Kimball would have embraced the diverse prerogatives of the "new preservation" after the enactment of the National Historic Preservation Act in 1966.

Conclusion

Fiske Kimball was certainly larger than life, expressing a plethora of contrasts in his dominating presence, in person and in the field.[54] He was generally not subtle, and his academic prowess was best used sparingly. As noted by Charles Peterson, Kimball was "so much brighter than anybody else" that it was his burden to "be nice to a lot of people that bored him to death." When confronted by self-important people, he was known as the "world's leading insulter," and when dressed down by Kimball, one would "stay permanently insulted."[55] Because of his dramatic character, Peterson concluded that when it came to preservation controversies, Kimball should be saved for "heavy, quick axe-work when some weight is needed for special deals."[56] And yet NPS Historian Herbert Kahler characterized Kimball as a "kindly man" who had a "bluff and arrogant manner which offended some people," often acting like the proverbial bull in a china shop, resulting in exciting and stimulating Advisory Board meetings.[57] Although he was not always ultimately successful, in the final analysis, his skill as a negotiator when dealing with influential politicians and patrons was as advanced as his "almost unbelievable" scholarly understanding of American architectural history.[58]

Kimball's translation and importation of a three-part preservation philosophy continue to shape professional practice, legitimizing the values embedded within American architecture. His late-1930s list of nationally significant examples of American architecture set the stage for the expansion of architectural history as a profession within the United States. As the NPS implemented the provisions of the Historic Sites Act, Kimball's academic stature pushed the agency to adopt and adapt to its new role as the steward to an ever-growing list of historic places. His vision for the adaptive use of surplus architecture encompassed both a chain of colonial mansions within Fairmount Park and a Greek Revival temple in downtown Philadelphia. Serving on the National Park System Advisory Board, Kimball helped craft many of the criteria and conventions that continue to govern entry into the National Register of Historic Places.

Consensus and supremacy ruled Kimball's world, and privilege governed his social and intellectual environment. His persistence and bluster helped create a wider appreciation for American architecture and the conservation of the built environment, a legacy still going strong even a generation after his death. More than just a "restoration architect," Kimball stood as a signpost for the "nascent professionalism" in the stewardship of historic buildings during the first half of the twentieth century.[59]

It was always prudent to let Fiske have the last word. Writing from Shack Mountain to a NPS superintendent in 1945, he candidly acknowledged the perennial conflict between the impact of field research and the weight of public expectation and tradition:

> The questions you ask me are ones I cannot answer from this distance, nor even from Philadelphia, where my notes would not cover them. But I believe you can answer them by research, partly at the building. It ought to be perfectly possible to determine about the paint—by some scraping, or possibly by burning off in a small area of the brick work and trim.
>
> I happened to be going by Mount Vernon once when they were doing a routine repainting job which involved burning off some of the accumulated surface of paint. This made it perfectly clear that the trim of the front (if memory serves me) had been red—as we found the window frames to be at Stratford—and the main surface, if I recall, yellow. I wrote this to [Mount Vernon's Resident Director Charles] Wall, who was away at the time of this work, but I imagine the white paint is too sanctified in the

minds of the good ladies to be changed very soon. Scrape, flaking off the coats, and do a little burning—and then follow what you find!

It is as humid as Hades here, and I am ass-high in letters.[60]

Notes

1. Connecting "historic preservation" with "movement" recognized the various disciplines—history, architectural history, and archaeology—and the civic and educational goals that were a part of campaigns to preserve, restore, or rehabilitate historic buildings prior to World War II. Fiske Kimball, "The Preservation Movement," *Journal of the American Society of Architectural Historians* 1, nos. 3–4 (1941): 15–17. Charles Hosmer concluded that Kimball was the first to use the phrase "the preservation movement" in print. Charles Hosmer to Frederick L. Rath Jr., October 19, 1982, Charles Hosmer Papers, Special Collections, University of Maryland Libraries (hereafter CHP), series 1, Correspondence.

2. The "expression of policy . . . with respect to preservation repair, restoration, and reconstruction of historical structures" was "prepared and read" by Kimball at the third meeting, in October 1936, and distributed to the "field men" within NPS who would be "required to follow it." Charles B. Hosmer Jr., *Presence of the Past: A History of the Preservation Movement in the United States Before Williamsburg* (New York: G. P. Putnam's Sons, 1965), 274–75. *National Park Service Restoration Policy Statement* (Washington, DC: US Department of the Interior, 1956).

3. As noted by Calvin Tomkins, National Gallery of Art Director J. Carter Brown "decided to get a doctorate after all, more or less on the theory of Fiske Kimball, who used to say it was easier to get a Ph.D. than it was to explain why you hadn't." Calvin Tomkins, "For the Nation," *New Yorker*, September 3, 1990, 49.

4. The group was originally called the Advisory Board on National Parks, Historic Sites, Buildings, and Monuments. The name was changed in 1972.

5. John H. Sprinkle Jr., *Crafting Preservation Criteria: The National Register of Historic Places and American Historic Preservation* (New York: Routledge, 2014).

6. Frank K. Melvin (President, Swedish Colonial Society) to Fiske Kimball, June 17, 1940, Fiske Kimball Papers, Philadelphia Museum of Art Library and Archives (hereafter FKP), box 100, folder 14.

7. Melissa Houghton, *Pioneers in Preservation: Biographical Sketches of Architects Prominent in the Field Before World War II* (Washington, DC: American Institute of Architects, 1990), 47–49. Kimball was among four original Advisory Board members who served for over a decade before a system of rotation was adopted in the early 1950s. His candidacy was undoubtedly supported by

John D. Rockefeller Jr., one of the prime advocates for the Historic Sites Act, owing to Kimball's ongoing work with the board overseeing the work of the Colonial Williamsburg Foundation.

8. Because of its congressional mandate, the NPS focused only on places of national significance, while the Historic American Buildings Survey—another NPS program, administratively established in 1933—focused on those properties that were significantly characteristic of the American builder's art. Thomas Schneider's influential 1935 report to the Secretary of the Interior recognized that places of "superlative quality" with historical, archaeological, architectural, or scientific importance, or "some combination of these factors," could be nationally significant. J. Thomas Schneider, *Report to the Secretary of the Interior on the Preservation of Historic Sites and Buildings* (Washington, DC: Department of the Interior, 1935).

9. Advisory Board on National Parks, Historic Sites, Buildings and Monuments, Department of the Interior, Washington, DC, Meeting Minutes (hereafter Advisory Board Minutes), February 13–14, 1936, Park History Program Subject Files, NPS Headquarters, Washington, DC.

10. Advisory Board Minutes, February 13–14, 1936.

11. Advisory Board Minutes, February 13–14, 1936.

12. John H. Sprinkle Jr., "Fiske Kimball's National Park Service Memoir," *CRM: The Journal of Heritage Stewardship* 7, no. 2 (2010): 78. Kimball's three-year role (1923–25) as chair of the AIA's Committee on Preservation of Historic Monuments and Scenic Beauties set the stage for his work with the NPS Advisory Board. Hosmer, *Presence of the Past*, 207–8. There he focused on the conservation of buildings of "really national importance" and sought to develop guidance as to the "proper methods of treatment" for historic structures. *Proceedings of the Fifty-Sixth Convention of the American Institute of Architects* (Washington, DC: AIA, 1923), 103–5.

13. "Dr. Fiske Kimball's Annotated List of Structures of Outstanding Architectural Merit," Advisory Board Minutes, August 15–18, 1938; "Sites Classified as Eligible Under Arts and Sciences in the Historic Sites Survey (List Prepared by Dr. Fiske Kimball)," Advisory Board Minutes, October 28–30, 1940; "The Arts and Sciences: Architecture (13 Original Colonies)," Advisory Board Minutes, October 28–30, 1941, Park History Program Subject Files, NPS Headquarters, Washington, DC.

14. Kimball was well versed in current trends in architecture. Fiske Kimball, "American Architecture: Correspondence of Walter Pach, Paul Cret, Frank Lloyd Wright and Erich Mendelson with Fiske Kimball," *Architectural Record* 65 (1929); Fiske Kimball, "Builder and Poet—Frank Lloyd Wright," *Architectural Record* 71 (1932). He saw adopting modernism as sacrificing an opportunity for

Americans to create their own non-European style. Fiske Kimball, "The Arts," in *A Century of Progress*, ed. Charles A. Beard (New York: Harper & Brothers, 1933), 397.

15. Fiske Kimball (?), foreword to *Great Georgian Houses of America*, by the Architects' Emergency Committee, 2 vols. (New York: Scribner's, 1933).

16. Christy Anderson, "Writing the Architectural Survey: Collective Authorities and Competing Approaches," *Journal of the Society of Architectural Historians* 58, no. 3 (1999): 350.

17. Advisory Board Minutes, "Rough Draft of Dictaphone Recording," December 11–12, 1945, Park History Program Subject Files, NPS Headquarters, Washington, DC.

18. Criterion C is the most commonly listed of the four National Register Criteria; more than 50 percent of listings refer to the architectural significance of the historic property. Adopting Criterion C in 1969, the National Register of Historic Places formally recognized that the creation of architecture is not only an artistic endeavor but also a historical act.

19. Finley's interest in Hampton evolved from his desire to acquire Thomas Sully's large painting of Elizabeth Ridgely, *The Lady with a Harp*, that hung at the estate for a postwar exhibition at the National Gallery of Art.

20. Architects' Emergency Committee, *Great Georgian Houses*, vol. 1.

21. Kimball added: "I know of no other 18th century house of equal importance which is apt to be given to the nation in any near future, and I think, if offered as a gift, it should by all means be accepted." Fiske Kimball, "Hampton, Maryland," July 9, 1946, Park History Program Subject Files, NPS Headquarters, Washington, DC. In 1940, he said much the same thing about the Vanderbilt Mansion in New York, which was controversial because of its recent design, but owing to Franklin Delano Roosevelt's influence, it was designated a National Historic Site. "Obviously the place, with its furnishings, is an extremely characteristic and complete example of the millionaire style of the gilded age, and we were right in endorsing its acceptance and preservation. There are doubtless other examples equally characteristic, but I do not imagine that, in any other case, we would be apt to receive a house equally complete with all its furnishings." Fiske Kimball to Francis Rolands, December 20, 1940, FKP, Historic Preservation Projects, National Park Service, New York, Hyde Park, Vanderbilt Mansion, box 99, folder 32.

22. Just prior to debating Hampton's recognition, the Advisory Board had heard about issues at James Monroe's home, Oak Hill. In 1945, knowing of FDR's interest in the property, Kimball had recommended that NPS use the Historic Sites Act to declare Thomas Jefferson's Monticello as a National Historic Site. Charles Hosmer to Theodore Fred Kuper, September 3, 1970, CHP, series 1, box 1, Correspondence.

23. Advisory Board Minutes, December 11–12, 1945, 32–33.

24. Oral history interview with Beatrice Wood, August 26, 1976, 12, conducted by Paul Karlstrom for the Archives of American Art, Smithsonian Institution.

25. In 1936, John D. Rockefeller Jr. asked NPS to prepared measured drawings and photographs of the church, a project that was overseen by former NPS Director Horace Albright on behalf of FDR's mother, who was interested in restoring the church.

26. Fiske Kimball to [NPS Director] Hillory Tolson, October 7, 1938, Park History Program Subject Files, NPS Headquarters, Washington, DC. Kimball prepared a list of a dozen more architecturally significant churches. He continued, "I am sorry to give these negative opinions, as the people concerned in each recommendation include friends of mine, and people of great influence."

27. Fiske Kimball to [Acting NPS Director] Arthur Demaray, May 16, 1941, Park History Program Subject Files, NPS Headquarters, Washington, DC. Despite continued NPS resistance, the property was eventually incorporated into the National Park System in 1978.

28. Charles B. Hosmer Jr., *Preservation Comes of Age: From Williamsburg to the National Trust, 1926–1949* (Charlottesville: University of Virginia Press, 1981), 736–38.

29. Fiske Kimball, *American Architecture* (Indianapolis: Bobbs-Merrill, 1928), 43–44. Advisory Board Minutes, December 7–9, 1944.

30. Sprinkle, "Fiske Kimball's National Park Service Memoir," 78.

31. Since the mid-1930s, more than 60 percent of park units have been cultural or historical in association, with the rest reflecting natural, scenic, or recreational values.

32. Harlan D. Unrau and G. Frank Williss, *Expansion of the National Park Service in the 1930s* (Washington, DC: National Park Service, 1983).

33. Charles Porter interview by Charles Hosmer, April 20, 1970, 27–28, draft transcription with annotations, Archives of American Art, Smithsonian Institution. Kimball was "mainly responsible for the original Advisory Board restoration policy."

34. Oral history interview with Erling Pedersen, September 14, 1972, 29, conducted by Charles Hosmer for the Archives of American Art, Smithsonian Institution.

35. Charles Hosmer to Austin Porter Leland, April 11, 1970, President, Robert E. Lee Memorial Foundation, CHP, series 1, Correspondence.

36. Hugh C. Miller, "Preservation Technology Comes of Age in North America: Part 1," *APT Bulletin: The Journal of Preservation Technology* 37, no. 1 (2006): 55–59. As translated by Julia Jokilehto in *A History of Architectural Conservation* (Oxford: Butterworth-Heinemann, 1999), Didron's philosophy was: "Regarding ancient monuments, it is better to consolidate than to repair,

better to repair than to restore, better to restore than to rebuild, better to rebuild than to embellish; in no case must anything be added and, above all, nothing should be removed" (271) (En fait de monuments anciens, il vaut mieux consolider que réparer, mieux réparer que restaurer, mieux restaurer que refaire, mieux refaire qu'embellier; en aucun cas, il ne faut rien ajouter, surtout rien retrancher).

37. At the first meeting of the Advisory Board, Chief Historian Verne Chatelain quoted from Henry James's "A Little Tour of France": "For myself, I have no hesitation; I prefer in every case the ruined, however ruined, to the reconstructed, however splendid. What is left is more precious than what is added; the one is history, the other is fiction; and I like the former the better of the two,—it is so much more romantic. One is positive, so far as it goes; the other fills up the void with things more dead than the void itself, in as much as they have never had life." Advisory Board Minutes, February 13–14, 1936.

38. Kimball, "Preservation Movement," 16.

39. Hosmer, quoting Kimball: "AIA Hosts Preservation Conclave," *Preservation News*, March 1990.

40. See Hosmer, *Preservation Comes of Age*, 9. Kimball presented his restoration policy in a letter to the stewards of Virginia's Stratford Hall: "In a precious old building the dominant thought, no doubt, should be preservation—and the greatest conservation should be exercised as to changing anything, even if this is believed to be changing it back the way it is supposed formerly to have been." Kimball, "The Fundamental Problems and Principles of 'Restoration' in American Buildings," 1930. Charles Porter to Hosmer, March 3, 1976, CHP, series 1, Correspondence. See Thomas Waterman's recommendations for restoration work in *The Mansions of Virginia, 1706–1776* (New York: Bonanza Books, 1945), 409–10.

41. Fiske Kimball to Ronald Lee, December 18, 1941, quoted in Seth C. Bruggeman, *George Washington Birthplace National Monument: Administrative History* (Williamsburg, VA: College of William and Mary, 2006), 53–54.

42. Advisory Board Minutes, November 7–9, 1939. NPS subsequently turned down several PWA projects that did not comply with the agency's restoration policy. NPS requested that interpretive markers at Pennsbury Manor identify the building as a reconstruction.

43. In 1940 Kimball had convinced the leadership of the Association for the Preservation of Virginia Antiquities (APVA) not to undertake the reconstruction of buildings through guesswork but rather to allow NPS archaeologists to conduct excavations within Jamestown to identify the remains of the seventeenth-century settlement. Fiske Kimball to David Finley, April 26, 1954, National Gallery of Art, Finley, box 38, F-19.

44. "AIA Hosts Preservation Conclave."

45. In the mid-1970s, Parks Canada referred to the phrase and the American National Trust axiom. Advisory Council on Historic Preservation, "The National Historic Preservation Program Today," Committee on Interior and Insular Affairs, United States Senate, January 1976, 110. See also *Department of the Interior and Related Agencies Appropriations for Fiscal Year 1969* (Washington, DC: GPO, 1968), 2650.

46. Robert E. Stipe, "The Next 20 Years," in *The American Mosaic: Preserving a Nation's Heritage* (Washington, DC: Preservation Press, 1987), 283. "By 1966, our basic guidelines . . . were from the days of William Morris." Charles Hosmer, interview with Robert Utley, June 17, 1986, 9, CHP.

47. National Park Service Director's Order 28: Cultural Resource Management was adopted on June 11, 1998, and still governs how the agency addresses the long-term stewardship and treatment of historic properties. See also *NPS Restoration Policy Statement*.

48. Kimball was also familiar with alternative forms of federal designation. Following the Antiquities Act of 1906, he lobbied for the creation of a National Monument for the ca. 1725 Mathew Jones House located on Mulberry Island within the US Army installation at Fort Eustis, Virginia. Hosmer, *Presence of the Past*, 207–8.

49. Sprinkle, "Fiske Kimball's National Park Service Memoir," 79.

50. Saul Kussiel Padover, "Confidential Report on the Carl Schurz Memorial Foundation (June 24, 1940)," Library of Congress, Papers of Harold Ickes, box 143. Padover (1905–1981), a political scientist and wartime intelligence officer, was Assistant to the Secretary of Interior from 1938 to 1943.

51. Supervisor of Historic Sites, "Memorandum for Mr. Demaray," May 27, 1939, Park History Program Subject Files, NPS Headquarters, Washington, DC.

52. Charles Peterson to Hon. Edwin O. Lewis, November 13, 1951, Charles E. Peterson Papers, Special Collections, University of Maryland Libraries, box 130.

53. Hosmer, *Presence of the Past*, 695.

54. See the comment by John Canaday quoted in the introduction to this volume.

55. Charles Peterson, interview by Charles Hosmer, February 9, 1972, Philadelphia, Pennsylvania, 40, Charles E. Peterson Papers, Special Collections, University of Maryland Libraries, box 141, Peterson Memoirs 2 folder. Peterson noted that Kimball's domestic architecture survey book was "still solid as a rock" nearly fifty years after its publication.

56. Charles Peterson to Mrs. John M. Gilchrist, November 21, 1950; Fiske Kimball to Charles Peterson, November 22, 1950, FKP, box 41, folder 12.

57. Herbert Kahler to Charles Hosmer, January 26, 1976, CHP, series 1, box 1, Correspondence.

58. Erling H. Pedersen to Charles Hosmer, May 24, 1974, CHP, series 1, box 1, Correspondence.

59. Hosmer, *Presence of the Past*, 300.

60. Fiske Kimball to Francis S. Ronalds, August 1, 1945, (Charlottesville, VA) Coordinating Superintendent, Morristown National Historical Park, Park History Program Subject Files, NPS Headquarters, Washington, DC.

"AS IT IS ACCURATE HISTORICALLY"

Fiske Kimball and the Restoration of Monticello

GARDINER HALLOCK

For a remarkable thirty years, Fiske Kimball (1888–1955) led the Thomas Jefferson Foundation's Restoration Committee and oversaw the restoration of Monticello's buildings and landscapes.[1] His chairmanship started just two years after the Foundation purchased Monticello in 1923 and ended only with his death. During this time, he was a fierce advocate for the careful, evidence-based restoration of Monticello's main house, wings, and surrounding landscapes. Kimball's philosophy—that it is "better to preserve than to repair; better to repair than to restore; better to restore than to construct or reconstruct"—continues to guide the Foundation's preservation philosophy.[2] Kimball's devotion to the physical and documentary evidence is his primary legacy at Monticello, and the work undertaken during his lifetime demonstrates the immense value of this approach.

Kimball's extensive impact on Monticello is most clearly illustrated by comparing three different restoration eras at the site. The first era spans from the Foundation's purchase of Monticello in 1923 up to 1937. It includes the early repairs and changes to the main house, the landscape, and other surviving Jefferson-era buildings. Because of the Foundation's limited funds, these projects generally did not focus on ensuring historical accuracy. The second, more active period dates to between 1937 and 1955. It encompassed a time of rising prosperity at the Foundation and resulted in important, large-scale restoration projects that Kimball both advocated for and directed. The third period is defined by the relatively sharp decline in restoration activity at Monticello after Kimball's death and before the professionalization of the Foundation's preservation and garden staff in the 1970s.

A comparison of these eras illustrates that in the years before Kimball started to direct the Foundation's restoration efforts, projects involving Monticello's architectural fabric rarely re-created Jefferson-era features faithfully. Similarly, during the twenty years after Kimball's death, the Foundation focused on education and land acquisitions. Without Kimball's strong advocacy and vision for architectural and landscape restoration projects, significant restoration work on the mountaintop largely stopped. However, in the middle period, when Kimball was the driving force of the restoration, work to restore the main house and the surrounding landscapes to the Jefferson era progressed rapidly. More importantly, Kimball insisted that the Foundation use an evidence-based methodology to ensure that the reconstructed elements were as accurate as possible.

Kimball recruited Milton Grigg (1905–1982), a Colonial Williamsburg–trained and Charlottesville-based consulting architect, to help him pursue this high level of accuracy. Together, they worked diligently to ground restoration and reconstruction projects at Monticello in the documentary and physical evidence. Along with Kimball's wife, Marie Goebel Kimball (1889–1955), who served as Monticello's first curator, they implemented a fourfold restoration methodology: using the vast Jefferson archive to uncover lost details, investigating and closely documenting the surviving Jefferson-era building fabric, undertaking archaeological investigations at a time when the field of historical archaeology was just being established, and referencing surviving period elements from other historic houses in the region for missing features with no known physical or archival traces. The purpose of this process was, in Kimball's words, to allow the new work to "get the old character" by being as authentic as possible.[3] As a result, Kimball's dramatic changes to Monticello's buildings and landscapes can be directly tied to his insistence on a meticulous restoration process. This rigorous process often, but not always, led Kimball to make the best choice possible with the available evidence.

Kimball's correspondence from this period also reveals that along with his knowledge and standards, he supplied something just as significant to Monticello's restoration: an expansive and exciting vision for the direction of the restoration program. As documented in a 1940 letter to the Foundation's founding president, Stuart Gibboney (1877–1944), Kimball proposed a series of major projects that included restoring the North and South Wings, excavations at Shadwell (Jefferson's birthplace), the installation of Jefferson-era objects in the house, a modern heating plant to reduce the risk of fire in the main house, a new superintendent's house to allow for the restoration of the Jefferson-era stone workmen's house, reconstructing the nailery and other "shops" along Mulberry Row, and replanting the orchards and vineyard. Many of these projects and others, such as the restoration of parts of the roof and repairs to major structural failures, were completed owing to his energetic leadership. Notably, his vision was compelling enough that many of the projects he envisioned that were not completed during his lifetime would be accomplished posthumously.

Nonetheless, contemporary historians can also find compelling criticisms of Kimball's pathbreaking accomplishments. For example, despite a consistent argument for achieving historic accuracy through evidence-based restorations, he occasionally allowed his own aesthetic preferences for refined classical ornament to override the evidence, as the examples of the Chinese railings and the monopteros will illustrate. More significantly, those preferences led to a focus on Jefferson and the main house. As a result, Kimball gave less attention to spaces associated with the plantation's enslaved population. While there is no evidence that he actively suppressed the restoration and interpretation of these features, the historical record clearly shows that they were largely ignored and overlooked.

Monticello Before the Foundation

Fortunately, Monticello was spared dramatic, large-scale alterations in the years after Jefferson died. Still, several yearslong periods of neglect were redeemed by successive campaigns of significant repair and renovation by two generations of the dedicated Levy family.[4] Visitor accounts from the 1820s reveal that the first period of neglect started even before Jefferson's death in 1826. In these letters, Monticello is described as "old and going to decay" and surrounded by "slovenly" grounds.[5] The decline was principally caused by Jefferson's crushing debts, the widespread impacts of the Panic of 1819, and a last-minute campaign to complete the house—including finishing the Southwest and Northeast Porticoes, installing marble around the fireplaces, and initiating a reroofing campaign—in the years just before his death. These late-life projects channeled the last of Jefferson's funds and energy, leaving little of either for much-needed basic maintenance and repairs. The state of Jefferson's finances also left his family heavily in debt after he died, and the pattern of neglect continued of necessity. As Jefferson's daughter Martha Randolph wrote to her daughter in 1831, "the debts are pressing the place going to ruin."[6] Ultimately, it took five years to find a buyer: an eccentric local druggist and silkworm enthusiast named James Turner Barclay (1807–1874).

Barclay never lived in the house, and Monticello sank further into decay during his three-year ownership. Smitten with the nationwide silkworm and mulberry tree craze of the 1830s, Barclay propagated silkworms in the interior of the main house and replaced Jefferson's carefully curated ornamental plantings around Monticello with caterpillar-nourishing mulberry trees. Barclay's sericulture experiment quickly failed, and Monticello was left to molder.

Redemption came with the arrival of Monticello's subsequent owner, Commodore Uriah Levy (1792–1862). Commodore Levy—the first Jewish Commodore of the United States Navy, a crusader against corporal punishment, and an ardent admirer of Jefferson's work to establish religious liberty—purchased the estate in 1834. After he officially gained the title in 1836, he used free and enslaved labor to save Monticello by repairing the damage caused by decades of deferred maintenance. Levy was dedicated to Monticello, and the property was his well-maintained summer residence until he died in 1862.

Unfortunately, his passing and the American Civil War instigated a second extended period of neglect and near abandonment at Monticello. A protracted inheritance lawsuit exacerbated these problems, and the estate was not settled until 1879, when Commodore Levy's nephew—the fittingly named US Congressman Jefferson Monroe Levy (1852–1924)—secured the purchase of Monticello and 218 acres at auction. The younger Levy initiated another major campaign of repair and renovation. While a private group advocating for the federal government to purchase Monticello as a shrine to Jefferson launched an antisemitic attack on Jefferson Levy's stewardship of the estate in the early twentieth century, photos and visitor accounts show that his preservation efforts were equal to his uncle's.

By the 1910s, Levy's fortune and health were failing him, and he listed Monticello for sale in 1919. Even with his financial troubles, Levy diligently cared for Monticello until 1923, when he sold it to the Thomas Jefferson Memorial Foundation in the year before his death.[7] Many members of the local community especially appreciated Levy's efforts. Near the end of his life, the Albemarle County Chapter of the Daughters of the American Revolution proclaimed "cheerful testimony to the care with which Monticello is preserved by Mr. Levy and to the zeal which he evinces in the protection of this sacred shrine. It desires to express its belief that no other individual could show more solicitude for the place or more lavishly expend time and money in its preservation."[8]

However, even with the Levys' excellent stewardship of the main house, many Jefferson-era elements were either missing or altered by 1923. The effect on Monticello's wings was the most noticeable. The South Wing had largely been rebuilt, and the North Wing was in even worse condition, with only the Jefferson-era fieldstone retaining wall and North Pavilion surviving. Because of the missing terraces, Levy had Thomas Rhodes, a longtime Monticello manager hired in 1889, move the Pavilion's doorways to face the West Lawn. Rhodes also built small Tuscan porticoes in front of the relocated doorways to tie the alterations to Monticello's neoclassical aesthetic. The workmanship was not strong, and Kimball, in his typical and unsparingly blunt style, would describe them

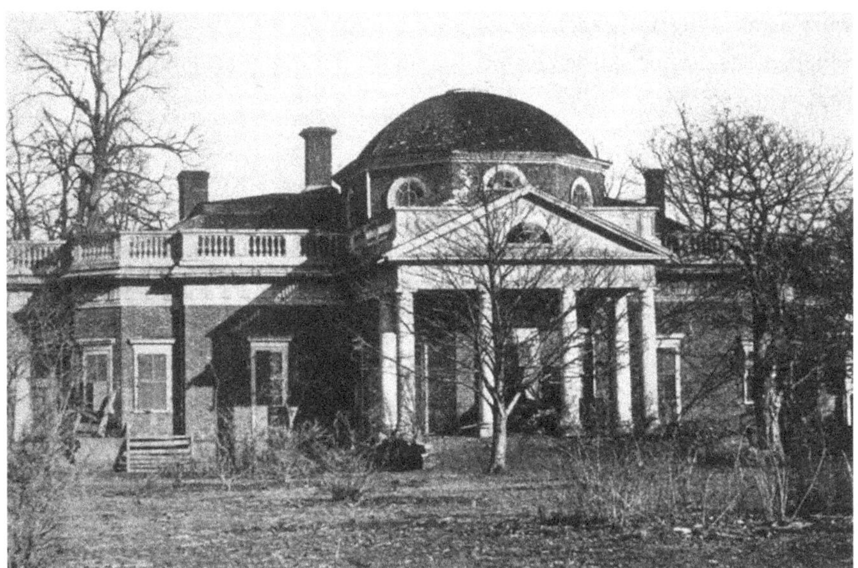

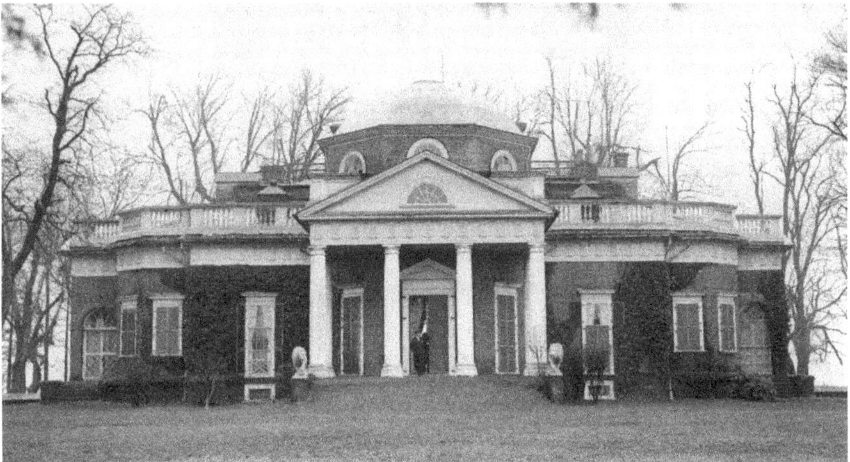

FIGURE 1. Monticello in the 1870s (*top*) and in 1921 (*bottom*) after repairs by Jefferson Monroe Levy. (© Thomas Jefferson Foundation at Monticello)

in 1937 as "wretched and should be removed."⁹ Similarly, Jefferson's carefully designed gardens and grove surrounding the house had largely vanished, as had almost all the buildings along Mulberry Row. While some of Jefferson's trees survived and matured into defining elements of the early twentieth-century landscape and a road trace still defined Mulberry Row—Monticello plantation's once-busy "main street" found just to the south of the main house—it took painstaking and exacting fieldwork to recover even the faintest remnants of Jefferson's original garden features when the landscape around the house was restored in the early 1940s.

Monticello, 1923 to 1937

Kimball's strong ties to Jefferson scholarship and Charlottesville meant that he was involved with the effort to turn the Monticello plantation into a historic site even before 1923. In fact, he communicated with both Congressman Levy and the Foundation before the sale. Levy, frustrated by the lack of interested buyers, contacted Kimball in the hope that he could find a buyer and help negotiate a sale. Similarly, the Foundation's president, the New York City lawyer Gibboney, also sought advice from Kimball in 1923.[10]

The thirty-five-year-old Kimball, though young, was a natural choice. His groundbreaking *Thomas Jefferson, Architect* (1916) and his role as the founding head of the University of Virginia's McIntire School of Fine Arts in Charlottesville, Virginia (1919–23) both made him the perfect candidate. The relationship between Kimball and the Foundation was formalized in May 1924, when Kimball accepted the board's invitation to oversee the restoration. Unlike his later work at Stratford Hall, Kimball volunteered his architectural services because of his deep interest in the preservation of the house. Over the three decades he was associated with the Foundation, devoting many hours to the restoration of Monticello, he only requested reimbursement for travel expenses.[11]

While the position appears to have been primarily honorary at first, Kimball further elevated the reputation of the Foundation's restoration activities by establishing the Restoration Committee in 1925.[12] The inaugural committee was chosen from an august group of cultural leaders, including R. T. Haines Halsey from the Metropolitan Museum in New York and Charles Moore, the Chairman of the United States Commission of the Fine Arts. Although members of the committee changed over time, Kimball remained chair of the committee until his death. The various groups he assembled to serve on the Restoration Committee would eventually bring academic rigor and oversight to the Foundation and ensure the work was done to the best standards of the period.

The first projects undertaken by the Foundation immediately after the 1923 purchase provide a helpful context with which to highlight the impact of Kimball's influence on Monticello's later restoration projects. Importantly, these early projects appear to have been done without Kimball's oversight, perhaps because they were seen as largely utilitarian (and, at the time, he was also transitioning to his new role as director of the museum in Philadelphia). While photos reveal the house as generally well maintained, immediate repairs were needed in 1923 to preserve and transform the mountaintop into a public history site before the hundredth anniversary of Jefferson's death. The most significant of these projects was the 1924 replacement of the Levy-era roof. Similarly, in 1927, the earthen ramp in front of the Southwest Portico was replaced with a simple stair made from unadorned bricks.[13] While historians and archaeologists have discerned from period drawings and notes found on a Jefferson land survey that stairs likely led up to the Portico in the Jefferson era, it does not appear that the Foundation intended to re-create these older steps.[14] Instead, as with most projects from this period, utility was the goal rather than beauty or historical accuracy.

The Foundation's repairs to the North and South Wings and on Mulberry Row during this early period were also focused on serviceability. These projects, likely overseen by Thomas Rhodes, included the "restoration" of a slave quarter under the South Wing and the rebuilding of the Mulberry Row stable after a devastating windstorm in 1927. As with the main house roof and Southwest Portico stairs, both projects were utilitarian. Interestingly, if the Foundation had accurately restored the slave quarter, it would likely have been one of the earliest restored slave dwellings in the United States. However, what little documentation survives about this project suggests that the space was most likely repaired only for use as the neighboring gift shop's storeroom or converted into bathrooms. The stable "restoration" followed a similar pattern. Although the new stable did incorporate and preserve two fieldstone structures from 1809, the rest of the design largely reflected early twentieth-century vernacular precedents rather than what Jefferson's free and enslaved craftsmen initially constructed. Other work from this era included repainting the main house's interior and a project to restore the icehouse that is only hinted at in the archives. In both instances, the work was again largely done without consulting physical or documentary evidence. Kimball found the painting unsatisfactory and had the interior repainted in 1936 under Grigg's direction. Kimball and Grigg would also engage in a second restoration of the icehouse in 1939. (An accurate restoration of the stable would not be completed until 2018.)

Letters between Kimball and Gibboney reveal that the primary reason for the simple, ahistorical nature of the work during this early period was financial. "Knowing the lack of funds, I don't press matters of restoration at Monticello," Kimball wrote in 1935.[15] In fact, Kimball was being generous. Owing to the Great Depression and the need to service the large loan required to buy the plantation, the Foundation was close to bankruptcy by February 1934. At that time, the organization only had $108 cash in hand against $120,000 of outstanding obligations. The situation did not improve in the near term, and at the February 1935 board meeting, the trustees seriously debated offering Monticello to the National Park Service. Happily, the Foundation's finances improved with the nation's fortunes. Two years later, after the crisis, Gibboney writes with an almost palpable sense of relief that the financial situation was "very satisfactory."[16] This improvement would finally allow Kimball to begin implementing his transformative vision of a mountaintop restored to its Jefferson-era appearance.

Monticello, 1937 to 1955

The first signs in the archives of Kimball's growing influence over the physical appearance of Monticello and its landscape appear in 1935, during a New Deal–era entrance road project. Significantly, Kimball's opinion of the work illuminates why he felt it was vital for the Foundation to undertake well-researched restorations by professionals. While Kimball approved of the new road and wrote Gibboney that "in general everything seems to me very excellent," he found a major fault in the brick steps built by the Bureau of Public Roads to connect Mulberry Row to the main house. These steps replaced Levy-era marble stairs and grass paths. After the work was completed, Kimball bluntly wrote to Gibboney in 1935 that "the brick steps which have been substituted are really themselves pretty terrible in treatment."

However, Kimball's concern was not just for the appearance of the stairs but also for how they affected the reputations of both the Foundation and Kimball himself. In the same letter to Gibboney, he adds that the steps "really tend to disqualify our judgment in matters of restoration." In Kimball's mind, unprofessional projects would lead the general public to question the Foundation's (and Kimball's own) ability to properly care for a house that was, for many people, a secular shrine to the republic. To ensure that this did not happen, Kimball concludes in his letter to Gibboney that he "would appreciate enormously if you would give me notice, so that we could design what is to be done in handling of the old work."[17] While Kimball did not know it, his words initiated twenty years of what was the most intense period of construction at Monticello since the Jefferson era.

As an outgrowth of Kimball's request for more control, and because he was off-site in Philadelphia, Grigg was hired as the architect of record in 1935. The two architects formed a very close partnership, and Grigg continued to work at Monticello after Kimball's death. Grigg and Kimball made a strong team. Grigg's

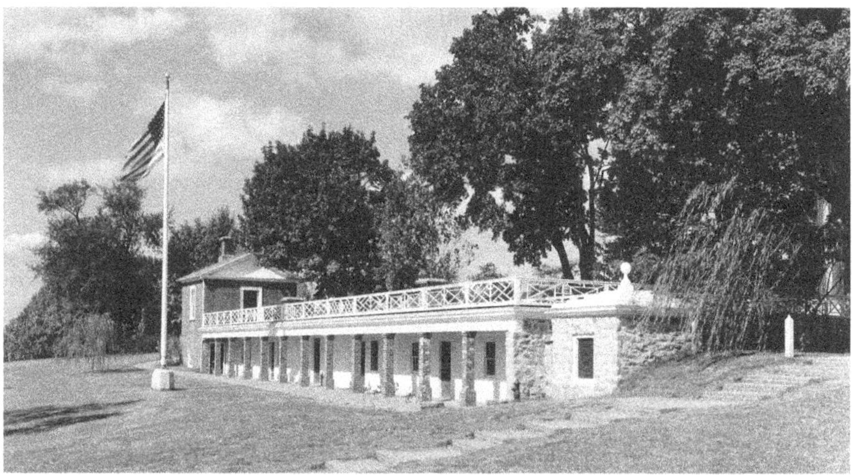

FIGURE 2. Monticello's restored South Wing around 1941. The Bureau of Public Roads steps are in the foreground. (© Thomas Jefferson Foundation at Monticello)

knowledge of eighteenth- and early nineteenth-century buildings in Virginia's Piedmont often served as a valuable vernacular counterweight to Kimball's overriding appreciation of classical design and extensive knowledge of high-style colonial architecture in British North America. Grigg was Kimball's trusted collaborator, helping with research, physical investigations, design development, and construction administration.

The partnership worked because the two men had similar restoration philosophies. These shared values were documented in 1941, when Kimball defended Grigg against an attempt by an influential friend of the Foundation to replace him with Floyd Johnson, another local architect. At the time, Kimball wrote Gibboney, "I respect Floyd Johnson's abilities also, but he was not at Williamsburg and has no experience with archaeological work or restoration."[18] So, in Kimball's mind, the combination of prior experience using an evidence-based restoration process and the proven ability to perform physical investigations made Grigg the right person. In the years that followed, Kimball would also repeatedly protect Grigg from Gibboney's Depression-influenced cost-consciousness. Just before the United States entered World War II and restoration work stopped at Monticello, Gibboney wrote to Kimball regarding what he saw as outrageous expenses for archaeological excavations at what was believed to be Jefferson's birthplace at Shadwell. "[A]s you know, we have to watch Grigg carefully," Gibboney warned Kimball in January 1941, and then again the following October: "If you leave Grigg alone, we will never get anything—you will have to keep after him."[19] Kimball characteristically ignored this advice and worked productively with Grigg for the next two decades.

The North Wing and the Main House

Kimball and Grigg first put their shared restoration philosophy into practice by starting the second, and much more ambitious, era of restoration at Monticello. In 1938, the pair began the first major project of this new era with the restoration of the North Wing. Unlike the South Wing, which was reroofed several times in the years after Jefferson's death, very little of Jefferson's North Wing survived aboveground. The documentary evidence was similarly slim at the time. All Kimball and Grigg knew was that horses and carriages occupied the North Wing in Jefferson's era.

To solve this problem, the architects brought the full force of their many years of restoration practice and theory to the project. The pair diligently pursued physical investigations, archaeological excavations, and a thorough analysis of the documentary record to flesh out the major elements of the lost structure. When these failed them, they sourced details from an excellent example of a surviving early nineteenth-century stable at the nearby Bremo Plantation in Fluvanna County. Even though a Jefferson memo uncovered by the historian Edwin

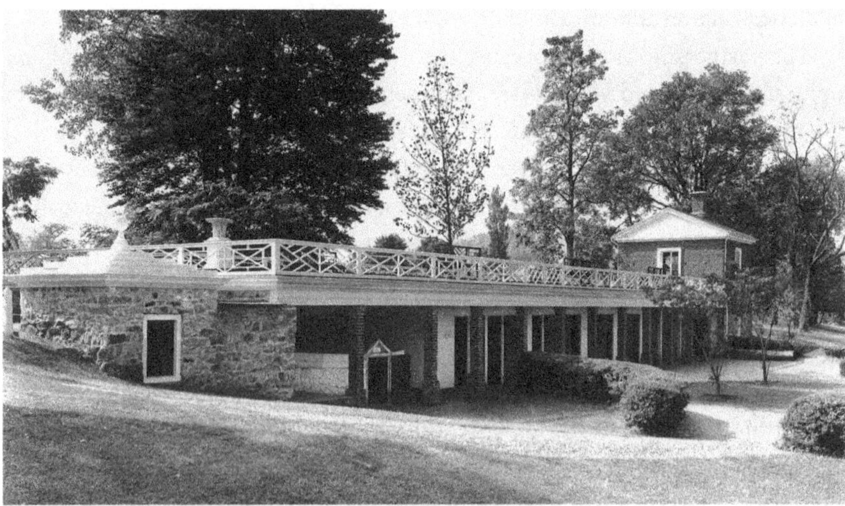

FIGURE 3. Monticello's North Wing after restoration by Kimball and Grigg. (© Thomas Jefferson Foundation at Monticello)

Betts (1892–1958) in 1941 proved that the result of their painstaking work was largely inaccurate, the project provides a telling example of their diligent consideration of the evidence available at the time.

Aside from the North Wing reconstruction project, smaller changes were simultaneously made to the main house. These important changes helped preserve the structure as Monticello experienced an ever-expanding number of visitors. Kimball's work included removing the Levy-era diamond-patterned window sashes enclosing the North Piazza and rebuilding the four corner terraces that provided access to the piazzas from the East and West Lawns. While these projects were minor compared to the North Wing, the changes allowed visitors to understand Jefferson's original design more fully. The work also helped articulate a house that used classically inspired architectural features to negotiate the traditionally abrupt transition between a building's interior and its surrounding landscape. Kimball had started the transformation that would once again make Monticello a house *in* a garden rather than a house *with* a garden.

The Landscape

Kimball had studied Monticello's designed landscapes for several years before he arrived at Monticello. As with Monticello's architecture, the understanding of Jefferson's designed landscapes largely started with Kimball. While W. A. Lambeth and Warren Manning's *Thomas Jefferson as an Architect and Designer of Landscapes* set the stage in 1913, Kimball's 1916 *Thomas Jefferson, Architect* revealed through documentary evidence the strikingly expansive plans Jefferson had developed for Monticello's grounds. Kimball's interest in Jefferson as a landscape architect only grew, and he eventually published two articles in *Landscape Architecture Magazine:* "The Grounds at Monticello in 1809" (1918) and "The Gardens and Plantations at Monticello" (1927).[20]

Kimball's expertise allowed him to play a role in the restoration of the landscape similar to his work with the architecture. Under his guidance, the plans for the restored landscapes immediately around the house displayed the same reliance on physical and documentary evidence. As he wrote Susanne Williams Massie (1861–1852), a prominent local resident involved with the influential Garden Club of Virginia, "I think today we all feel more kindly to the idea of putting things back the way they were, irrespective of whether we ourselves wanted to do them just that way or not." Kimball's coaching would prove effective, and the structure of the landscape as reconstructed was, in general, faithfully based on their understanding of Jefferson's drawings and the physical evidence. As Kimball wrote to Grigg about the design at the time, "I like it very much indeed. As it is accurate historically, it is certainly the right thing to do."[21]

As with much of their work together, Kimball and Grigg believed they had authentically restored the landscape. However, research in the decades after the West Lawn's restoration has found that important Jefferson-period elements were either left out or incorrectly re-created. For example, the iconic fishpond is largely fictional. Jefferson did excavate a fishpond, but he appears to have filled it in shortly afterwards, perhaps because he did not learn of an effective method of waterproofing masonry until 1818.[22]

Progress on the landscape was initially slow, and it would take many years of research and advocacy before the restoration of the grounds was completed. The University of Virginia's Department of Engineering started the work in the mid-1920s with a survey and a 1926 project by the Garden Club of Virginia to stabilize Jefferson-era trees.[23] The following year (and, coincidentally, the same year *Landscape Architecture Magazine* published "The Gardens and Plantations at Monticello"), Kimball's untiring advocacy finally convinced the Garden Club of America to sponsor the West Lawn's restoration. Their one condition was that the Foundation hire Amy Cogswell, a pioneering Connecticut-based landscape architect who specialized in Colonial Revival designs, to produce the plans. Cogswell is thought to have developed her design by combining a Jefferson plan for Monticello from the 1770s that includes formal, if restrained, rectangular garden beds with a view of the West Front painted around fifty years later by Jane Braddick Peticolas. A single drawing showing a portion of Cogswell's design survives.[24] It delineates an informal cottage garden–type planting plan inserted into the beds delineated by Jefferson in the 1770s.

While Kimball initially supported her work, Cogswell's plans were harshly rejected by the local members of the Garden Club of Virginia. Trying to make peace, Kimball sought Susanne Williams Massie's blessing to someday restore the landscape and "put it all back as it was in his [Jefferson's] day." Massie replied curtly, however: "I would be delighted to see the gardens restored properly." The reasons for Massie's disapproval appear to be cultural as well as professional, and time did not heal the bitter rift caused by the Garden Club's harsh criticism of Cogswell's initial design. When Kimball invited Cogswell back to restart the work in 1938, she refused. Her own brusque reply reveals her experience of the Garden Club's regional and gender biases: "Would not a southern woman be more acceptable than a Yankee? I think so. Or—better still—a Man."[25]

After the aborted attempt in the late 1920s, Morley Williams (1886–1977) arrived at Monticello in 1932 to complete the next serious physical investigation of the Jeffersonian landscape. Williams was a trained engineer and meticulous landscape architect whose work at Stratford Hall, Mount Vernon, and Tryon Palace, as well as Monticello, emphasized the careful recording of the existing landscape before developing restoration plans. To document the existing conditions, Williams had an exacting datum floated over the West Lawn by stretching strings into a grid. Using this fixed plane, he recorded minute changes in the lawn's elevation by measuring down to a hundredth of a foot. He also checked his findings using car headlights at night. The bright, raking lights revealed subtle variations in the West Lawn's topography, and the resulting deep shadows materialized long-lost elements of the original landscape for the assembled onlookers. His careful fieldwork revealed a hidden serpentine path circumnavigating the West Lawn. When Williams recorded his findings in a drawing, the result was very similar to a sketch of a garden path Jefferson drew for the West Lawn in 1807.[26]

Williams's discovery turned out to be the key that unlocked an interpretation of the documentary evidence. It was this combination of physical evidence with the documentary record that ultimately led Kimball, the Foundation, and the Garden Club to approve the plans for restoring the West Lawn. Interestingly, Kimball would not invite Williams back to Monticello to help with other landscape restoration projects, including the restoration of the North Wing in 1938. Kimball's opinion of Williams is unknown. While he may have sensed a rival, he may also have been reluctant to have Williams return to Monticello because of his reputation for being difficult and argumentative.[27]

By 1938, Kimball's many years of cajoling and lobbying the Garden Club of Virginia members paid off when they voted to provide a "substantial" gift of $10,000 to the garden restoration project at their January 1939 meeting.[28] University of Virginia professor Edwin Betts joined the Restoration Committee in 1938 to help ensure the accuracy of this work. At the time, Betts was carefully compiling and editing Jefferson's "Farm Book" and "Garden Book." His work provided an exciting view into Jefferson's gardens, and this new source of information was eagerly incorporated into the landscape restoration efforts. Ultimately, Kimball, Grigg, Betts, Floyd Johnson, and local Garden Club of Virginia member Hazlehurst Perkins developed the West Lawn's final design after a long period of debate and discussion. Landscape architect Gordon Wood assisted with plant specifications and the production of scaled drawings.[29] The same passionate and knowledgeable team developed plans to restore the East Lawn's landscape the following year, with the help of the Garden Club of America.

South Wing

With the lawn restoration projects underway, Kimball began to work with Grigg on a comprehensive restoration of the South Wing. In Jefferson's time, the South Wing held many of the workspaces needed to sustain life at Monticello, including the kitchen, smokehouse, dairy, and three slave quarters. Kimball and Grigg were helped in their work by the evidence for partitions found on the wing's surviving circa 1802 fieldstone walls and brick chimneys. The architects combined this physical evidence with Jefferson's wonderfully detailed 1796 floor plan of the South Wing to re-create an accurate interpretation of the wing's Jefferson-era form.

Kimball and Grigg pored over the evidence to ensure the accuracy of the kitchen, smokehouse, and dairy; however, the three slave quarters received little attention. While it is true that the architects attempted to faithfully articulate the quarters' exterior (although documents found later would reveal that different materials were used), Kimball and Grigg gave little thought to restoring the interiors to interpret slavery at Monticello. The few relevant documents found in the archive suggest that Kimball's views on race were typical of his class in the mid-twentieth century. In a 1934 letter to Gibboney, for instance, he writes about the Black guards who also served as the custodians: "One has always to keep after that race."[30]

The indifference to the interiors of the slave quarters sheltered by the South Wing resulted in the decision to continue to use two of them as public restrooms. Toilets were first installed in these quarters before the 1940 restoration, most likely prompted by their proximity to the primary visitor parking area. Kimball and Grigg's choice to not relocate them may have been driven by the cost associated with moving the infrastructure. Many restorations today are similarly constrained by budgets, existing conditions, and serving the needs of visitors, so leaving the restrooms where they were could be seen as a necessary compromise.

However, the fate of the third quarter, identified by Jefferson's plan as the "cook's room," is less understandable. If Kimball and the Foundation had been intent on interpreting the contributing role of the enslaved population at Monticello, the interior would have been meticulously restored along with the kitchen, smokehouse, and dairy. Instead, Grigg described this space as "an unimportant room from the standpoint of exhibition facilities," and they determined that its best use was as a shelter for the night watchman.[31] Nothing found to date in the archives suggests that this lapse was malicious or meant to advance a deeper political or philosophical agenda. Kimball and Grigg also put spaces more closely associated with the Jefferson family to modern use, as with a gift shop in the South Pavilion. However, the almost complete silence on the issue of the slave quarters suggests that they saw no significance in re-creating the experience of the enslaved population. This is especially clear in light of the extreme lengths to which Kimball and Grigg went to accurately restore what they believed were Jefferson's horse stalls in the North Wing.

Kimballization at Monticello

The diligent search for documentary or archeological evidence did not always win out. Kimball's taste for classical architecture and particular passion for high-style eighteenth-century details are expressed in the term "Kimballization." It describes restored architectural features designed after documented examples taken from the correct period but sourced from buildings grander than anything that existed at the site.[32] This is not an uncommon tendency in restoration work. As noted above, Grigg's knowledge of local building traditions served as a counterweight to Kimball's impulses, although Grigg, too, could push too hard for what Kimball dismissively called the "piedmont vernacular."[33]

The chimney breast of the South Pavilion serves as a good example of their exchanges. In their considerations of how it should be paneled, Kimball turned to his knowledge of published sources available to Jefferson and to his knowledge of local traditions: "The major question is whether the old wall would not have been paneled. Why should we assume that Jefferson, who already possessed Gibbs' *Rules,* and who was familiar with everything in the Tidewater, would not have attempted, in his own room, to have something as elegant as practicable? Even elsewhere in the Piedmont by 1768–1769 [the approximate construction date of the South Pavilion] they were paneling chimneybreast walls, and I cannot imagine he would really have sheathed this wall in the main story." Grigg replied, "I agree that a system of structural panel treatment may be indicated but respectfully suggest one with detail less Georgian."[34]

Similarly, the design of the Chinese railings once installed on top of the wings clearly shows how Kimball's aesthetic preferences colored decisions made at Monticello. In 1939 and 1940, Kimball and Grigg reconstructed the Chinese railings around the terraces over the North and South Wings. In this instance, the choice was between an almost purely conjectural Chinese railing and a simpler railing designed by Jefferson in 1824. Jefferson's well-developed specifications for this simpler railing featured pyramidal-topped vertical pales clinched to plain-sawn horizontal boards with wrought-iron nails. Jefferson's notes included lumber dimensions, notes on the special hardware needed to join the fence panels, and detailed construction information. He even calculated the total amount of material required to fully encircle both terraces.[35] Furthermore, the Peticolas, Vail, and Martha Woodward renderings of Monticello's west and east elevations from around 1825 and 1826 all illustrated a section of this railing on the short leg of the L-shaped South Terrace.

Kimball and Grigg closely studied Jefferson's specifications and knew that the railing was shown installed in the Peticolas painting. They also found no physical evidence of a Chinese railing surviving on the house. However, they still preferred the more complicated and higher-status Chinese railing. Going against his own dogged advocacy for documentary evidence, Kimball let his own taste intercede—referring to the vernacular origins of Jefferson's design as "that wretched railing" as he turned to other potential sources for a design.[36]

Kimball located an 1838 engraving of Monticello that showed a Chinese railing with a simple, single-braced X pattern on the North Terrace. While the engraving appears to be fairly accurate, it was made at least a decade after Jefferson's death and after Uriah Levy renovated Monticello. Examples of this Levy-era railing, or its successors, survived until the 1920s. Still, Kimball grasped at this meager evidence for the Chinese railing. He dismissed the evidence found in the period Peticolas painting as indicative of a small section of railing executed by Jefferson's enslaved workers as a trial. Even more unusual for Kimball and Grigg, the version of the Chinese railing they reconstructed was not based on any surviving physical evidence and was only marginally based on information found in surviving Jefferson documents relating to Monticello. Instead, they used drawings of Monticello and the University of Virginia completed after Jefferson's death. Kimball had convinced himself that Jefferson would have assuredly abandoned the vulgar paled railing in favor of an elaborate Chinese rail.[37] The resulting Chinese rails on the North and South Terraces became an iconic architectural element at Monticello and survived until they were replaced with a reproduction of Jefferson's simpler railing between 2016 and 2018.

One final project demonstrates Kimball's taste for high-style ornament over the practical and vernacular: the construction of a monopteros at the wellhead near the South Pavilion. In this instance, the complete lack of documentation on the appearance of the Jefferson-era well provided Kimball an opportunity

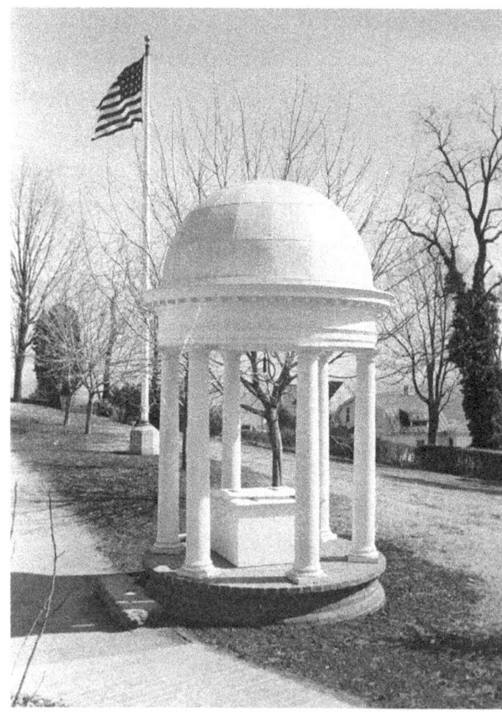

FIGURE 4. The completed monopteros constructed over the Jefferson-era well. (© Thomas Jefferson Foundation at Monticello)

to create a classically inspired design. By the time Kimball arrived at Monticello, the original Jefferson-era wellhead was long gone. Only a sixty-foot-deep, brick-lined circular shaft survived from Jefferson's time. Instead, the well was covered by an awkwardly proportioned, hexagonally roofed monopteros from the Levy era.[38] As with the amateur porticoes built on the Pavilions during the same period, this temple-form well house appears to have been an attempt to create a new architectural feature in the Jeffersonian spirit. Kimball and Grigg recognized that this inaccurate re-creation of a monopteros was not the right choice for a well house and had it demolished in 1940 at the start of the South Wing restoration project.

The architects started planning the new wellhead soon after the old one was demolished. The Jefferson-era archival record was scant, and research only revealed to the architects that the well was excavated in 1769, used a windlass, and often failed.[39] The archaeological evidence was also largely missing because the Levy-era monopteros's foundation erased any belowground Jefferson-period evidence that could have provided the wellhead's size, shape, and foundation materials. In response, Kimball and Grigg turned to Jefferson's drawings for inspiration.

Their first plan adapted a striking dovecote with a stepped pyramidal roof that Jefferson drafted but never built. It was considered because it was a documented Jefferson design and conformed to Kimball's belief that Jefferson would have used classically inspired high-style buildings whenever possible. Later, Kimball found fresh inspiration in another Jefferson drawing that depicted a more standard temple form. This time, it was a Tuscan monopteros—most likely a sketch for a clock—that Jefferson drew after 1804.[40] This proved too compelling for the two architects, and Grigg completed a design for a monopteros based on the sketch. With Kimball's backing, the plans were accepted, but the fanciful structure was not constructed until after Kimball's death in 1955.

Later Projects

Kimball's influence in the Foundation increased between 1938 and 1941 with the completion of the large-scale projects at the wings and West Lawn. His growing importance is signaled by his election as a trustee of the Foundation in 1939. Kimball then used his board seat, which he held until his death, to sustain the momentum of the restoration program, except for a long pause during World War II. Kimball's influence was further solidified after Marie Goebel Kimball was named Monticello's first curator in 1944. With his position secure, Kimball would continue to press the Foundation aggressively to focus on the restoration of Monticello and its grounds until his death fifteen years later.

Kimball tenaciously advocated for many projects he conceived in the 1920s and 1930s until they were brought to fruition. These projects included the restoration and stabilization work carried out on the main house in the 1950s. Combined, these projects were the most significant preservation and restoration work undertaken at Monticello during his lifetime. Kimball's argument for the projects was primarily driven by a report written by Grigg exposing the dangerously deteriorated condition of the main house's masonry-embedded joist ends—a condition Grigg blamed on the ivy that was allowed to grow on the walls in the late nineteenth century and early twentieth. As these critical joists supported the floors and ceiling, Grigg gave Kimball the cudgel he needed to advocate for a major restoration of the house. Kimball ultimately won the apparently contentious debate on whether to undertake this costly work at a meeting of the trustees in 1953. The board made the decision just in time. Mere days after the meeting, several of the North Octagon Room's joists abruptly failed, and the floor dropped several inches before coming to a precarious rest.

No one was injured, but the need for the work was now undeniable and started soon after the floor's failure.[41]

Kimball and Grigg produced a comprehensive stabilization plan to direct the work. The project included supporting the cellar ceiling framing with steel I-beams; replacing many of the second-floor joists with steel beams; installing a groundbreaking heating and air conditioning system; restoring the terrace roof, dome roof, and skylights; reconstructing the roof's Chinese railing; repairing and replacing water-damaged sections of the Parlor floor; and repainting the interior. Notably, most of this work occurred in the relatively short period between 1953 and 1955 and was finished under budget and ahead of schedule.[42]

Legacy

Kimball died in August 1955, just as these large projects approached completion. After his death, architectural restoration work at Monticello quickly came to a halt. Ultimately, like Jefferson before him, Kimball was the animating spirit that gave life to ambitious projects that improved Monticello's buildings and landscapes. While important research and an expansion in programs to bolster the Foundation's educational mission were undertaken in the decades after Kimball's death, no significant restoration projects were accomplished. Perhaps the best marker of this new phase in the Foundation's history occurred in 1967, when the Board of Trustees disbanded Kimball's cherished Restoration Committee.

It was not until the 1970s that significant restoration work was undertaken at Monticello again. The timing largely reflected the expanding influence of the historic preservation movement and the rapid revenue growth caused by an increase in visitation in the years before the Bicentennial of the Declaration of Independence. These two events allowed the Foundation to hire and promote talented professionals who specialized in architectural history as well as curatorial, archaeological, and horticultural history. These often young and ambitious new staff members, led by Resident Director James Bear, advocated for reconsidering Monticello's built environment and how it was interpreted using a fresh understanding of the physical and archival resources. Although the professional staff's depth of knowledge in their respective fields would eventually grow to be greater than that of Fiske and Marie Kimball's, the couple's extensive, decades-long record at Monticello established a baseline of research that remains relevant today.

Far from disparaging Kimball's and Grigg's work, succeeding generations of scholars have found that the process of reanalysis and re-restoration at Monticello

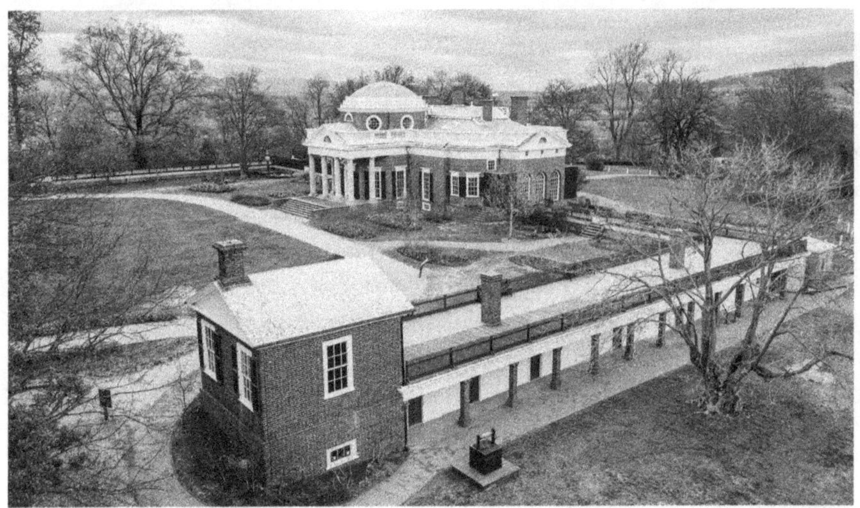

FIGURE 5. Monticello in 2018, after a second restoration of the North and South Wings. (© Thomas Jefferson Foundation at Monticello)

is as vital to the interpretive process as the original restorations were in their time. In fact, the current reconsideration of Kimball's legacy parallels the completion of a multi-decade program to thoroughly reanalyze—and largely replace—his and Grigg's work. The reevaluation of Kimball's restoration projects at Monticello started in earnest with the removal of the domed temple and columns of the well-head monopteros in 1974.[43] (The brick base was demolished in 2018.)

In the early 1990s, much of the restored roof designed by Kimball and Grigg was replaced with the current, meticulously reconstructed roof whose design drew on a much-expanded understanding of the physical and documentary evidence. Finally, the major reconstructions of the North and South Wings, as well as the main house's cellars, were reanalyzed and largely replaced between 2001 and 2018. The restorations of the West and East Lawns—now firmly in their eighth decade—are also being reinvestigated.

Notably, the resulting work is not only more accurate but also more responsive to the questions being brought to these sites by contemporary visitors, including those focused on race and slavery. Visitors now see how the enslaved people lived and worked on Mulberry Row and the South Wing, experience parklike landscapes that are closer to Jefferson's ideal, and walk through a reimagined vegetable garden that Monticello's longtime Director of Gardens and Grounds Peter Hatch described as the "Ellis Island of introduced economic plants."[44] Kimball, however, would still take satisfaction in seeing that the tools he used to ensure the greatest possible accuracy of his restoration projects at Monticello—carefully considering the documentary record, thoroughly investigating the architectural and archaeological evidence, and referencing surviving period examples when all else fails—have only been improved and expanded in the decades since his death. In this very real sense, Monticello's restored spaces remain a product, and a legacy, of Fiske Kimball.

Notes

1. The Foundation was known as the Thomas Jefferson Memorial Foundation until 2000, when the name was changed to the Thomas Jefferson Foundation.
2. William Hildreth to Milton Grigg, 1961, Thomas Jefferson Foundation Archives (hereafter TJF Archives), Jefferson Library, Thomas Jefferson Foundation, Inc.
3. Fiske Kimball to Milton Grigg, July 15, 1955, TJF Archives.
4. For more information on the history of Monticello in the period between Thomas Jefferson's death and the Foundation's purchase of the estate in 1923, see the very detailed description in Marc Leepson's *Saving Monticello: The Levy Family's Epic Quest to Rescue the House That Jefferson Built* (New York: Free Press, 2001).
5. Margaret Bayard Smith, *A Winter in Washington* (New York: Bliss & White, 1824); Samuel Whitcomb Jr., "An Interview with Thomas Jefferson," May 3, 1824, Accession #2816, Special Collections, University of Virginia Library. A transcription of Whitcomb's memorandum is available in Merrill D. Peterson, ed., *Visitors to Monticello* (Charlottesville: University of Virginia Press, 1989), 93–96.
6. Martha Jefferson Randolph to Ellen Wayles Randolph Coolidge, August 15, 1831, Harold J. Coolidge Collection, Washington, DC.
7. A complete history of the Levy ownership of Monticello can be found in Leepson's comprehensive *Saving Monticello.*
8. Mary Amanda Norwood Lyons, Resolution of the Albemarle County Chapter of the Daughters of the American Revolution, Presented at the Chapter Meeting, University of Virginia, November 13, 1912, Special Collections, Jefferson Library, Thomas Jefferson Foundation, Inc.
9. Fiske Kimball to Stuart Gibboney, 1937, Special Collections, Jefferson Library, Thomas Jefferson Foundation, Inc.
10. Hugh Howard, *Dr. Kimball and Mr. Jefferson: Rediscovering the Founding Fathers of American Architecture* (New York: Bloomsbury, 2006).
11. Howard, *Dr. Kimball and Mr. Jefferson,* 178.
12. Letters and minutes from the board meetings, Thomas Jefferson Memorial Foundation, box 14, folder 2.

13. 1930 memorandum, TJF Archives, box 9–23: series 9, folder 24. The cost of the stairs is listed as $691.78.

14. Recent research undertaken by Foundation research archaeologist Derek Wheeler has uncovered evidence that Jefferson documented the West Portico stairs in survey notes. These stairs can also be seen in watercolors made in 1825 by Jane Braddick Peticolas and Aaron Vail.

15. Fiske Kimball to Stuart Gibboney, July 15, 1935, Special Collections, Jefferson Library, Thomas Jefferson Foundation, Inc.

16. Thomas Jefferson Memorial Foundation Board minutes from 1934, 1935, and 1937.

17. Two letters written by Fiske Kimball to Stuart Gibboney, both dated July 15, 1935, TJF Archives.

18. Fiske Kimball to Stuart Gibboney, May 12, 1940, TJF Archives.

19. Stuart Gibboney to Fiske Kimball, January 13, 1941, TJF Archives; Stuart Gibboney to Fiske Kimball, October 24, 1941, TJF Archives.

20. Fiske Kimball, "The Grounds at Monticello in 1809," *Landscape Architecture Magazine* 8, no. 3 (1918); Fiske Kimball, "The Gardens and Plantations at Monticello," *Landscape Architecture Magazine* 17, no. 3 (1927). The latter article was later reprinted by the Thomas Jefferson Memorial Foundation as the monograph *Jefferson's Grounds and Gardens at Monticello*.

21. Fiske Kimball to Milton Grigg, January 12, 1939, TJF Archives.

22. The artist William Coffee wrote to Jefferson about the naturally hydraulic "Roman" cement on November 7, 1818, and Coffee came to Monticello in 1820 to instruct the mason on how to install it.

23. This would be the Garden Club's first project at Monticello. Garden Club members continue to be involved at Monticello and have done more than any other group to advance the restoration of Jefferson's designed landscape.

24. Amy Cogswell, *A Planting Plan for Monticello: Bed #1*, April 1927 (blueprint), Jefferson Library, Thomas Jefferson Foundation, Inc.

25. Peter Hatch, "Restoring Monticello's Landscape, 1923–1955," *Magnolia* 23 (Fall 2009–Winter 2010).

26. Morley Williams, "The Gardens at Monticello," *Landscape Architecture* 24, no. 2 (1934). Kimball's design for the restored landscape at the North Wing is an example of the problems that arise when features are re-created using only documentary evidence. Kimball sought to manifest a Jefferson drawing that sketched out a carriage turnaround in front of the North Wing without any corroborating physical evidence and in a location that was compromised by modern infrastructure. The resulting design was limited by a modern road that was essential to navigating around the mountaintop; this required that the turnaround be expressed using a half-scale re-creation delineated by waist-high privet hedges. To add to the confusion, later archaeological excavations at

the North Wing determined that the carriage turnaround never went beyond Jefferson's drafting table. The privet hedges also made it difficult to navigate around the North Wing and likely left Monticello's visitors confused rather than informed. Much of the privet that defined this fanciful landscape feature was removed in the 1980s.

27. Fiske Kimball to Milton Grigg, May 4, 1938, TJF Archives.

28. Milton Grigg to Fiske Kimball, January 19, 1939, TJF Archives.

29. Hatch, "Restoring Monticello's Landscape." This article provides a much deeper exploration of the West Lawn's restoration. Also see Milton Grigg to Fiske Kimball, January 11, 1939, TJF Archives. Several other letters between the two men survive that describe Grigg's development of his thoughts on how the gardens should be laid out.

30. Fiske Kimball to Stuart Gibboney, May 23, 1934, TJF Archives.

31. Milton Grigg to Stuart Gibboney, January 6, 1941, TJF Archives.

32. Jonathan A. Farris, "Fiske Kimball, The Robert E. Lee Memorial Foundation, and the 'Museumification' of Stratford Hall," paper delivered at Fiske Kimball: Creator of an American Architecture symposium, University of Virginia School of Architecture, November 19, 1995.

33. A good example of this tension is seen in the Kimball-Grigg correspondence concerning the restoration of the South Pavilion, TJF Archives, restoration, box 92–11: series 92, folder 45.

34. Memorandum to Milton L. Grigg, January 10, 1941, and Grigg's response in "Memorandum to Dr. Kimball," January 11, 1941, both in Jefferson Library, Thomas Jefferson Foundation, Inc.

35. Jefferson, "Notes for railings on the Terrasses," 1824 (N147bb), Massachusetts Historical Society.

36. Fiske Kimball to Milton Grigg, February 1, 1938, TJF Archives.

37. Milton Grigg to Fiske Kimball, January 29, 1938, TJF Archives.

38. A monopteros is a dome-roofed, circular structure in the form of a temple. Photographs of the Levy monopteros that covered the Jefferson well are found in the "iconography" collection at the Jefferson Library outside of Charlottesville, Virginia.

39. P. Gardiner Hallock, memorandum on wellhead reconstruction, unpublished manuscript, 2014, TJF Archives.

40. The sketch includes numbers in the frieze and architrave, with multiples of five up to the number sixty in the frieze and roman numerals I through XII on the architrave. "Monticello: Tuscan monopteros, recto, 1804 or later," Thomas Jefferson Papers, Massachusetts Historical Society, http://www.masshist.org/thomasjeffersonpapers/doc?id=arch_N183.

41. Milton Grigg to Fiske Kimball, February 2, 1953, TJF Archives.

42. Fiske Kimball to Milton Grigg, June 7, 1954, TJF Archives.

43. TJF Board of Trustees minutes, April 1974. Interestingly, directly after the temple's completion, it was found to be so out of place in its modest setting that board member William Hildreth voiced his criticisms using Kimball's own mantra that it is better to "preserve than to restore and restore rather than re-construct." William Hildreth to Milton Grigg, 1961, TJF Archives.

44. Peter Hatch, *A Rich Spot of Earth: Thomas Jefferson's Revolutionary Garden at Monticello* (New Haven, CT: Yale University Press, 2021), 4.

THE MONTICELLO IMAGE IN THE AMERICAN MIND

Fiske and Marie Kimball Curate Thomas Jefferson's Home

ANN M. LUCAS

In his classic study of Thomas Jefferson's legacy, *The Jefferson Image in the American Mind,* Merrill Peterson reminds us that "greatness, once it has been exhibited in works and ideas, invites approach . . . to the human being." Jefferson's reputation enjoyed a resurgence in the first decade of the twentieth century, while Fiske Kimball was studying architecture at Harvard. Democrats "refurbished" the political Jefferson and, as Peterson writes, "others discovered in Jefferson ingratiating personal traits and civilized values that had little to do with politics."[1] It would be Fiske Kimball and his wife, Marie Goebel Kimball,[2] who would come to define the public's newfound understanding of Jefferson's creative powers and contributions to the artistic world. The Kimballs codified, interpreted, and publicized Jefferson's "scientific" approach to architecture and the decorative arts, putting to rest contemporary doubts that Jefferson himself was capable of designing works like Monticello and the University of Virginia and setting the bar for Jefferson scholarship that continues to shape Monticello today.[3] Fiske and Marie Kimball firmly fixed the *Monticello* image in the American mind.

Even seventy-five years after Jefferson's death—and long before the Thomas Jefferson Memorial Foundation existed—a curious public recognized that the political and personal threads of Jefferson's life were combined at Monticello. By some estimates, thousands of visitors were making the pilgrimage there each year,[4] including the Reverend Peter Fossett, who was once enslaved by Jefferson but visited as a free man in 1900.[5] Fossett and others were welcomed to the property by its private owner, Jefferson Monroe Levy, whose uncle, Commodore Uriah Levy, had purchased Monticello in 1834. Though interrupted by the Civil

War, the Levy family's almost ninety-year tenure at Monticello far exceeded Jefferson's own.[6] Members of the Coleman and Henderson families greeted visitors at Monticello's gate and gave tours. With the Jefferson Memorial on Washington, DC's tidal basin still forty years in the future, Monticello—and Jefferson's grave there—served as a de facto memorial to Thomas Jefferson.

The Kimballs, Jefferson Research, and the Coolidge Family

Fiske Kimball was among those who visited Monticello during Levy's ownership. He arrived in 1914 to examine the building as part of his study of a newly uncovered collection of architectural drawings by Jefferson. Fiske had come upon evidence of Jefferson as an architect when he was working on his first major book, *A History of Architecture* (1918), but it was Marie who pursued the topic.[7] She discovered that Jefferson had in fact made drawings and surmised

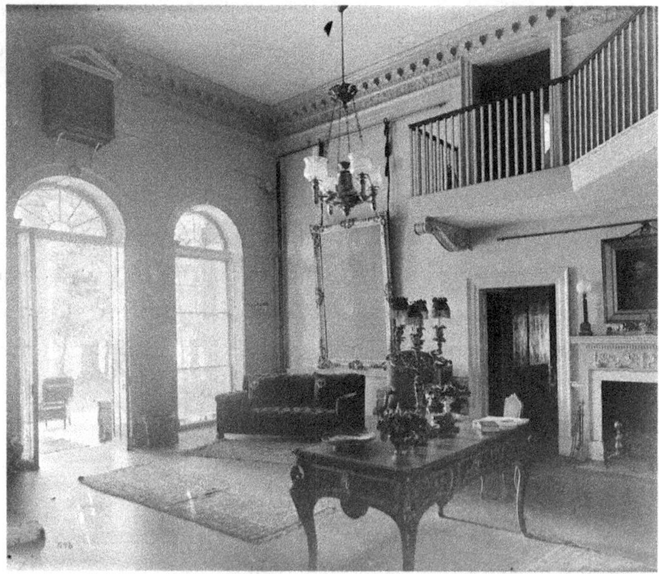

FIGURE 1. Monticello's entrance hall during the Levy era, as Fiske Kimball would have first seen it on his visit in 1914, was a mixture of Jefferson-era fixtures, such as the Great Clock, wall brackets, and entablatures, and items collected and displayed by Jefferson Monroe Levy, including a portrait of his uncle Uriah P. Levy. (Rufus W. Holsinger, September 17, 1912, Holsinger Studio Collection, MSS 9862, Albert and Shirley Small Special Collections Library, University of Virginia)

that some of these had likely survived in his papers. (This would come to be a pattern with their scholastic partnership. Marie's work was fundamental to Fiske's study of Jefferson, but Fiske's name would dominate publications on the topic, especially in the early years.[8]) This initial scholarly investigation would transform their lives. Thus began a lifelong association for both Marie and Fiske with Thomas Jefferson, Monticello, and the nascent Thomas Jefferson Memorial Foundation.[9]

Fiske Kimball was commissioned by Clara Amory Coolidge to study and publish what came to be known as the Coolidge Collection of Jefferson's architectural drawings as a tribute to her late husband, Thomas Jefferson Coolidge Jr.[10] The grand folio *Thomas Jefferson: Architect,* published in 1916, was the acclaimed result.[11] When Fiske first saw the drawing collection, he realized it was monumental. "It was marvelous," he recalled, adding that "there were three or four hundred drawings, many highly competent, some mere scraps. Most were in outline only, a few were rendered in wash, their technique indicating more than a single authorship. They constituted a wilderness of the most obscure kind. There was scarcely a signature in the lot, rarely any title, and but few dates, though many of the drawings were covered with notes and calculations in Jefferson's handwriting."[12]

While Fiske examined hundreds of Jefferson's drawings, memoranda, and library lists, Marie sifted through Jefferson's correspondence and account books. Fiske described their partnership: Marie "plowed through" some fifteen thousand manuscripts at the Massachusetts Historical Society, turning up those that "had a bearing, identifying, dating, and illuminating various designs." She likewise examined twenty-five thousand Jefferson papers at the Library of Congress, "with equally rich finds. . . . Marie undertook also the dull work of comparing these [water] marks with those of the papers used in Jefferson's correspondence, and thus dated almost all of them." Together they conquered cryptic notations, cramped handwriting, and mouse-eaten drawings. The Kimballs were even allowed to take the drawings with them to Michigan, where Fiske was teaching, for further study.[13]

The collection convinced Fiske that "Jefferson's interest and influence in architecture appear as notable as his services in politics and science. Instead of a few drawings, hitherto in dispute, we have now a great mass of studies, designs, and memoranda, unquestionably his, in which the extent of his activity and the development of his architectural knowledge, draughtsmanship, and creative power are clearly shown. . . . Nowhere else can the mental processes of an early American architect and the inner development of his designs be followed so closely."[14]

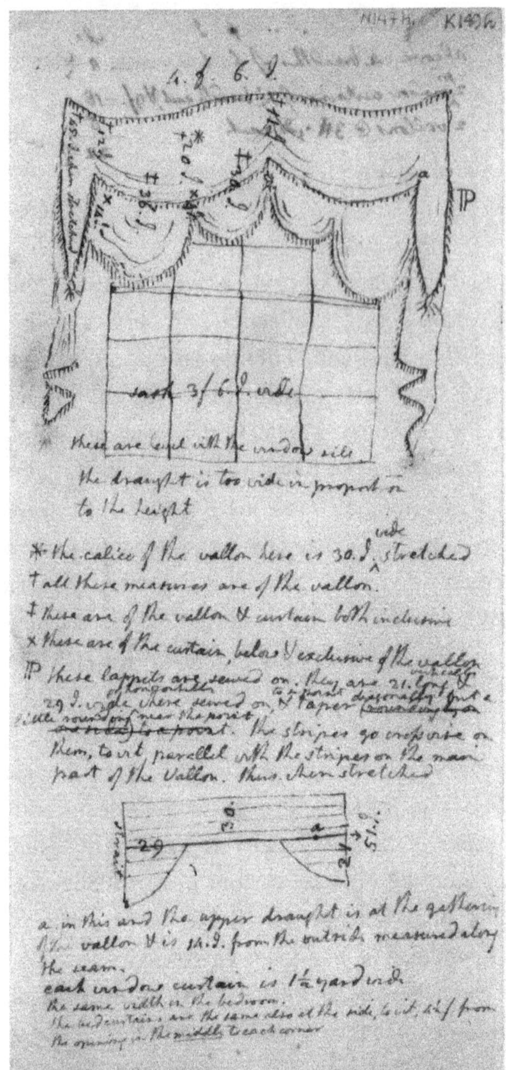

FIGURE 2. Thomas Jefferson's sketch and specifications for curtains, ca. 1803, are an example of the type of architectural drawing that the Kimballs published in the 1916 folio *Thomas Jefferson, Architect* and that informed their furnishing of Monticello. (Courtesy of the Massachusetts Historical Society, Coolidge Collection, N147h; K149h)

In their attempt to put Jefferson's drawings in order by chronology and project, the Kimballs made what Fiske termed a "scientific study" of each drawing. Marie analyzed them as artifacts, looking at the paper, examining the ink, pencil, and washes. This evidence allowed the Kimballs to reunite documents, firmly establish authorship, and, most importantly, estimate dates. Similarly, they compiled a list of architectural books in Jefferson's library as a way of understanding Jefferson's design processes and influences. The completed *Thomas Jefferson, Architect* incorporates information from Jefferson's letters, account books, memorandum books, and journals to create a framework and numbering system for his architectural efforts that is relied upon by scholars to this day.

The Kimballs occupied Jefferson's mind in a way that rendered them the ultimate authority on not only the drawings themselves but also their contents. Of the more than 400 drawings in the Coolidge Collection, 245 of them—including pages of specifications from Jefferson's building notebook—are for Monticello. These include garden designs, surveys and plats, library lists and furniture, curtains, outbuildings, observation towers, clocks, parquet flooring, entablatures, garden pavilions, a brewhouse, slave dwellings, and domes.[15] This flood of discoveries, scholarship, and publishing happened while Monticello remained the private residence of Jefferson Monroe Levy.

The Kimballs and the Acquisition of Monticello

As the foremost scholar on Jefferson's architecture, Fiske naturally became involved in discussions surrounding various efforts in the late teens and early twenties that were aimed at making Monticello a public institution. Fiske acted as a go-between when Levy had hoped to sell the house to members of the Coolidge family in 1917, and in 1921 his essay, "Thomas Jefferson as an Architect," was part of the real estate brochure for Monticello.[16] When asked by a Harvard classmate what he thought of the property, Fiske replied that he was "greatly interested that Monticello shall be purchased either by some quasi-public body like several with which I am connected, or by some private individual who will not exploit it but treat it with suitable care and public spirit."[17]

Fiske expressed his desire for public ownership in March 1923 in a published American Institute of Architects report of the Committee on Preservation of Historic Monuments and Scenic Beauties:

> The private ownership of Monticello continues to be regrettable; but much more so is the bad condition into which the house and especially the outbuildings have fallen during the last few years of relative neglect. The roofs of the terraces have been left without proper painting, and are now fenced off with barbed wire. Although no doubt the owner is doing all his resources permit, it is greatly to be hoped that the efforts to purchase the house for the public may be prosecuted with greater success than they have been since it came publicly on the market, and that the much-needed work of maintenance and repair should then be undertaken at once. Various extraneous additions of modern date should be removed.

Fortunately, this could easily be effected. Beyond this, Jefferson's drawings for parts which have long disappeared are all available, even to the planting plans, and it would be perfectly feasible to put the place back exactly in the form which it had in his lifetime.[18]

The Thomas Jefferson Memorial Foundation

On April 13, 1923, mere weeks after this report was published, the Thomas Jefferson Memorial Foundation was incorporated in Albany, New York, "for the purpose of establishing Monticello as a memorial to the Author of the Declaration of Independence and for the purpose of inculcating through patriotic education a better understanding and appreciation of the life and service of Thomas Jefferson."[19] Fiske immediately wrote to the Foundation's president, Stuart Gibboney, sending a copy of the AIA report and offering his assistance: "Some passages in the enclosed report of this Committee may be of interest to you in connection with your admirable effort to purchase and preserve Monticello. At the time it was written, only a few weeks ago, there seemed no prospect of any such movement, and now has come your great success, as an answer to our wish. You can readily imagine how delighted the architectural profession of the country will be at the prospect of rescuing this precious monument."

In just three paragraphs Fiske lays out what will become his life's work with the Thomas Jefferson Memorial Foundation. He will make connections with national organizations like the American Institute of Architects; he offers his services based on the "very detailed study" he has made of Jefferson's architectural drawings; and he will use "any influence I possess with the Coolidge family, the principal owners of Jefferson's relics, to aid you in securing gifts of these for the refurnishing of the house." Finally, he includes a gift of twenty-five dollars "as my personal contribution toward the purchase of Monticello, and wish my means permitted this to be a great deal more."[20] In the end, both Fiske and Marie Kimball would go on to donate their services to the Foundation for more than thirty years. In 1953 he commented to a publisher, "Marie and I love Monticello, the Foundation, for which we have given thousands of dollars worth of services."[21] The Kimballs were never compensated for their work at Monticello, merely reimbursed for expenses such as shipping, blueprints and photocopies, long-distance telephone calls, and travel. Even travel expenses were minimized by the Kimballs' eventually taking up residence near Monticello over the summers.[22]

Fiske quickly earned a seat at the table with the Foundation's leaders. Gibboney's reply to Fiske's offer, dated just two days later, is covered with Kimball's notes and annotations. In much the same way that Kimball analyzed Jefferson's drawings and memoranda, generations of scholars have also been discerning Kimball's thought process from his own notes. His tick marks on the list of the board of directors indicates those people whom he knows, such as Edwin Alderman, President of the University of Virginia, and Lady Astor. His pencil notes indicate that he clearly had a phone call with Gibboney in which they discussed the finances of the Foundation; Jefferson Monroe Levy had proposed an asking price of $500,000, with $100,000 due at the end of 1923, leaving a $400,000 balance to mortgage.[23] The two make plans to meet when Kimball is in New York in the coming week, and Gibboney follows up with an urgent telegram, asking Kimball to confirm the offering price Levy gave to Charlottesville philanthropist Paul Goodloe McIntire.[24]

At nearly the same moment that the Foundation was formed in New York, the Kimballs were moving to that city as well, leaving Charlottesville after Fiske's four years serving as the head of the University of Virginia's McIntire School of Fine Arts to join the Institute of Fine Arts at New York University. In 1924 the Foundation's board of directors unanimously voted to ask Fiske to chair its Restoration Committee. The Foundation had very limited funds for anything other than paying off Monticello's mortgage. There were no funds for substantial work on the buildings—as noted in Gardiner Hallock's essay for this volume, "'As It Is Accurate Historically': Fiske Kimball and the Restoration of Monticello"—but the Kimballs could begin their work to restore Monticello's interiors.[25]

The Search for Artifacts

In January 1827, following Jefferson's death the year before, much of Monticello's contents and most of the people enslaved there were auctioned off to help satisfy Jefferson's debts.[26] While the people and the estate's contents had been scattered across the country, Jefferson Monroe Levy had managed to acquire several important pieces and preserve some that were fixtures of the house, such as the Great Clock in Monticello's Entrance Hall and the brackets in the Tea Room. These were surrounded by later Victorian pieces. Through sales and auctions, the Kimballs would rid Monticello of anything they deemed to be "non-Jefferson"—sometimes in error, as was the case with the removal of carved wooden brackets from Monticello's Entrance Hall. Even today the various sales and auctions of items associated with Monticello can lead to confusion. Curators still use the techniques and resources identified by Fiske and Marie Kimball as their guides.[27]

Marie's first documented work for the Foundation came in 1927, when she traveled to the Library of Congress to consult Jefferson's manuscripts and account books. The two articles she published that same year under her own name about the furnishing of Monticello make evident that she was clearly doing much more than legwork for Fiske's research. In a two-part article in *Magazine Antiques,* Marie firmly established her methodology. She began by recounting a recent "front-page story" about one artifact of most significance to Americans: the desk on which Jefferson wrote the Declaration of Independence. It had apparently left the country and was owned by the Bismarck Museum in Berlin, with whom there had been negotiations for its return for fifteen years. The conundrum involved an American ambassador and the State Department, and it had even escalated to the Oval Office. In Marie's words, "the matter was fortunately referred to a Jefferson expert, familiar with the true history of the desk," which was revealed to be safely in the national museum in Washington, DC, having never left home. It had been given to the United States in 1888 by Jefferson's descendants, who realized that an object with such historic importance should not be in private hands. The Berlin museum owned a convincing copy, given by one of those same descendants to Otto von Bismarck, complete with a reproduction of a note in Jefferson's handwriting authenticating its provenance from him to his granddaughter Ellen Randolph Coolidge's husband, Joseph Coolidge Jr.[28]

In one fell swoop, Marie established that artifacts related to Jefferson and Monticello were matters of national, if not international, interest and that their authentication should be left to the experts. Her two articles detail her method of reliance on primary sources to authenticate and exhibit items at Monticello: Jefferson's correspondence, account books, lists of art, packing lists, drawings, floor plans by descendants, inventories, accounts by family members, and descriptions by visitors to Monticello. At the same time, she named key figures aside from Jefferson whose stories contributed to and could be told through Monticello: the enslaved joiner John Hemmings and the master joiner with whom he trained, James Dinsmore; family members, including Jefferson's wife, Martha Wayles Jefferson, daughter Martha Jefferson Randolph, and "favorite" granddaughters; and visitors of historic importance, such as the Marquis de Lafayette. Marie outlined the types of furniture and artifacts that had originally furnished Monticello, illustrating the articles with examples ranging from the Chippendale furniture rescued from the fire at Jefferson's birthplace, Shadwell, to French lighting as well as modest pieces she thought were most likely made in the joiner's shop on the

The Furnishing of Monticello*

By MARIE KIMBALL†

Part I

THE DECLARATION OF INDEPENDENCE DESK

ONE October day in the year 1925, the American papers carried a front-page story more than usually amazing. It was to the effect that the desk upon which Thomas Jefferson had written the Declaration of Independence had been found in the Bismarck Museum in Berlin, where it had been reposing for the past twenty-five years; and that now, thanks to the activities of an American pastor in the German city, the desk was about to return to its native country. No doubt, apparently, could be entertained as to the authenticity of the desk, the story continued. It had been given to the Iron Chancellor, Prince Otto von Bismarck, on the occasion of his eighty-first birthday, by Jefferson's great-grandson, the Honorable Thomas Jefferson Coolidge, to whom the desk had descended. A frayed and yellowed piece of paper, inscribed in Jefferson's own hand and pasted inside the desk, told its history to the year 1825:

Thomas Jefferson gives this writing desk to Joseph Coolidge, Jr., as a memorial of his affection. It was made from a drawing of his own, by Benjamin Randolph, cabinetmaker at Philadelphia, with whom he first lodged on his arrival in that city, in May, 1776, and is the identical one on which he wrote the Declaration of Independence. Politics, as well as religion, has its superstitions. These gaining strength with time, may one day give imaginary value to this relic, for its associations with the birth of the Great Charter of our Independence.

Monticello, Nov. 18, 1825.

For fifteen years, our story went on, attempts had been made to induce the Bismarck family to part with this rare treasure. During the war the attention of the State Department was called to it, but with no success.

A letter had subsequently been directed to the President of the United States. The Department of State now turned to its files and reported that, in 1877, the desk upon which Jefferson had written the Declaration of Independence had been offered the United States, but that no record of an acceptance could be found. With this reassurance, the question of the return of the desk to the United States was placed in the hands of the American Ambassador to Germany.

Rumors were current that the Bismarck family was about to be induced to part with the piece, for a consideration; and further action was imminent, when the matter was fortunately referred to a Jefferson expert, familiar with the true history of the desk. He informed the authorities that, at that very moment, the original desk was in the National Museum at Washington, D. C.; indeed that it had been there for the last fifty years.

The story of Jefferson's desk was not so mysterious as the newspapers would have had us believe. The desk had wandered, to be sure; but it had never left its native land. In 1825, when Ellen Randolph, the grandchild to whom Jefferson was most devoted, married Joseph Coolidge, Jr. of Boston, she took with her a handsome inlaid desk made by John Hemmings, Jefferson's skillful negro carpenter. Along with her other luggage, this desk was shipped in a packet sailing from Richmond, and was lost at sea. All Ellen's mementoes and the letters of her beloved grandfather were carried down with it. As a consolation, the venerable statesman determined to send the despairing Ellen a substitute, "not claiming the same value from its decorations, but from the part it has borne in our history and the events with which it has been associated."

In his usual modest fashion Jefferson wrote:

Fig. 1 — DECLARATION OF INDEPENDENCE DESK (closed)
Made by Benjamin Randolph, the Philadelphia cabinetmaker, for Thomas Jefferson, after the latter's own specifications. On this desk the Declaration of Independence was written.
By permission of The United States National Museum, Washington

FIGURE 3. Beginning in 1927, Marie Kimball published seminal articles in *Magazine Antiques* and other popular magazines detailing the Kimballs' methodology for the furnishing and interpretation of Monticello. (Marie Kimball, "The Furnishing of Monticello, Part I," *Magazine Antiques,* November 1927)

plantation. Jefferson's role in America's independence, his political life, love of music, passion for science, movements up and down the East Coast and abroad, shopping, collecting habits, labor-saving contrivances, and daily way of life were all revealed by the objects and architecture at Monticello. What better memorial could there be?

"No hunt for antiques can compare in interest," Marie wrote, "or in thrill to the search that has been going on, these past several years, for the furniture that

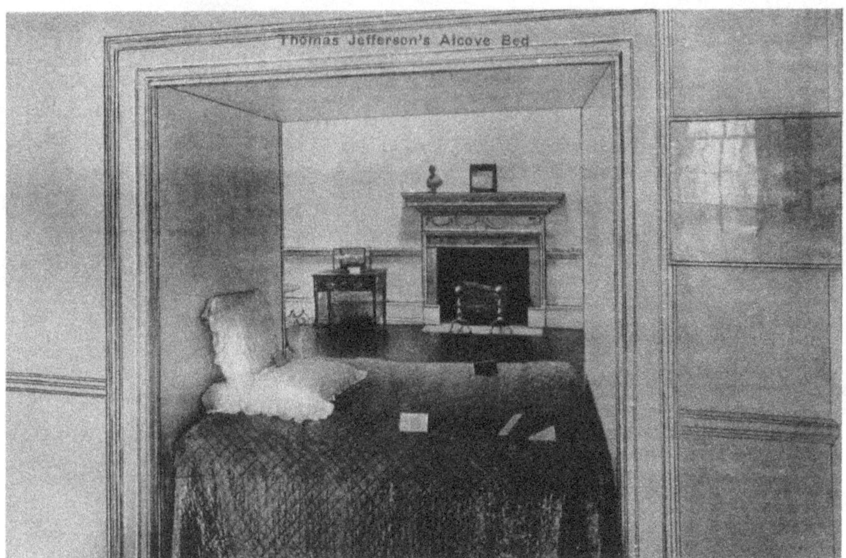

FIGURE 4. In 1926, three years into Fiske Kimball's tenure, Monticello commemorated the nation's centennial with a postcard of the sparsely furnished Jefferson bedchamber. The postcard caption highlighted the type of authentic relics the Kimballs sought in order to furnish Jefferson's home, describing this as "the original Alcove Bed at Monticello showing the two original pillows which were under Jefferson's head when he died July 4, 1826—the 50th Anniversary." (Thomas Jefferson Foundation Archives, © Thomas Jefferson Foundation at Monticello)

formerly stood in Monticello; yet the problem of separating the true from the false, and of putting the mansion back as it was in Jefferson's day is not an easy one."[29] It was slow going. The Kimballs nurtured meaningful relationships with descendants and local families whose ancestors attended Monticello auctions. They joined the Monticello Association of Jefferson's descendants and faithfully attended their annual gatherings at Monticello. In correspondence with the Garden Club of Virginia, Fiske made clear that personal taste was to be set aside in favor of facts: "I think today we all feel more kindly to the ideal of putting things back the way they were, irrespective of whether we ourselves wanted them just that way or not."[30] The Kimballs' resolve rendered Monticello's early interiors barren, drawing complaints from visitors. The situation was exacerbated by the opening of Colonial Williamsburg in 1935. As Fiske complained to Gibboney, "the gold-plated character of Williamsburg has raised the standard of everything about period houses, and tends to make anything on the old, amateur standards look shabby."[31]

In 1937, Fiske wrote to a Jefferson descendant from whom he hoped to acquire some original furniture, "As you may know, there is a good deal of criticism of the bareness of Monticello, and that in view of this it has taken a great deal of courage to hold out for the principle that nothing should be shown at Monticello which did not belong to Jefferson or his immediate family. Of course this means that we are almost entirely dependent upon the generosity of surviving members of the family who own the pieces, to secure some day a sufficient number of such pieces to furnish Monticello adequately."[32] He similarly lobbied another family member that same year, saying that "the Foundation has now been able to curtain the house, and you will see it looks much more attractive. This has done something to relieve the bareness of which visitors complain, but there is constant pressure to furnish the house with reproductions."[33]

Every object the Kimballs accepted and exhibited added depth to the nation's image of Thomas Jefferson. Unexpected items from the family, such as a music rack and Martha Jefferson Randolph's sheet music from Paris, led to consideration of Jefferson as a musician and his family's stay in France; a manuscript cookbook with French recipes revealed Jefferson the epicure and the influence of the cuisine created by enslaved chefs at Monticello. A revolving chair, adaptable furniture, and an architect's table reinforced Jefferson's reputation as an innovator. The facets of Jefferson's life at Monticello multiplied. Offers of "Jefferson relics," as they were called, continued to stream in. Owners were motivated by the hope of monetary gain, nostalgia, a sense of duty, or a combination of the three. Gibboney would often receive the details, some happily accompanied by a photo, and send them off to Fiske—sometimes several in one letter—and await his verdict.[34] Marie was doubtless also involved in these deliberations, as she continued to publish articles about the search for Jefferson's furnishings in the popular press.[35] Fiske's rejections were brisk and decisive—Victorian was a four-letter word to him—but he did on occasion reverse his decision. In such a case he wrote to Gibboney, "The photograph alters the whole face of the situation, for the chair shown in it can be at once recognized by its style, as not being Victorian at all, but of the very period when Jefferson was securing his furniture in Paris."[36] In his excited reply to the owner, he added, "It is, as you of course appreciate, a remarkably fine piece, and we would give our eyes to have it at Monticello."[37]

As the Kimballs sought out objects, they visited descendants in their homes, gently probed about cousins who might have "relics," and circulated Marie's articles to the Monticello Association.[38] Fiske was patient but persistent in his correspondence with those who owned artifacts, and the line "I suppose there is absolutely no chance that you would part with . . ." was often employed, especially in the 1940s, once the Foundation had satisfied the mortgage and funds were more readily available for acquisitions.[39] In a letter inquiring about the value of an oval table she owned, a descendant wrote that "the mahogany was brought from South America and the table made at Monticello by Jefferson's slaves under his directions. It was used at Monticello in the tea room, so I have always been told." As if he needed reminding, she added that when Fiske and Marie had lunched with her, that was the table they had used! Monticello is still in conversation with the owners of this table today and happily have a reproduction of it on display.[40] As Diane Ehrenpreis, Monticello Curator of Decorative Arts and Historic Interiors, has observed, the pool of artifacts retained by Jefferson's family members skewed toward items that were unique or exceptional, such as those that Jefferson designed or adapted, which reinforced the Kimballs' interpretation of Jefferson's "genius."[41]

Curating Monticello from Philadelphia

Once Fiske accepted the directorship of the Pennsylvania Museum (now Philadelphia Museum of Art) in 1925, the Kimballs conducted their work for Monticello at a distance, living primarily at Lemon Hill in Philadelphia. Correspondence documents their role managing Monticello's public relations from afar, coordinating photographers and juggling "exclusives" with outlets like *Magazine Antiques* and *Town and Country*.[42] They launched a furniture reproduction program, selected items for the gift shop, wrote Monticello's brochures and guidebooks, composed scripts for the guides, and wrote the copy for labels to accompany art and artifacts. In the case of the 1823 James Westhall Ford portrait of Martha Jefferson Randolph, Kimball excitedly submitted revised label copy, when, as he put it, "By a coincidence little short of marvelous, papers have just turned up in private hands here which establish the authorship of the smaller portrait of Martha Jefferson Randolph we have at Monticello." When a hapless graphic designer suggested flattering Jefferson by adding a line to a brochure asserting that Jefferson alone built Monticello, Kimball was unequivocal in his response: "No, I certainly do *not* approve the retention of the line 'with no builder nor craftsmen other than his own.' There were numerous builders and craftsmen employed by Jefferson at Monticello: notably James Oldham, James Dinsmore and John Neilson, not to speak of others."[43] This, in itself, was a first—to give the name of the white workmen who had built Monticello. Still, the "others" Kimball omitted were men such as the enslaved carpenters John Hemmings and his nephews Madison and Eston Hemings. Like the impermanent buildings many occupied, the enslaved people at Monticello left a type of record that the Kimballs and their peers were ill-equipped to process.

As art, artifacts, and furniture arrived, the Kimballs would send directives on their placement from Philadelphia; when they were on-site at Monticello, stories persisted that Fiske would go through rooms rearranging the furniture only to have Marie follow and put it back.[44] Fiske wrote Gibboney in advance of one visit to ask him to ease the way for him with the on-site staff: "I am going to be down there a good deal this summer and am prepared to put some time on arranging and labelling relics there if you would like me to. If so, will you please notify Mr. Rhodes and Mrs. Waterman, so that they won't object." Gibboney responded, "I never knew anybody objected to anything you did at Monticello for I don't know how we would get along without you."[45] Thomas Rhodes was the superintendent at Monticello, a position he continued from his employment with Jefferson Monroe Levy, and he supervised house tours.[46] Marie was officially named Curator of Monticello in 1944, and Fiske was her supervisor. "The curator hears that a number of new display cases are about to be ordered for Monticello," she wrote to Foundation President Frank Houston. "She would like to say that she is not entirely in agreement with this." In his response, Houston advised that this was something Marie and Fiske should "get together on."[47] Display cases aside, examples of the couple working in harmony far outweigh any apparent discord. The restoration of Monticello's curtains exemplified the couple's lifelong ability to complement one another's scholarship and resulted in the coauthored article "Jefferson's Curtains at Monticello" for *Magazine Antiques* in 1947.

Missed Opportunities

One of the most remarkable exchanges surrounding a group of artifacts came through President Franklin D. Roosevelt's office in 1938. Nellie Jones, a descendant of Madison Hemings, wrote to Stuart Gibboney with the offer of an inkwell, shoe buckle, and spectacles—the "personal property [of] Thomas Jefferson, President of the USA" that he had given to Madison's mother, who we now know was Sally Hemings. Gibboney passed the letter along to Kimball, who replied,

> This very respectable colored woman writes a letter much more intelligently than many of our own race. Her story was very straight (except that I am not aware that Jefferson took any slave with him to France—but that is not the crucial point). I see no harm in letting her send on the things, for inspection, as she is willing to do. It might be that the buckle

is identical with one of the buckles we have, which would thus authenticate the whole lot. As to purchasing them, and fixing a price, we really have quite enough of these little mementoes so that it would be indifferent whether we bought any more. . . . we certainly wouldn't be willing to pay much. If you ask her to send them on for inspection, let them be sent to Monticello, and inform me so that I can make comparison when I am down there at Thanksgiving.[48]

Kimball never got the opportunity to make the assessment of these, as Gibboney declined Jones's offer. We still seek them—and their owner's story—today.[49]

Despite meticulous research—or, in some cases, because of literal adherence to such research—mistakes were made. As authoritative and abrasive as Fiske could be, he equally relished legitimate corrections, responding to one clever writer with a cheerful "Touché!" when she pointed out an error in his thinking about Jefferson's curtain designs.[50] Another mistake wasn't resolved in his lifetime, but Kimball's recordkeeping made it possible for later scholars to revisit the question. Twice, Mrs. Henry Dooley offered to donate to Monticello a painting called "Harper's Ferry," which had a label on the back indicating that it had been purchased from an auction of Jefferson's art. Both times Fiske refused the gift, insisting that Jefferson never owned a painting by that name. Thankfully, he kept the correspondence, filed with other rejected offers in the non-Jefferson files. Fifty years later, in preparation for an exhibition celebrating the 250th anniversary of Jefferson's birth, researchers at Monticello recognized that this painting was, in fact, very likely an original painting called *The Junction of the Potomac and Shenandoah Rivers* by William Roberts, which the artist had sent to Jefferson in 1804 along with a painting of Natural Bridge. Jefferson's art inventory indicated that both hung in the Dining Room as examples of what Jefferson called "the most sublime of Nature's works."[51] After years of dead ends, Monticello Curator of Arts and History Emilie Johnson re-engaged the search in 2020 and found Mrs. Dooley's granddaughter. Remarkably, the painting was still in her possession, and she graciously fulfilled her grandmother's wish to donate it to Monticello, where it now hangs in the Dining Room.

Legacy

With the arrival of each new object at Monticello during the Kimballs' tenure, the image of Jefferson in the American mind became richer and more nuanced. By the time President Roosevelt dedicated the Jefferson Memorial in 1943 on the occasion of the bicentennial of Jefferson's birth, Jefferson had, in Peterson's estimation, "transcended politics to become the hero of civilization. He had come to stand for ideals of beauty, science, learning, and conduct, for a way of life enriched by the heritage of the ages yet distinctly American in outline. The range of his appeal, if not its intensity, increased with the disclosure of his varied and ubiquitous genius."[52] Through their efforts to authentically restore Monticello's interiors, Fiske and Marie Kimball not only informed the nation's image of Jefferson in their lifetime but also set the standard the Foundation relies upon today to "follow truth wherever it may lead."[53]

Notes

1. Merrill D. Peterson, *The Jefferson Image in the American Mind,* rev. ed. (Charlottesville: University of Virginia Press, 1998), 230–31. Peterson is among the colleagues and mentors whom I wish to acknowledge for their influence on my research and writing. Thanks to Anna Berkes, William Beiswanger, Megan Brett, Peggy Cornett, Andrew Davenport, Diane Ehrenpreis, Peter Hatch, Emilie Johnson, Susan Kern, Jeff Looney, Cinder Stanton, Susan Stein, and Endrina Tay for their encouragement and assistance.

2. An exceptional biography of Marie Kimball, "Marie Kimball: Pioneering Scholar and First Curator of Monticello" by Anna Berkes, is included in *Virginia Women: Their Lives and Times,* vol. 2, edited by Cynthia A. Kierner and Sandra Gioia Treadway (Athens: University of Georgia Press, 2016), 202–21.

3. Richard Guy Wilson, ed., *Thomas Jefferson's Academical Village: The Creation of an Architectural Masterpiece* (Charlottesville: University of Virginia Press for the Bayly Art Museum of the University of Virginia, 1993), 80–82.

4. Peterson, *Jefferson Image,* 381. Peterson reports that between forty thousand and fifty thousand visitors came to Monticello annually, but I agree with Marc Leepson that the number seems to be a gross exaggeration. Accounts of twenty-five people a day would result in fewer than ten thousand annual visitors. In her 1912 testimony before the House Rules Committee, Maud Littleton reports being told that on average, sixty people a day visited Monticello. See "A Pilgrim Turns Crusader" in Merrill D. Peterson, *Visitors to Monticello* (Charlottesville: University of Virginia Press, 1989), 183, and Marc Leepson, *Saving Monticello: The Levy Family's Epic Quest to Rescue the House That Jefferson Built* (New York: Free Press, 2001), 149.

5. Lucia Stanton, *Free Some Day: The African-American Families of Monticello* (Charlottesville, VA: Thomas Jefferson Foundation, Inc., 2000), 154–55. Peter Fossett (1815–1901) had been born into slavery at Monticello, was sold on the

auction block on Monticello's West Lawn in 1827, and returned seventy-three years later a free man. Fossett recalled the warm welcome he received from Levy and his sister, Amelia Levy Mayhoff.

6. Melvin I. Urofsky, *The Levy Family and Monticello, 1834–1923* (Charlottesville, VA: Thomas Jefferson Foundation, Inc., 2001), passim.

7. Fiske related in his memoir, "Among my papers there was a little slip on which I had jotted 'Jefferson as an Architect.' . . . Marie saw this slip and said, 'That looks like a good subject. Can I have it?'" Fiske Kimball, Memoirs, Fiske Kimball Papers, Philadelphia Museum of Art Archives (hereafter FKP), box 159, folder 5, pp. 4, 6, as quoted in Berkes, "Marie Kimball," 208.

8. Berkes, "Marie Kimball," 210ff.

9. The discovery came in 1912, when he began writing *A History of Architecture*. Berkes, "Marie Kimball," 208. George Roberts and Mary Howland Roberts, *Triumph on Fairmount: Fiske Kimball and the Philadelphia Museum of Art* (Philadelphia: J. B. Lippincott, 1959), 32–33, is a less reliable source. "Memorial" was dropped from the name of the Foundation in 2000.

10. Thomas Jefferson Coolidge Jr. (1863–1912) was a descendant of Jefferson's granddaughter Ellen Wayles Randolph Coolidge and her husband, Joseph Coolidge Jr. He grew up in Boston surrounded by relics from Monticello and engaged Charles McKim to design a house in Manchester-by-the-Sea that was inspired by Jefferson's home. While on a visit to Monticello and the University of Virginia in 1911, Coolidge found "almost by accident" a cache of architectural drawings owned by his cousins Mary Walker Randolph and Cornelia Jefferson Taylor, descendants of Jefferson's grandson Thomas Jefferson Randolph, who lived in Charlottesville. The drawings had been "forgotten," his biographer noted, and "bore evidence of having suffered from damp and mice." Coolidge obtained the entire collection and brought them to the Massachusetts Historical Society, to which his father and grandfather had also given Jefferson manuscripts. The drawings were in the process of being conserved when Coolidge died at age forty-nine. See Thomas Jefferson Coolidge, *The Autobiography of T. Jefferson Coolidge, 1831–1920* (Boston: Houghton Mifflin, 1923), 277–78. Fiske Kimball, *Thomas Jefferson, Architect: Original Designs in the Coolidge Collection of the Massachusetts Historical Society*, intro. Frederick Doveton Nichols, Da Capo Press Series in Architecture and Decorative Art 5 (New York: Da Capo Press, 1968), 8.

11. "For the first time it became possible to comprehend Jefferson's tastes and skill in architecture, and so happily associated with the name of his descendant who had saved the drawings from possible loss or injury." Coolidge, *Autobiography*, 279.

12. Roberts and Roberts, *Triumph on Fairmount*, 32.

13. Fiske Kimball, Memoirs, FKP, box 159, folder 5, p. 8, as quoted in Berkes, "Marie Kimball," 210. See also Marie Frank, "Fiske Kimball and the Genesis of *Thomas Jefferson, Architect,*" *Classicist* 13 (2016): 56–64.

14. F. Kimball, *Thomas Jefferson, Architect,* 13.

15. Thomas Jefferson, Architectural Drawings, [manuscript], circa 1772–1819, from the collections of the Massachusetts Historical Society, Boston, Massachusetts, accessed 15 March 2021, http://www.masshist.org/thomasjeffersonpapers /arch/.

16. "Historic Monticello for Sale," H. W. Hilleary, Washington, D.C., [1921], Thomas Jefferson Memorial Foundation Archives (hereafter TJMF Archives), Special Collections, Jefferson Library, Thomas Jefferson Foundation, Inc.

17. Leepson, *Saving Monticello,* 215.

18. Fiske Kimball, Chair, "AIA Report of Committee on Preservation of Historic Monuments and Scenic Beauties," March 14, 1923, TJMF Archives, box 1, folder 1, n.p.

19. Stuart Gibboney, Report of the President of the Thomas Jefferson Memorial Foundation, September 25, 1926, TJMF Archives.

20. Fiske Kimball to Stuart Gibboney, April 18, 1923, FKP, box 78, folder 4.

21. Fiske Kimball to Alice Winchester, March 14, 1953, FKP, box 78, folder 12.

22. Kimball's 1939 letter to Gibboney regarding his expenses is indicative of his caution when charging the Foundation for his travel and other incidental expenses: "I don't know whether you would regard the travelling expenses on the enclosed as a legitimate charge against the Foundation, as I did get a couple of days pleasure down south after the meeting. So please pay all of them, half of them, or none of them as you think fit. The 'phones and wires ought to be taken care of in any case." Fiske Kimball to Stuart Gibboney, April 24, 1939, TJMF Archives, series 9, box 20, Kimball Correspondence. The Kimballs' home, Shack Mountain (Albemarle County, Virginia), which Fiske designed in a Jeffersonian style, was completed in 1935.

23. Stuart Gibboney to Fiske Kimball, April 20, 1923, FKP, box 78, folder 4.

24. Stuart Gibboney to Fiske Kimball, April 27, 1923, FKP, box 78, folder 4.

25. It should be noted that Fiske Kimball's surviving archive greatly exceeds that of Marie Kimball. See Berkes, "Marie Kimball," 212–13, 215.

26. Lucia Stanton, *"Those Who Labor for My Happiness": Slavery at Thomas Jefferson's Monticello* (Charlottesville: University of Virginia Press, 2012), 195–98. Jefferson's family retained select items from the sale, such as the furniture from Jefferson's private suite, which the Kimballs, and subsequent curators, tracked. I was fortunate to be part of a team led by Susan Stein, Thomas Jefferson Foundation Gilder Senior Curator, that built upon Kimball's research and successfully located and exhibited more than 150 objects from Monticello in their original

locations for the landmark exhibition and catalog *The Worlds of Thomas Jefferson at Monticello* (New York: Abrams, 1993).

27. "Catalogue: art furnishings from Monticello, Va., the home of Thomas Jefferson by order of the Thomas Jefferson Memorial Foundation," 1928, Special Collections, Jefferson Library, Thomas Jefferson Foundation, Inc.

28. Marie Kimball, "The Furnishing of Monticello, Part I," *Magazine Antiques* 12, no. 5 (1927): 380–81.

29. M. Kimball, "Furnishing, Part I," 381.

30. Fiske Kimball to Sue Massie, May 1938, as quoted in Peter J. Hatch, "Restoring the Monticello Landscape, 1923–1955," *Magnolia* 23, no. 1 (2009–10): 5.

31. Fiske Kimball to Stuart Gibboney, October 13, 1939, TJMF Archives, series 92, box 4.

32. Fiske Kimball to Hollins Randolph, April 8, 1937, TJMF Archives, series 92, box 4.

33. Fiske Kimball to Jefferson Randolph Kean, May 27, 1937, TJMF Archives, series 92, box 4. Fiske's correspondence with Gibboney reveals their concern over the perceived value of a Monticello ticket when the house had little furniture. Fiske offered two solutions: open the second and third floors, furnishing them with reproductions of furniture owned by descendants, and restore the North and South Wings with their terraces leading to the pavilions. Fiske Kimball to Stuart Gibboney, August 29, 1937, TJMF Archives, series 92, box 4.

34. For example, Stuart Gibboney to Fiske Kimball, October 11, 1938, FKP, box 78, folder 3.

35. See Marie Kimball, "Thomas Jefferson's French Furniture," *Magazine Antiques* 15, no. 2 (1929): 123–28; "The Original Furnishings of the White House, Part I," *Magazine Antiques* 15, no. 6 (1929): 481–86; "The Original Furnishings of the White House, Part II," *Magazine Antiques* 16, no. 1 (1929): 33–38; "Jefferson's Furniture Comes Home to Monticello," *House Beautiful* 66, no. 2 (1929): 164–65, 186, 188, 190; "More Jefferson Furniture Comes Home to Monticello," *Magazine Antiques* 38, no. 1 (1940): 20–22.

36. Fiske Kimball to Stuart Gibboney, September 20, 1928, FKP, box 79, folder 3.

37. Fiske Kimball to Cameron Clark, September 20, 1928, FKP, box 79, folder 3.

38. For example, Fiske Kimball to George Esser, April 7, 1953, and Esser to F. Kimball, April 23, 1953, FKP, box 78, folder 3.

39. See FKP, box 79, folder 5, for several examples.

40. Elizabeth Randolph Betts to Fiske Kimball, November 27, 1928, FKP, box 79, folder 3.

41. Ehrenpreis also credits the Kimballs for gathering together furniture that told important stories, such as the revolving chairs, revolving-top table, sofas, and polygraph that constitute Jefferson's reading and writing arrangements. See

Diane Ehrenpreis, "Every Convenience for a Man of Letters: Thomas Jefferson's Writing Suite," in *The Material Culture of Writing*, ed. Cyndey Alexis and Hannah J. Rule (Louisville: University Press of Colorado, 2022), 141–42. In Ehrenpreis's work on Monticello's recent Mountaintop Project, which restored spaces in Monticello's second and third floors, she drew inspiration from Marie's willingness to illustrate in her articles objects that looked like those that had been at Monticello, in the hope that a keen reader might recognize them and come forward with missing items. Ehrenpreis prepared a virtual tour of the Kimballs' Monticello, available at https://www.youtube.com/playlist?list= PLjRnhUjPwbM3nmDfex_uZUKfR0V3ynN19 (number 13).

42. See TJMF Archives and FKP, especially box 78, folder 12.

43. W. E. Thomsen to Fiske Kimball, March 1, 1948, and F. Kimball to W. E. Thomsen, March 2, 1948, FKP, box 78, folder 12.

44. "It is still remembered in Charlottesville how Fiske used to go through the rooms with a colored boy, giving instructions for moving the furniture, and how Marie would follow one room behind, giving directions to another for putting it all back." Roberts and Roberts, *Triumph on Fairmount*, 167.

45. Fiske Kimball to Stuart Gibboney, June 23, 1933, and Gibboney to F. Kimball, June 28, 1933, TJMF Archives, series 92, box 4.

46. If anyone would object to the Kimballs' work rearranging furniture, writing tours, and making labels, it would be Thomas L. Rhodes. Rhodes was the author of *The Story of Monticello* (Baltimore: Pridemark Press, 1928; repr., 1947) and supervised Monticello's tours and its guide staff, which initially was composed of Black men who had worked for the Levy family and given tours during their ownership, including Robert Sampson, William Page, Benjamin Carr, and Willis Henderson. Theodore Fred Kuper, one of the first employees for the Thomas Jefferson Foundation, described Rhodes as a "worshiper of Thomas Jefferson. He had read and reread an early biography of him until it was a dog-eared wreck. Rhodes was also a passionate supporter of the Lost Cause," flying the Confederate flag above his home on the property until instructed otherwise by the Foundation. Thomas Fleming, "Monticello's Long Career—From Riches to Rags to Riches," *Smithsonian Magazine* 4, no. 3 (1973): 66. In 1951 Monticello's Board of Trustees moved to replace Black guides with white female hostesses. TJF Senior Fellow Niya Bates is at work on scholarship surrounding Monticello's early guides, including descendants of the Coleman and Henderson families who worked for the Levy family and lived in the gatehouse. See "Coleman and Henderson," Getting Word: African American Oral History Project, https:// gettingword.monticello.org/families/coleman/.

47. Marie Kimball to Frank Houston, May 28, [1948], and Houston to M. Kimball, June 2, 1948, TJMF Archives, box 24.

48. Fiske Kimball to Stuart Gibboney, October 28, 1938, FKP, box 79, folder 3.

49. Nellie Jones to Stuart Gibboney, August 10, 1938, TJMF Archives. See also Annette Gordon-Reed, *The Hemingses of Monticello: An American Family* (New York: W. W. Norton, 2008), 374–75.

50. Fiske Kimball to Nancy McClelland, December 14, 1945, FKP, box 78, folder 17.

51. Ann M. Lucas, "Junction of the Potomac and Shenandoah," in Stein, *Worlds*, 190.

52. Peterson, *Jefferson Image*, 378.

53. Thomas Jefferson to William Roscoe, December 27, 1820. Thomas Jefferson, *The Papers of Thomas Jefferson: Retirement Series*, vol. 16, ed. J. Jefferson Looney (Princeton: Princeton University Press, 2022), 499.

ARCHITECTURAL IMAGINATION

Fiske Kimball's Modern Museum

JOHN VICK

Between the years 1925 and 1955, Fiske Kimball was director of the Philadelphia Museum of Art, one of the country's preeminent cultural institutions and a celebrated landmark of the city. His impact on the museum would be extensive and enduring, unmatched by any successors, and a cornerstone of Kimball's own remarkable career. He oversaw not only the completion of the museum building but also the installation of well over one hundred galleries for the display of the permanent collection and special exhibitions, drawing on his talents as an architect and art historian alike. His three decades as director also demonstrated an adept handling of the varied and often competing interests of museum stakeholders—from trustees, collectors, and artists to public visitors, city officials, and contractors. For his staff, small by today's standards, Kimball was demanding and determined, yet he led by example, delegating some tasks to others but doing many himself.

Kimball's tendency to take matters into his own hands is no better evidenced than in his vision and strategy for establishing a permanent place for modern art at the museum. A proponent of the art of his lifetime, Kimball spent much of the 1940s and early 1950s developing what he would call the "Modern Museum" in galleries at the end of the building's north wing, an area known internally as Section 7. This effort was characteristic of Kimball's tenure in Philadelphia for its focus on three priorities: finishing the building, growing the collection, and developing a canonical presentation of art. Though Kimball rarely considered these priorities in isolation, all three were uniquely interconnected during the years he created the Modern Museum. Balancing them, while simultaneously pushing them forward, would take patience, diplomacy, and practicality but also quick thinking, boldness, and creativity. To borrow a compliment paid to Kimball by the collectors Louise and Walter Arensberg, it would also take "architectural imagination," an ability to conceive of new and exciting solutions that stand the test of time.

The Philadelphia Museum of Art, originally called the Pennsylvania Museum and School of Industrial Art, was still a fledging institution when Kimball became its director in 1925. Although founded nearly fifty years earlier, during the nation's 1876 Centennial Exposition, the museum had outgrown its original home, Memorial Hall, in west Fairmount Park. Construction of a larger building, sited along the east bank of the Schuylkill River at the end of the recently developed Benjamin Franklin Parkway, had begun in 1919 after decades of planning. Yet six years later, the new museum remained far from finished. Only the south and north pavilions, known as Section 1 and Section 7, were built. They stood disconnected atop the rise of land that had once held the city's reservoir, waiting for the rest of the museum to join them. For Kimball, the challenge of completing the building and filling it must have been both daunting and alluring.[1]

Another three years would pass before the museum officially opened to the public on March 26, 1928. Though this date marks a significant milestone for the institution, it hardly meant the end of construction. A photograph taken almost six months later, on October 3, 1928, shows workers on the museum's east terrace, busy completing the central fountain and paved areas surrounding it. Beyond them is the columned Section 7, the eventual home of Kimball's Modern Museum, with Section 6 to the left connecting back to the rest of the museum, which sits out of frame. The exterior of Section 7 remains unfinished, the distinctive bronze finials and terracotta sculptures not yet adorning its roofline and pediment. Moreover, three large windows, set behind columns atop a lower level, reveal an equally unfinished interior. No gallery walls divide the space, allowing for a clear view through to the windows on the building's opposite side. The first floor of Section 6 is also unfinished. Inside Section 7, the second floor has not even been built yet, leaving a single cavernous space, ripe with potential.

This is the irony of the museum's construction history. Although Section 7 was among the first parts of the building erected, it was among the last to be completed. Only a small handful of galleries on the second floor were installed for the 1928 opening. Expanding the footprint of public space by converting raw interiors into completed galleries became the primary goal for Kimball and his staff over the next several years. It was an immense and arduous task, as he acknowledged in 1939: "More [galleries] will follow rapidly, although the vastness of the enterprise still places the installation of many features months or years in the future."[2] By the early 1940s, nearly 150 galleries were open, with European,

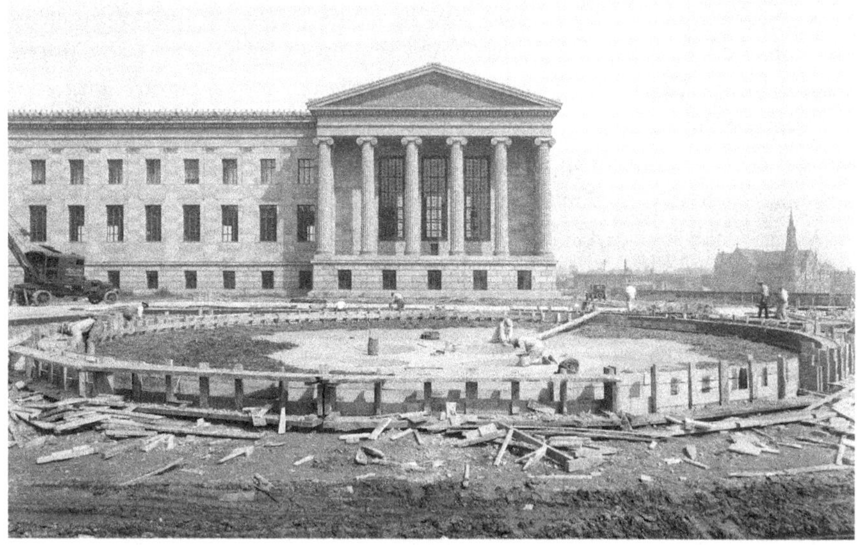

FIGURE 1. Philadelphia Museum of Art, East Terrace with view of Sections 6 and 7, south façades, October 3, 1928. (Courtesy of the Philadelphia Museum of Art, Library and Archives, Special Format Records, Photographs, SFP_B002_F007_002)

American, and Asian art and architecture on the second floor, and the collections amassed by John G. Johnson and William P. Wilstach on the first. The first floor also included galleries dedicated to specific material areas of the collection, like textiles, ceramics, glass, and prints. Yet visitors consulting a gallery map in 1942 would have found Section 1—today home to the Japanese Tea House and the American Art collection—designated "Future Expansion," while Section 7 promised "American" but was in fact closed to the public and installed with hanging screens for painting storage.[3]

The A. E. Gallatin Collection

By the end of 1942, the future of Section 7 and the Modern Museum began to take shape, owing to an unexpected series of events and some quick action from Kimball. In December, the American collector and artist Albert Eugene Gallatin received notice that his Museum of Living Art would be evicted from its home at New York University. Opened in 1927, this museum was the first public venue dedicated to showing modern art in the United States outside of commercial galleries and temporary exhibitions. Gallatin's holdings represented many leading European artists of the time, such as Pablo Picasso, Piet Mondrian, Jean Arp, and

Joan Miró, as well as several American modernists, including those in Gallatin's own circle of "Park Avenue Cubists," Suzy Frelinghuysen, George L. K. Morris, Charles Green Shaw, and himself. Hearing of the impending closure during the Christmas holidays, Kimball contacted Gallatin to see if the unfortunate circumstances might provide an opportunity for a temporary exhibition in Philadelphia, and maybe even a donation to the museum.

Kimball had known Gallatin for more than a decade. They met in 1930 in Philadelphia (Gallatin was born in nearby Villanova), and they soon discovered their mutual connections to New York University. Kimball had taught at the university in the early 1920s and remained a consulting architect there. At this first meeting, Kimball told Gallatin his works deserved a better space than the one provided by the university—perhaps an early indication of his intentions to bring the collection to Philadelphia.[4] Seven years later, in 1937, Kimball borrowed a small Joaquín Torres-Garcia painting, *Street* (1930), from Gallatin for a show called *Forms in Art*. Gallatin donated the painting to the museum when the show closed and offered to lend more works if Kimball was willing to commit to a stand-alone exhibition of his collection. But Kimball had to decline. With many of the galleries still unfinished, he had no room for a show of such magnitude.

By late 1942, however, as Gallatin confronted the final days of his collection at New York University, the situation in Philadelphia had changed. Not only had more galleries opened, but Kimball had even designated a specific area of the first floor just off the central stair hall for "Transient Exhibitions." Kimball offered to exhibit the collector's works there as an overture to an eventual acquisition. The two met in mid-January 1943 to hash out a gift agreement. Gallatin had three major demands. First, exhibit the entire collection that summer; second, by fall, create new galleries for the collection in the unfinished Section 7; and third, display the works together at least until his death (Gallatin was sixty-one at the time). On January 28, just over a month since Kimball's outreach and two weeks after the closing of the New York University space, the agreement was signed.

Gallatin's works arrived in Philadelphia in early February to be stored until the exhibition, which debuted to the public on May 14, 1943. Gallatin attended the opening events, as did some artists in his collection, like Fernand Léger and Marcel Duchamp, who had both left France earlier that decade to live out the war in New York. Even before the celebrations began that evening, the museum had already hosted a variety of artist talks, avant-garde film screenings, and related programs (which continued through the run of the exhibition). The institution had relatively little track record of showing modern and abstract art, but Kimball seemed intent on ensuring that the Gallatin collection would be received by an informed public. The events provided an opportunity for visitors to understand the new works in the context of current art movements—from Cubism and De Stijl to Dada and Surrealism—and not simply against the backdrop of the museum's older, more traditional collections. It may also be that Kimball hoped these programs would attract interest and win favor from some of the more conservative members of the museum's board and staff who did not share his enthusiastic embrace of modernism.

Not long after the Gallatin exhibition closed on November 3, 1943, a selection of works from his collection began moving into new galleries in Section 7, just as Kimball had promised only nine months earlier. This area of the building had been nearly complete since the 1930s, when the empty shell seen in the 1928 photograph was transformed into a two-story block of approximately twenty-four galleries of varying sizes and proportions. Both floors were divided into nine galleries, with the largest in the middle, aligned with the tall windows. On the first floor, the smaller side galleries were topped with mezzanines. The west mezzanine was accessible by stairs on the building's north side where Sections 6 and 7 meet, while the east mezzanine could be reached by stairs set against the east wall of Section 7. Because of this arrangement, the smaller galleries on the first floor had lower ceilings, resulting in an even more varied sequence of spaces than on the floor above, where the ceiling height was consistent throughout.

Kimball appears to have taken advantage of this range in architecture when laying out the Gallatin collection during the final months of 1943. Visitors would have entered from Section 6 into a little square anteroom (today a portion of Gallery 280), then turned right to find a long, narrow gallery (today 281) hung with small paintings and works on paper, interspersed with a few sculptures on pedestals and furniture for visitor seating.[5] This intimate introduction then gave way to a larger, high-ceilinged gallery (282) with the three tall windows facing south toward the terrace. Adorned with exterior bronze grilles designed by Louis Comfort Tiffany, these windows flooded the space with natural light and cast geometric shadows that rhymed with the modernist compositions on the walls.[6] Here Kimball installed the most ambitious and important pieces from the acquisition. On the north side, opposite the windows, hung Léger's *The City* (1919) beneath a bold sans serif heading: "A. E. GALLATIN COLLECTION 1920–1940." Picasso's *Three Musicians* (1921) and Miró's *Painting* (1933) were among the notable works installed on the east and west walls, respectively, while smaller paintings, drawings, collages, and sculpture were displayed on the south, where the low windowsills meant less room for art. In the middle of the floor

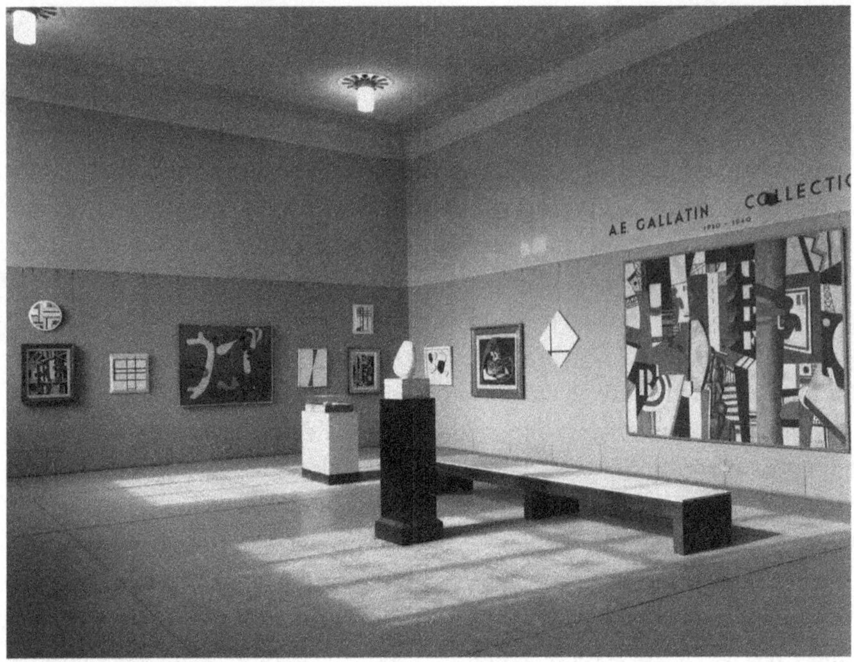

FIGURE 2. A. E. Gallatin Collection (current Gallery 282), Philadelphia Museum of Art, 1946. (Courtesy of the Philadelphia Museum of Art, Library and Archives, Rights and Reproductions Photograph Collection, RNR_B077_Gallatin_1946_v002)

was Constantin Brancusi's *Torso of a Young Girl [II]* (ca. 1923), with assemblages by Picasso and Miró nearby. Another small, low-ceilinged gallery (283) of nearly the same dimensions as the first concluded the collection installation, but no photographs of it survive.

Although these three galleries together displayed an estimated seventy to eighty works and represented a range of artists and styles, the installation only scratched the surface of the nearly three hundred works Gallatin donated to the museum. If this partial display bothered Gallatin, he did not mention it to Kimball. Their correspondence throughout this period was cordial and showed enthusiasm on both sides for the collection's presentation. Surely Gallatin understood that the Section 7 galleries were a work in progress. When the three galleries for his collection opened in 1943, the rest of the section remained unfinished and shut. Moreover, if he thought their eventual completion would mean an expanded display of his collection, Kimball must have set him straight. The section's partial vacancy and untapped potential for future installations were key to the director's long-term plans to establish the Modern Museum, as he would later call it, as a place for the museum's expanding modern art holdings to be shown together and thereby balance in quality and quantity the more historic areas of the collection.

Throughout the 1940s, Kimball sought out other collections for temporary exhibitions in hopes they might translate, like Gallatin's, into gifts that could be shown more permanently in Section 7. Immediately before the Gallatin exhibition opened, the Transient Exhibition spaces hosted *Mexican Art Today,* a display of more than three hundred works by artists including José Clemente Orozco, Diego Rivera, David Alfaro Siqueiros, and Rufino Tamayo. A year later, in 1944, the same galleries presented an exhibition of some four hundred works from the collection of photographer Alfred Stieglitz, featuring Arthur Dove, Marsden Hartley, John Marin, Georgia O'Keeffe, and Stieglitz himself, among others. Select works from both exhibitions were later shown in Section 7 and other areas of the building, leading to around three hundred new acquisitions of paintings, drawings, prints, and photographs by the end of the decade.

The Louise and Walter Arensberg Collection

Kimball would cap off his drive to acquire art for the Modern Museum with the pursuit of the collection of Louise and Walter Arensberg. Though living in Los Angeles by the 1940s, the couple had started collecting art in New York three decades earlier. They, like many Americans, had been introduced to modern art through a visit to the 1913 Armory Show, but the Arensbergs were relatively unique in wanting to immerse themselves in this newfound interest and having the financial means to do so. In 1914 they relocated from Cambridge, Massachusetts, to Manhattan's Upper West Side, to a building fittingly called The Atelier. Over the next few years, they became part of a circle of American and European artists, writers, performers, and other avant-garde creatives, among them Duchamp, who for much of that time lived and worked in an adjoining studio also owned by the Arensbergs. As the couple's passion for modern art grew, so did their collection, until their walls were stacked with works by the likes of Georges Braque, Henri Matisse, Francis Picabia, Henri Rousseau, Charles Sheeler, Joseph Stella, and, of course, Duchamp.[7] They also acquired Fang and Aztec sculptures among other examples of Indigenous art from Africa and the Americas. Such older works were then in vogue among collectors, in part for their perceived affinities with the abstracted styles of some European modern artists.

The Arensbergs moved to Los Angeles in 1921, and in 1927 they bought a two-story, three-bedroom house at the base of the Hollywood Hills that would allow their art collection to further grow.[8] Remaining on top of developing art movements—in part thanks to Duchamp, who stayed a close friend and informal art advisor—they collected paintings by Salvador Dalí, René Magritte, and Paul Klee, among others, as well as a trove of sculptures by Constantin Brancusi. They also greatly expanded their collection of pre-Columbian art, a term used to encompass work of Aztec, Mayan, Teotihuacan, and other Indigenous cultures of Mexico and Central America made before European contact. Photographs of the Arensbergs' home taken in the mid-1940s and early 1950s show walls bursting with paintings and works on paper, while tables, dressers, and shelves overflow with sculpture and pottery. The installation took advantage of not only the home's generous square footage but also the natural light that poured in through its many windows and the compelling sightlines gained from doorways connecting the main rooms of the first floor. One of the most stunning spaces was the sunroom, designed by Richard Neutra and completed in 1933 as one of several additions the Arensbergs made to the original 1920 structure.[9] A ribbon of eight windows lined one corner of this room, offering views of Aztec sculptures in the garden and a lush backdrop for the works displayed inside, among them

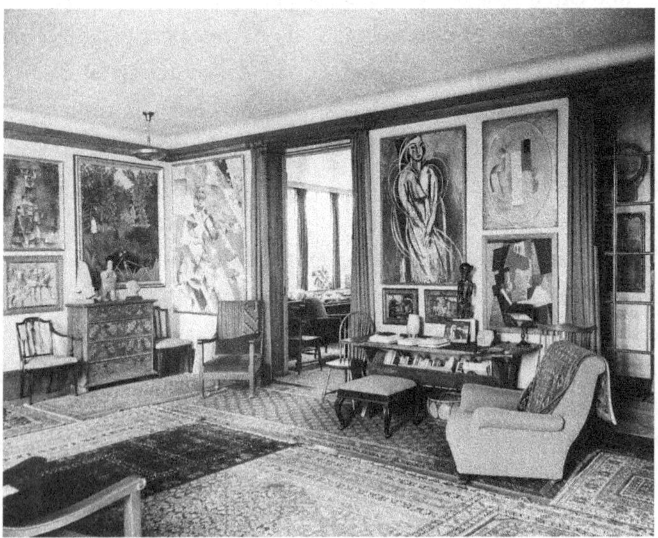

FIGURE 3. Living room of the home of Louise and Walter Arensberg (7065 Hillside Avenue, Hollywood, California), with view into sunroom (gallery room), photo by Fred R. Dapprich, ca. 1944. (Courtesy of the Philadelphia Museum of Art, Library and Archives, Arensberg Archives, WLA_B054_F012_002_001)

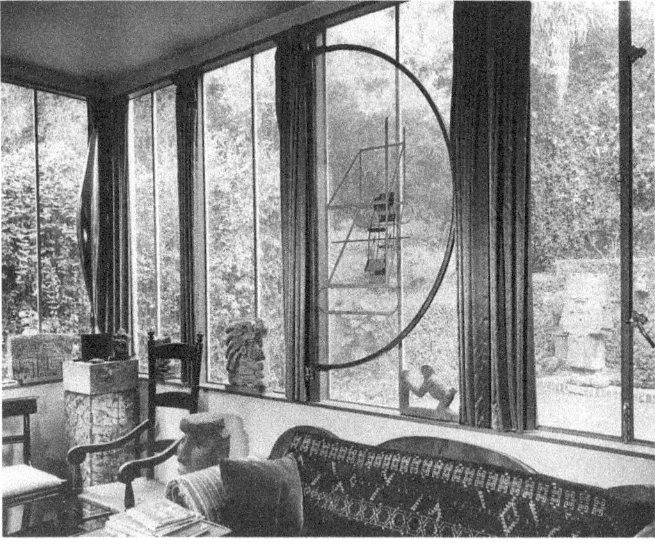

FIGURE 4. Sunroom (gallery room) of the home of Louise and Walter Arensberg (7065 Hillside Avenue, Hollywood, California), photo by Fred R. Dapprich, ca. 1944. (Courtesy of the Philadelphia Museum of Art, Library and Archives, Arensberg Archives, WLA_B054_F021_002_001)

Duchamp's glass *Glider Containing a Water Mill in Neighboring Metals* (1913–15) and Brancusi's glistening bronze *Bird in Space* (1924).

Kimball first visited the home on February 10, 1947, to meet the Arensbergs and discuss a possible donation of their collection to the museum. Kimball had no prior acquaintance with the couple, and in fact he reached out to them only on a recommendation from Gallatin. Yet the meeting went very well. The Arensbergs had already promised their collection to the University of California, Los Angeles, under the condition that a new building be constructed to house it, but the university was having second thoughts around the time Kimball visited and would eventually cancel the deal later that year.[10] As Walter told Kimball during their first meeting: "They are trying to get out of it: the conservative Trustees of the University hate the stuff. I am thinking of using you as a wastebasket." To which the museum director replied, "We are no wastebasket, but we like fine collections like yours."[11]

Unlike Gallatin, who finalized his gift to the museum in less than two months, Walter and Louise were hesitant to commit. First, when the UCLA agreement fell apart, they began receiving competing offers from many other museums and schools, including the Art Institute of Chicago, the National Gallery of Art, the Metropolitan Museum of Art, Stanford University, Harvard University, and the University of Minnesota. Second, they had concerns about sending their collection to Philadelphia, which they felt already had a strong collection of modernism in the works from Gallatin and in the nearby collection of Albert C. Barnes, whom Walter openly detested.[12] Finally, unlike the Gallatin collection, which had been shown in a public gallery before going to Philadelphia, the Arensbergs' collection was installed in their private residence, and they were very intent on finding ways to translate their carefully designed domestic space to any permanent institutional home. It was a challenge well suited to Kimball's skills as an architect and architectural historian as well as to his experience installing dozens of period rooms at the museum. He understood how to conceptualize and outfit a space to approximate the style and feel of a certain time or place—only in this situation it was not English rococo, French medieval, or Chinese Ming dynasty but California midcentury.

When Kimball returned to Hollywood in February 1949, two years after his first visit, he brought drawings he had drafted himself to illustrate how the Arensbergs' collection might be displayed at the museum. An installation plan shows the first floor and mezzanines of Section 7. Gallatin's collection occupies the south galleries overlooking the terrace, as it had for the past five years, and the west mezzanine, too. Works from the Arensbergs are distributed throughout the remaining galleries and the east mezzanine, following a roughly chronological and monographic organization. The presentation begins with "Forerunners" (Gallery 280), likely suggesting Rousseau, adjacent to early works by Matisse, Marc Chagall, Giorgio de Chirico, and others (284). In the large space at the heart of the section (288) are cubists, including Duchamp, leading to smaller galleries featuring surrealists Dalí, Yves Tanguy, André Masson, and Miró; "Americans," later identified as Sheeler, Marin, and others of their circle; and then a corner gallery (286) devoted to Klee.[13] The second-largest gallery allocated to the Arensbergs (285) was on the north side of the section, with windows facing the city's Fairmount neighborhood. There Kimball appears to have placed the Arensbergs' most abstract works—sculptures by Brancusi and paintings by Léger, Picabia, Wassily Kandinsky, and more.

Kimball also drew up longitudinal and cross sections of the north gallery, which he designated the "central gallery" out of importance rather than its situation within the section. His drawings prominently highlight an inventive architectural feature: a raised balcony, approximately five feet in height, running beneath the windows on the north wall. This clever response to the Arensbergs'

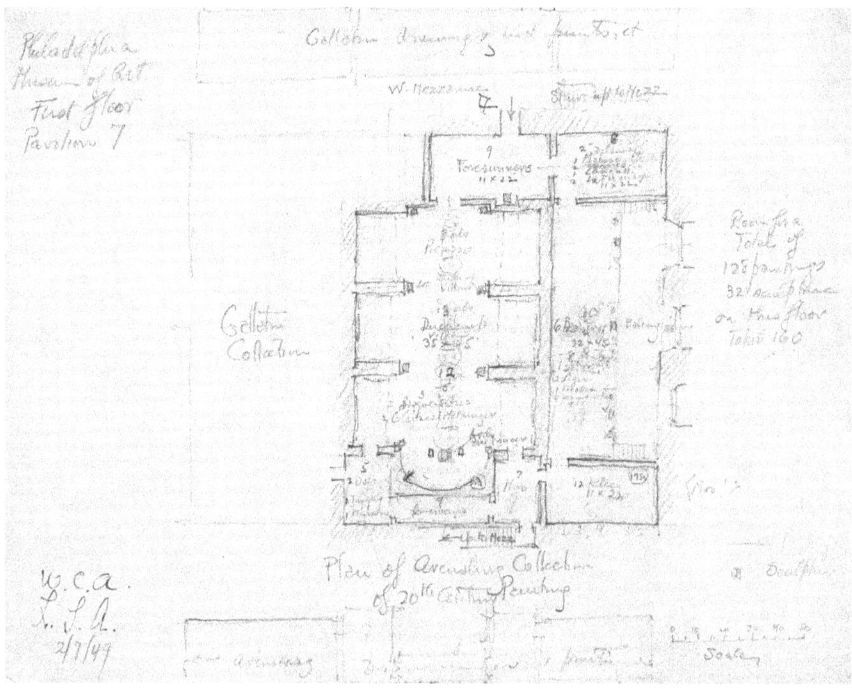

FIGURE 5. Fiske Kimball's installation plan of the Louise and Walter Arensberg Collection (current Galleries 280, 284–88), February 7, 1949. (Courtesy of the Philadelphia Museum of Art, Library and Archives, Fiske Kimball Records, FKR_B181_F003_004_001)

demand for galleries with large windows like they had in Hollywood raised the visitor to the level of the windows while also changing the scale of the room to better mimic the proportions of the Arensbergs' home. The cross section in particular—showing the varied heights of the first-floor galleries and the mezzanine above—evokes a space more domestic than institutional. Just in case that was not enough to convince the Arensbergs that Philadelphia would provide a true home for their collection, Kimball drew in sofas and chairs with relaxing visitors as well as specific works installed against the windows, like *Bird in Space,* as he had found in the couple's Hollywood sunroom.

When Louise and Walter initialed Kimball's drawings of Section 7 in approval, they also signed off on a slightly less detailed drawing showing how their pre-Columbian sculptures might be displayed. Keeping their entire collection together was a nonnegotiable point for the couple, even if the modern portion attracted more attention from vying museums and universities. Kimball knew this well and annotated his drawing for their pre-Columbian collection: "4 Galleries

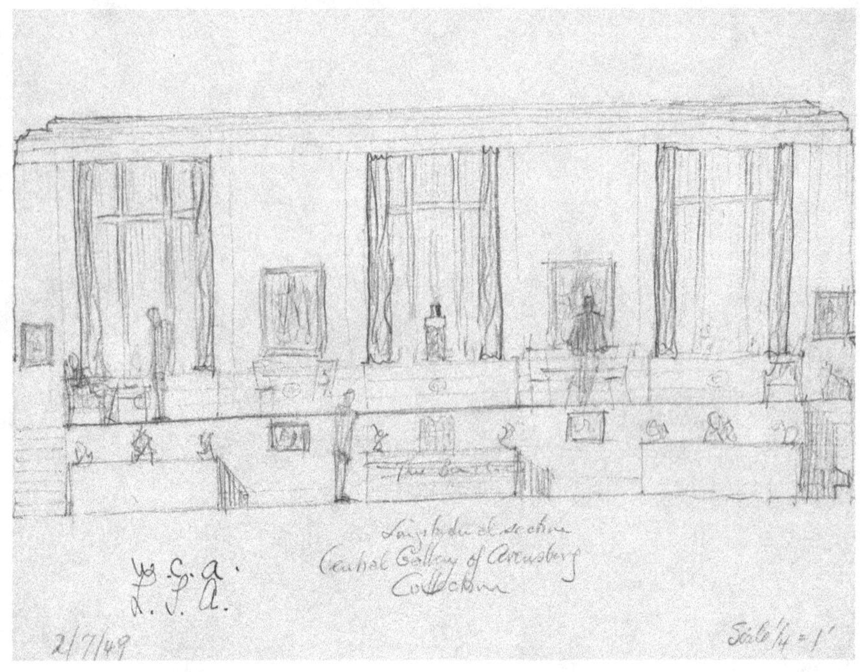

FIGURE 6. Fiske Kimball's longitudinal section of the central gallery (current Gallery 285) for the Louise and Walter Arensberg Collection, February 7, 1949. (Courtesy of the Philadelphia Museum of Art, Library and Archives, Fiske Kimball Records FKR_B181_F003_003_001)

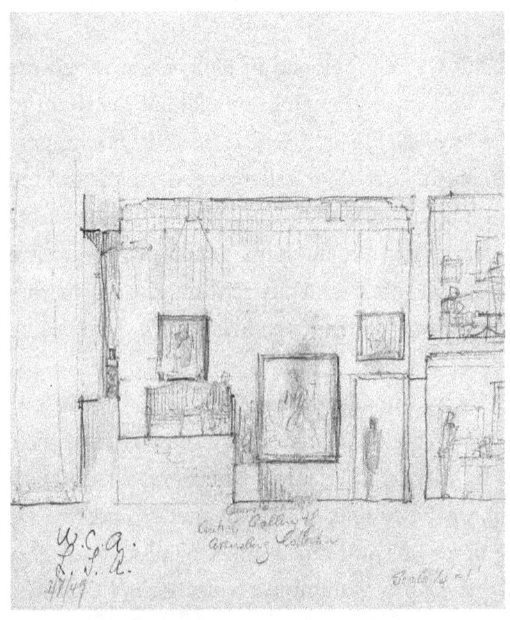

FIGURE 7. Fiske Kimball's cross section of the central gallery (current Gallery 285) for the Louise and Walter Arensberg Collection, February 7, 1949. (Courtesy of the Philadelphia Museum of Art, Library and Archives, Fiske Kimball Records, FKR_B181_F003_005_001)

like this . . . Grand total 144–160 pieces."[14] It is telling of his desire for the Arensberg collections that Kimball made such a grand offer. Just earlier that decade, Kimball had formalized an agreement with the University of Pennsylvania Museum of Archaeology and Anthropology, located about two miles away on the other side of the Schuylkill River, that should have precluded him from pursuing any pre-Columbian works of art. The two institutions had delineated their respective collecting areas to prevent competition and resolved to exchange existing collections accordingly. Kimball wrote, in a memorandum he presented at a June 1941 board meeting, "The scope of the University Museum includes not only ancient peoples (archaeology) but also primitive peoples (ethnology). The line here, in America, Africa, and Polynesia, is obviously that of contact with European civilization. Thus in America the pre-Columbian civilizations of Mexico, Peru, etc., as well as the art of the American Indians, etc. would be in the field of the University Museum, while the Philadelphia Museum of Art would cover the colonial and national arts since the European conquest."[15] However evident the Eurocentric impulses and colonialist logic of that earlier agreement, Kimball's unflinching willingness to now ignore its terms in hopes of winning the Arensbergs' bequest was just as apparent.

Not long after reviewing Kimball's drawings, the couple committed to bequeath their collection to Philadelphia, albeit with the stipulation that during their lifetime the agreement would remain open to negotiation and could be revoked if they received a better option. While not ideal, Kimball was thrilled by the prospect of bringing another major collection to Philadelphia's growing Modern Museum. He quickly shared the news with Gallatin, who both deserved credit for suggesting the possible acquisition in the first place and remained invested in any expanded presentation of modern art at the museum. "With this prospect as bait," Kimball wrote, "we shall now go to City Council for money to finish the whole of Section 7 (where your main galleries are), so that, if successful as I hope, we can then bring up your other things and show all our 20th century adjacent."[16]

But just a couple months later, with new offers coming in from Stanford and Minnesota and plans underway for an exhibition in Chicago, Walter called Kimball to express concerns about the bequest. He outlined the main problems of gallery size and design in a follow-up telegram: "The tentative arrangement of the pictures as illustrated in your drawings makes a masterly use of the available space but we still feel that the available space is inadequate and unsatisfactory for circulation and perspective. Also lacking and of paramount importance as we feel is the spatial extension and release from Museum confinement obtainable by means of large wall windows." Walter continued by sharing the lengths to which other museums were willing to go to win the collection: "The two principal alternatives are institutions which have offered to raise the funds for a new building in which the collection could be housed in accordance with certain ideals that we have tried in a very limited way to exemplify in our own home."[17]

Ever knowledgeable of the inner workings of his peer institutions and resolutely committed to his own curatorial vision for Philadelphia, Kimball fired back an adroit reply.[18] Writing from Shack Mountain, his Charlottesville retreat, where he and his wife, Marie, were spending the Easter holiday, he began with an admission of the joy he would find in designing a new building for the collection that would "embody artistic creativeness in a modern spirit, analogous to that of the works themselves."[19] But he then warned against such impulses, making the case for his vision of an encyclopedic and adaptive art museum by citing three rival institutions as cautionary tales. First, he said a new building would isolate the collection from the valuable art-historical context found elsewhere in the museum and would also "boot away" younger visitors "up to age fifty" primarily interested in modernism. He claimed this was already happening at the Metropolitan, calling it a "mausoleum of masterpieces." Second, Kimball doubted the ability to fundraise for such a specialized building, pointing to operating deficits at the Museum of Modern Art. (On that point, the history of MoMA's many building expansions since the 1940s would prove Kimball wrong.) And third, invoking the Isabella Stewart Gardner Museum, he delicately cautioned that the collection might grow static on its own, becoming a "museum [of] the history of Taste." By contrast, and in closing, Kimball promised that in Philadelphia the couple's collection "would never appear isolated or mysteriously disproportionate, nor ever fail to be maintained as it deserves."

Seeking a second opinion and not well enough to travel themselves, the Arensbergs asked their old friend Duchamp to visit Philadelphia to evaluate the museum's offer in person. Duchamp met with Kimball on May 6, 1949, toured the designated galleries, and sketched up two floor plans, which he later sent to the Arensbergs along with five pages of detailed notes. His report was generally favorable, approving of the overall area and distribution of the galleries, as well as their windows and mix of natural and electric light. The correspondence also reveals how the Arensbergs' hesitations evidently motivated Kimball to double his initial proposal, made just three months earlier, by adding an additional gallery on the first floor of Section 6 (271) plus half of the second floor of Section 7. Duchamp thought the museum would cede even more space, encouraging his friends to leverage the Chicago threat, writing that Kimball "is ready to give you complete satisfaction even though he might give the impression of bargaining on space."[20]

Throughout the spring and summer of 1949, the Arensbergs stayed focused on the Chicago exhibition, which opened that October and served as a test run for a possible donation there.[21] Just as Duchamp had been the couple's eyes and ears in Philadelphia, he also visited Chicago to see the collection on view, issuing a glowing assessment of the installation, complete with an annotated floor plan.[22] Less than two weeks later, Walter wrote to Kimball lamenting that he and Louise were feeling less and less sure about a donation to Philadelphia, again citing the proximity to Barnes as a concern but mostly faulting the size and architecture of the offered space. "The Chicago installation proves that it [the collection] needs a great deal of space," he wrote, and in what seemed to be the final blow, he added, "Forgive me. This is not an argument. It's just the way I feel."[23] In response, Kimball immediately detoured his curator of prints and drawings, Carl Zigrosser, to Chicago to size up the competition.[24] He also replied to Walter, offering to find more room for the collection in Section 7 and using humor as best he could to diffuse the tense situation: "There is space in that pavilion upstairs, downstairs, and in my lady's chamber."[25]

Kimball's correspondence with the Arensbergs ceased for the next several months, as meanwhile Walter and Duchamp weighed offers from other museums across the country. Then in May 1950, without much explanation, in a letter to Duchamp summarizing conversations with the National Gallery of Art, Walter added a casual yet ultimately fateful postscript: "P.S. And by the way, unless you think it inadvisable, wouldn't this be a very opportune time for you to see Fiske Kimball again[?]"[26] Two months later, on July 5, Duchamp returned to Philadelphia to find Kimball with a new proposal: twenty galleries on two floors of Section 7 and some of the adjoining Section 6, plus both mezzanines, estimated to be about three hundred feet more linear wall space than the Chicago exhibition. Moreover, with the second floor still unfinished, the Arensbergs could divide it as they liked—an opportunity Duchamp thought "should be taken up seriously." On the crucial question of windows, he told the Arensbergs they lend "an impression quite different from the usual cubicle effect of museum galleries."[27]

Feeling "all keyed up again," Kimball once more returned to Hollywood in hopes of finally ending the gift negotiations.[28] He did not, but two major breakthroughs resulted. At Walter's urging, Kimball decided not to split the Arensberg collection across the first and second floors of Section 7. It would instead cover the section's entire first floor, plus both mezzanines, bumping Gallatin upstairs. This move doubled the windows available to the couple's collection, adding those facing the terrace on the south side to those on the north. Consequently, Kimball and the Arensbergs decided against raising a balcony up to the height of the windows as shown in Kimball's 1949 drawings. Instead, Walter and Louise asked to extend the windows down to the floor to gain the desired views outside. Kimball was skeptical of this request, worrying that it would sacrifice precious hanging space on the walls. He also knew that extending the windows would mean extending the bronze Tiffany window grilles on the exterior, which in turn would require a special materials clearance, given postwar regulations on copper use. Not being in any position to argue, however, he did his best to entertain the idea while gently pushing back against it.

The predicament continued to vex Kimball throughout the summer and well into the fall of 1950. The Arensbergs wanted the lowered windows written into their gift agreement, while Kimball tried to convince them otherwise, warning that the bureaucratic nightmare to get copper for the grilles might jeopardize the entire project. By November, the Arensbergs grew willing to consider other options, asking Kimball again what he thought about lowering the windows and if Duchamp had any opinion. Kimball replied, "I personally judge the galleries are better as they are—as the high sills (7 feet) considerably increases the hanging space for the smaller pictures, and the light below these high sills is excellent. Marcel Duchamp thought so too, and did not think it necessary to lower the sills."[29] Understandably wary that this debate could go on forever—nearly four years had passed since his first Hollywood visit—Kimball devised a compromise, something between the Arensbergs' wish to extend the windows to the floor and his to leave them as is. "What I would do, myself," Kimball continued, "is cut a central door from gallery 1729 [282] to the large colonnaded portico outside it, facing south toward the great paved and planted court, so as to make a beautiful place to sit out, directly off your collection." Walter and Louise responded days later: "We withdraw entirely the condition about lowering the windows. We accept however with enthusiasm and with an acknowledgement of your architectural imagination the suggestion of a door in the middle of the south wall of the gallery opening onto the court."[30] The next month, Kimball returned to Hollywood to finalize the gift—ultimately more than four hundred modern works and nearly seven hundred pre-Columbian, African, and other Indigenous objects—wiring the museum on December 28: "Hurrah Hurrah for Mr. A contract signed sealed and delivered."[31]

Yet it appears Kimball's "architectural imagination" to transform galleries to the Arensbergs' liking was more of a practical repurposing. Returning to the 1928 view of the museum under construction (see fig. 1), a door on the first floor of the south façade of Section 7 is clearly visible between the columns and beneath the central window, more than two decades before Kimball's letter suggesting it. There is no indication that the door functioned or led anywhere, and all located photographs and blueprints, including alternate views of the Gallatin installation in the mid-1940s, show an uninterrupted interior wall. Whether this original doorway was purely decorative—possible given similar stonework on the corresponding façade of Section 1—or a functional design never fully realized, it clearly caught Kimball's eye as offering a potential exit from his stalemate with the Arensbergs.

After the gift agreement was signed, Kimball spent the next few years finalizing the unfinished interiors of Section 7 ahead of the official opening of the Modern Museum. In the central gallery (288), he cut a doorway in a niche leading to the south gallery that overlooked the terrace (282). This was another compromise with the Arensbergs, who were so enthused by Kimball's balcony door that they requested a line of doorways cut straight through the section to connect the three largest galleries.[32] They settled on just this one staggered doorway instead.[33] Kimball also used the central gallery to connect the mezzanines with overhead walkways, fitting them with railings of his own design that reveal his admiration for Frank Lloyd Wright. Correspondence suggests Kimball proposed other modernist interventions to this gallery, like opting for squared-off walls and ceilings instead of churchlike vaulting. However, Walter vetoed such plans as "too damn Wright-y," perhaps feeling the rounded ceilings better evoked the arched doorways that connected his dining and living rooms back home in Hollywood.[34]

The doorway from the south gallery to the terrace balcony was finally opened on March 23, 1953, and installed with a new glass door. Kimball described it glowingly in a letter written to the Arensbergs that very day: "They broke through out onto your great south balcony (portico) today. It is going to be *simply beautiful.* Now the azaleas, the rhododendrons, the paulownias, will be coming out, and we shall have a foretaste of what it will be some day, gay with reclining chairs, and porch furniture."[35] A second report arrived from Duchamp in October: "I saw the rooms prepared for the collection—They are completely finished except for some details in the electric lighting—and they are beautiful," he wrote. "Also, the outdoor terrace with a door from one of the rooms gives a pleasant feeling to the whole arrangement."[36]

Creating the Modern Museum was in some ways a race against time. Sadly, the Arensbergs never experienced the balcony for themselves. Louise passed away on November 25, 1953, just weeks after Duchamp's letter arrived, and Walter soon followed on January 29, 1954. Gallatin had died in 1952, but not before approving the reinstallation of his collection in more spacious galleries on the upper floor of Section 7, clearing the way for the Arensberg collection to take over the galleries below. Kimball's own health also deteriorated in these years, but he managed to keep the project on track. When the Arensberg collection opened on October 16, 1954, Kimball's vision of the Modern Museum was finally complete. Extending well beyond Section 7, it was also larger than first imagined, with works from the Arensbergs occupying even more galleries than had been promised.[37] Photography of this debut, though incomplete, shows Brancusi sculptures welcoming visitors in a long gallery of Section 6 (274), which led to a gallery installed with pre-Columbian objects. Perhaps this opening combination was intended to reference the display of some of these same works in the entry foyer of the Arensbergs' home.[38] Visitors then jumped to cubist paintings in the large central gallery (288), just as Kimball first proposed in 1949, though more pre-Columbian sculptures were included there, too. Works on paper covered the walls of the mezzanine walkways above the central gallery, while cubism continued in the large gallery to the north (285), where Kimball had once proposed the raised balcony along the windows. One of the small north galleries featured Klee. On the south side, a smaller gallery formerly dedicated to Gallatin focused on Duchamp, while the larger gallery in the middle, with the balcony door (282), held an eclectic mix of artists and styles.

The highlight of this last gallery, however, was a work not directly from the Arensbergs: Duchamp's *The Bride Stripped Bare by Her Bachelors, Even* (1915–23), also called *The Large Glass*. The artist had toiled away on this masterpiece during much of his time living in the Arensbergs' New York studio. It was destined for the couple's collection, like nearly everything else Duchamp made then, but he was still working on it when they moved to Hollywood. Thus, the Arensbergs sold *The Large Glass* to Katherine Dreier, another collector and friend of Duchamp's. She displayed the work in an exhibition at the Brooklyn Museum in 1926 and later in her homes in West Redding and Milford, Connecticut. The piece cracked while in transit following the Brooklyn exhibition, leading Duchamp to repair it in 1936.[39]

After Dreier passed away on March 29, 1952, Duchamp served as an executor of her will and helped realize the collector's wish to donate *The Large Glass* to the Philadelphia Museum of Art, where it could reside alongside the vast majority of the artist's oeuvre. Interestingly, less than one year earlier, Duchamp had confided in Walter that he thought Philadelphia would balk at the offer, writing: "I suspect that F.K. and the Trustees hardly like anything she has, including the glass as well. This is *strictly confidential:* I have a hunch that broken glass is hard

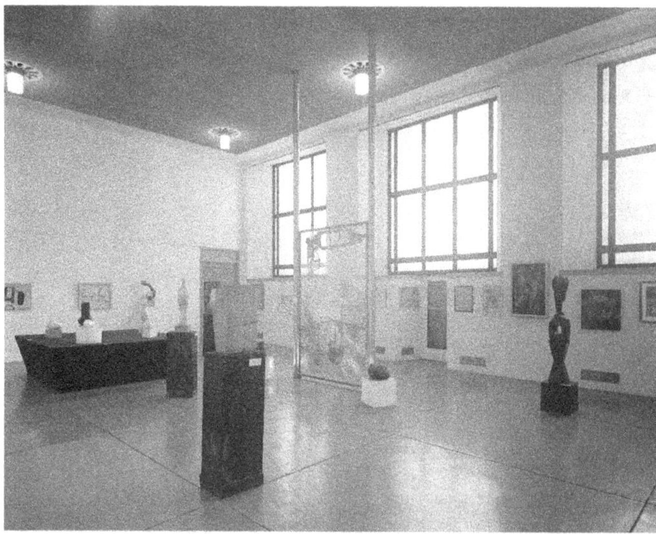

FIGURE 8. The Louise and Walter Arensberg Collection (current Gallery 282), Philadelphia Museum of Art, 1965. (Courtesy of the Philadelphia Museum of Art, Library and Archives, Rights and Reproductions Photograph Collection, RNR_B064_ArensbergCollection_001)

to swallow for a 'Museum.'"[40] Kimball, however, put those concerns to rest, accepting the work into the collection and inviting Duchamp to oversee its installation in July 1954. Echoing how he and Dreier had installed *The Large Glass* in Milford in front of a window overlooking her garden, Duchamp sited the work in the museum's south gallery of Section 7 directly on axis with Kimball's door to the terrace balcony.[41]

The Legacy of the Modern Museum

The acquisition of the Arensberg collection, and its opening in October 1954, was the last great "hurrah hurrah" for Kimball; he would pass away eight months later, in August 1955, while traveling in Europe. And yet the legacy of the Modern Museum remains. Visitors to the Philadelphia Museum of Art today still encounter *The Large Glass* in the center of this gallery, but it no longer aligns with a door. As it turned out, Kimball's pleasant description of an outdoor space directly off the room was something of a fantasy, an experience ultimately unavailable to the public. The door remained closed for nearly its entire existence, apparently not even opening when Duchamp returned for visits in the 1960s.[42] Moreover, likely as a security measure, the opening to the balcony was fitted with a solid exterior door beyond the inner glass door, so that the doorway—Kimball's compromise with the Arensbergs over the windows, and the key to finally securing their gift— was in practice neither a door nor a window.

This dilemma was not resolved until well after Kimball's death. In 1969, the museum received the bequest of *Étant donnés: 1. La chute d'eau, 2. Le gaz d'éclairage,* a final opus by Duchamp, who had passed away the previous fall. Duchamp created this work in near total secrecy from 1946 to 1966, and because its development coincided with Kimball's courting of the Arensbergs and the installation of their collection in Philadelphia, he designed it to fit in a small gallery next to the one with the balcony door and *The Large Glass.*[43] When *Étant donnés* was installed at the museum—a task overseen by Anne d'Harnoncourt, a curatorial assistant who later became director—the large south gallery was also renovated. *The Large Glass* was remounted, the walls below the windows raised to provide more hanging space, and "that door problem," as Duchamp's stepson Paul Matisse called it, remedied with a sheet of acrylic glass, transforming the opening into a window.[44] Although this meant the loss of Kimball's imaginative idea of walking out onto the balcony, the change unwittingly revived the Arensbergs' original request for a view of the outside from within the gallery, extending visually, if not physically, the experience of their collection beyond the walls of the museum.

Another change to the gallery in 1969 would precipitate a larger fragmenting of Kimball's Modern Museum. To celebrate Duchamp after his death and provide visitors with some context for viewing *Étant donnés,* d'Harnoncourt reconceived the gallery with *The Large Glass* to focus on Duchamp instead of the Arensberg collection more broadly. This shift away from the quasi-period room concept honoring the couple's artistic and architectural tastes would in time be felt elsewhere, too, so that none of the galleries today look as they did in 1954. The long gallery that showed Brancusi now has a ceiling painting by Sol LeWitt and is often hung with paintings by living artists. In the gallery where Kimball had once sketched out a balcony raised to window height, the windows are walled up to accommodate Cy Twombly's ten-painting cycle *Fifty Days at Iliam.* The central gallery that had been the core of the Arensberg collection shows Brancusi sculptures—most of them from the couple's collection—but the mezzanine is now closed to the public and, until recently, held offices for the Contemporary Art department. Directly above, where Gallatin's collection reopened in 1954, are early nineteenth-century French paintings and furniture. Nowhere in the galleries are the pre-Columbian sculptures to be found.[45]

Even though the Modern Museum has dissolved as each installation and exhibition, director and curator, artist and collector has left their mark on the galleries, Kimball's legacy for establishing a place for avant-garde art within the building remains. Paintings and sculptures from Gallatin and the Arensbergs—not to mention Stieglitz and other collectors—still appear throughout the museum. Some rarely go into storage, as they are so popular with visitors; others are so famous they seem to be forever cycling through loans to venues around the world. Yet perhaps the most enduring, if inconspicuous, evidence of Kimball's embrace of modernism is found not on the walls but in them: the door-turned-window in the Section 7 gallery overlooking the terrace. A dark film now covers the acrylic sheet, reducing UV light in the gallery, but the window still affords a view outside. The charming architectural quirk aligns so perfectly with *The Large Glass,* echoing its proportions and materiality, that common museum myth holds Duchamp designed the window himself. But really it was Kimball's doing. Or at least half his doing, a practical repurposing of an older building feature nearly gone to waste. His clever compromise put an end to years of negotiation over the Arensbergs' great collection of modern art, which needed a home—which Kimball was only too happy to provide.

Notes

The research for this essay began in 2015, when I received a letter from Lyne Limouse, a scholar in Aussillon, France, asking questions I could not answer about the "porte-fenêtre" in the gallery with Marcel Duchamp's *The Large Glass.* Nearly a year later I finally had a satisfactory response for Limouse, but in the process had turned up new questions about the gallery. I continued and expanded my research, presenting it in 2017 for the tour "Dark Ages to Duchamp: Doors in the Museum's Collection," co-led with Ainsley Cameron and Jack Hinton, and then in 2018 as a lecture for the annual Fiske Kimball Society Luncheon. I want to thank the organizers of these events for giving me the opportunity to share this obscure but consequential chapter in museum history. I also want to thank the many colleagues who provided feedback on my thinking and writing on this topic over the years, especially Matthew Affron, Alexander Kauffman, and Mark Nelson. Michael R. Taylor deserves credit as well for both inspiring my interest in Duchamp and encouraging me to pursue a career in museums. Yet above all this essay is indebted to the librarians and archivist at the Philadelphia Museum of Art who offered invaluable guidance as I sifted through photographs, letters, and maps I never would have discovered on my own. Here I single out Susan Anderson Laquer, who in addition to supporting my research introduced me to Marie Frank, which led to the publication of this essay.

1. As Kathleen Curran notes, the challenge of completing the museum's new building was a major factor in drawing Kimball to Philadelphia, where "all his experiences, careers, and fields of interest were employed." Kathleen Curran, *The Invention of the American Art Museum: From Craft to Kulturgeschichte, 1870–1930* (Los Angeles: Getty Research Institute, 2016), 187–88.

2. "Construction," *Philadelphia Museum Bulletin* 34, no. 180 (1939): 2.

3. "Handbook of the Museum," *Philadelphia Museum Bulletin* 37, no. 193 (1942): 65. See also Floor Plan One, Section 7, 1940 August 27, Special Format Records, Architectural Drawings, Philadelphia Museum of Art (hereafter PMA) Library and Archives.

4. On matters concerning the Gallatin acquisition, this essay is greatly indebted to Gail Stavitsky, "The A. E. Gallatin Collection: An Early Adventure in Modern Art," *Philadelphia Museum of Art Bulletin* 89, nos. 379–80 (1994): 38–39.

5. This essay refers to galleries by their current numbers, which should not be confused with prior numbering systems. The original gallery numbers, which appear here in some cited texts and drawings, used four digits to refer to floor, section, and gallery. A three-digit system indicating only floor and gallery was later implemented, but it needed to be updated in 2021 with the completion of the Core Project and the opening of public spaces on additional levels of the building.

6. Additional views of the A. E. Gallatin Collection in the 1940s are available in the Rights and Reproductions Photograph Collection, PMA Library and Archives.

7. See photographs of the apartment taken by Charles Sheeler sometime after May 1919, Philadelphia Museum of Art, The Louise and Walter Arensberg Collection, 1950, 1950-134-989, 990, 991.

8. For a comprehensive history of this house, including an archive of all known photography during the Arensbergs' ownership, see Mark Nelson, William H. Sherman, and Ellen Hoobler, *Hollywood Arensberg: Avant-Garde Collection in Midcentury L.A.* (Los Angeles: Getty Publications, 2020).

9. Nelson, Sherman, and Hoobler, *Hollywood Arensberg*, 35–41.

10. Nelson, Sherman, and Hoobler, *Hollywood Arensberg*, 58.

11. Fiske Kimball to R. Sturgis Ingersoll, February 10, 1947. Fiske Kimball Records (hereafter FKR), PMA Library and Archives. In this same letter, Kimball asks Ingersoll to gauge support for the potential acquisition, acknowledging, "I know we have crowded our own Trustees pretty hard on modernism."

12. Complaining to Kimball about the proximity of the Barnes Collection in Merion, Pennsylvania, Walter wrote: "I am obliged to confess to a slight reluctance to entering the region that is so infected by the pollution of Dr. Barnes,

and that will, somehow, as long as he continues, require to be quarantined. I should think that he would recognize that he is very bad advertising for his famous product, for he is himself a kind of running sore that even Argyrol cannot cure." Walter Arensberg to Fiske Kimball, July 8, 1948, FKR.

13. Marcel Duchamp to Louise and Walter Arensberg, May 8, 1949, Arensberg Archives, PMA Library and Archives.

14. Fiske Kimball, Proposed installation of pre-Columbian, etc, Arensberg Collection, February 8, 1949, FKR.

15. Fiske Kimball, Memorandum on the scope of museum collections, Board meeting minutes, June 1941, Board of Trustees Records, 299, PMA Library and Archives.

16. Fiske Kimball to Albert Eugene Gallatin, February 18, 1949, FKR. By "bring up your other things" Kimball is likely referring to works from Gallatin's collection on view on the lower level of the building, somewhere in the general proximity of today's galleries 150 to 157.

17. Walter Arensberg, telegram to Fiske Kimball, April 8, 1949, FKR.

18. See the chapter "From Craft to *Kulturgeschichte* in Philadelphia: The Pennsylvania Museum of Art, 1876–1928," in Curran, *Invention*, 173–201, for a fuller view of the Philadelphia Museum of Art's development and an analysis of how Kimball's repeated efforts to create architectural installations for the arts of a culture or period reflected his keen awareness of contemporary European and American museum practices.

19. Fiske Kimball to Walter Arensberg, April 12, 1949, Arensberg Archives.

20. Marcel Duchamp to Louise and Walter Arensberg, May 8, 1949, Arensberg Archives.

21. For more on this exhibition, see Naomi Sawelson-Gorse, "The Art Institute of Chicago and the Arensberg Collection," *Art Institute of Chicago Museum Studies* 19, no. 1 (1993): 81–111.

22. Marcel Duchamp to Louise and Walter Arensberg, October 21, 1949, Arensberg Archives.

23. Walter Arensberg to Fiske Kimball, November 3, 1949, FKR.

24. Fiske Kimball to R. Sturgis Ingersoll, November 9, 1949, FKR.

25. Fiske Kimball to Walter Arensberg, November 9, 1949, FKR.

26. Walter Arensberg to Marcel Duchamp, May 18, 1950, Arensberg Archives.

27. Marcel Duchamp to Louise and Walter Arensberg, July 8, 1950, Arensberg Archives.

28. Duchamp to L. and W. Arensberg, July 8, 1950.

29. Fiske Kimball to Walter Arensberg, November 23, 1950, Arensberg Archives.

30. Walter Arensberg to Fiske Kimball, November 30, 1950, FKR.

31. Fiske Kimball, telegram to Henri Marceau, December 28, 1950, FKR.

32. W. Arensberg to F. Kimball, November 30, 1950.

33. Kimball's preference for staggered doorways is evident throughout the museum building, including in the many period rooms on the floor above. See Curran, *Invention*, 198.

34. Although this quote comes from Kimball, it appears to be a reiteration of a previous conversation with Walter. Fiske Kimball to Walter Arensberg, June 7, 1951, Arensberg Archives.

35. Fiske Kimball to Walter Arensberg, March 23, 1953, Arensberg Archives.

36. Marcel Duchamp to Louise and Walter Arensberg, October 29, 1953, Arensberg Archives.

37. For the director's full accounting of this debut, see Fiske Kimball, "Opening of the Louise and Walter Arensberg Collection. The 'Modern Museum' of the Philadelphia Museum of Art," *Philadelphia Museum Bulletin* 50, no. 243 (1954). In addition, Alexander Kauffman spoke on Modern Museum in the lecture "Philadelphia's 'Modern Museum': Exhibiting Avant-Garde Art at Mid-Century," delivered at the Arthur Ross Gallery, October 5, 2011.

38. Nelson, Sherman, and Hoobler, *Hollywood Arensberg*, 22–24.

39. For more on *The Large Glass*, Duchamp, and Dreier, see Paul B. Franklin's "Marcel Duchamp, Katherine S. Dreier & La Société Anonyme, Inc," *Étant donné Marcel Duchamp*, no. 9 (Paris: Association pour l'Étude de Marcel Duchamp, 2009).

40. Marcel Duchamp to Louise and Walter Arensberg, April 19, 1951, Arensberg Archives.

41. Marcel Duchamp to Henri Marceau, April 7, 1954, FKR.

42. See photographs of Duchamp in the gallery taken by Gianfranco Baruchello, 1966, Alexina and Marcel Duchamp Papers, PMA Library and Archives, 13-1972-9(432, 435, 436).

43. For a comprehensive history of this work, its installation, and its interpretations, see Michael R. Taylor et al., *Marcel Duchamp: "Étant donnés"* (Philadelphia: Philadelphia Museum of Art, 2009).

44. Paul Matisse to Anne d'Harnoncourt, April 1, 1969, *Étant donnés* Curatorial Records, PMA Library and Archives.

45. At the time of this writing, several pieces of pre-Columbian sculpture from the Arensberg collection were on long-term loan to the Penn Museum and the Princeton University Art Museum.

SELECTED BIBLIOGRAPHY

Selected Archival Sources

HARVARD ART MUSEUM ARCHIVES, CAMBRIDGE, MA

Kimball, Fiske. Papers.

JEFFERSON LIBRARY, THOMAS JEFFERSON FOUNDATION INC., CHARLOTTESVILLE, VA

Grigg, Milton. Papers.
Thomas Jefferson Foundation Archives.

MASSACHUSETTS HISTORICAL SOCIETY, BOSTON, MA

Jefferson, Thomas. Architectural Drawings.

PHILADELPHIA MUSEUM OF ART LIBRARY AND ARCHIVES, PHILADELPHIA, PA

Arensberg, Walter and Louise. Papers.
Board of Trustees. Records.
Duchamp, Marcel and Alexina. Papers.
Étant donnés. Curatorial Records.
Kimball, Fiske. Papers.
Kimball, Fiske. Records.
Oral History Project. Interview with Anne Goebel Barkman.
Rights and Reproductions Photograph Collection.
Special Format Records.

ROCKEFELLER LIBRARY, COLONIAL WILLIAMSBURG FOUNDATION, WILLIAMSBURG, VA

Minutes of the Meetings of the Advisory Committee of Architects, 1928–1948. Transcriptions.
Williamsburg Journals of William G. Perry, 1927–1942 in Five Volumes. Transcriptions.

UNIVERSITY OF VIRGINIA LIBRARY, SPECIAL COLLECTIONS,
CHARLOTTESVILLE, VA

Kimball, Marie Goebel. Papers.

Published Sources

Allaback, Sarah. "Theodora Kimball: Defining a New Field—City Planning." *View* 23 (2023): 15–21.

Berkes, Anna. "Marie Kimball: Pioneering Scholar and First Curator of Monticello." In *Virginia Women: Their Lives and Times*, vol. 2, edited by Cynthia A. Kierner and Sandra Gioia Treadway, 202–21. Athens: University of Georgia Press, 2016.

Bricker, Lauren Weiss. "The Writings of Fiske Kimball: A Synthesis of Architectural History and Practice." In *The Architectural Historian in America: A Symposium in Celebration of the Fiftieth Anniversary of the Founding of the Society of Architectural Historians*, edited by Elisabeth Blair MacDougall, 215–35. Studies in the History of Art 35. Washington, DC: National Gallery of Art, 1990.

Brownlee, David Bruce. *Making a Modern Classic: The Architecture of the Philadelphia Museum of Art*. Philadelphia: Philadelphia Museum of Art, 1997.

Canaday, John. *Culture Gulch: Notes on Art and Its Public in the 1960s*. New York: Farrar, Straus and Giroux, 1969.

Cogliano, Francis D. *Thomas Jefferson: Reputation and Legacy*. Charlottesville: University of Virginia Press, 2006.

Curran, Kathleen. *The Invention of the American Art Museum: From Craft to Kulturgeschichte, 1870–1930*. Los Angeles: Getty Research Institute, 2016.

Ehrenpreis, Diane. "Kimball Tour of Monticello." Presented at Fiske and Marie Kimball: Shaping Our Experience of Buildings and Objects, virtual conference hosted by the Robert H. Smith International Center for Jefferson Studies, March 20, 2021. https://www.youtube.com/watch?v=pIwoPfQ2x5c&list=PLjRnhUjPwbM3nm Dfex_uZUKfR0V3ynN19&index=13.

Elwall, Robert. *Building with Light: The International History of Architectural Photography*. London: Merrell Publishers in association with the Royal Institute of British Architects, 2004.

Fleming, E. McClung. "Artifact Study: A Proposed Model." *Winterthur Portfolio* 9 (1974): 153–73.

Forty, Adrian. *Words and Buildings: A Vocabulary of Modern Architecture*. London: Thames & Hudson, 2000.

Frank, Marie. *Denman Ross and American Design Theory*. Hanover, NH: University Press of New England, 2011.

———. "Fiske Kimball and the Genesis of *Thomas Jefferson, Architect*." *Classicist* 13 (2016): 56–64.

———. "Fiske Kimball and the University of Virginia Architecture Program in the 1920s." *ARRIS* 18 (October 2007): 15–27.

———. "Object Lesson: Fiske Kimball and the Restoration of Moors End, Nantucket." *Buildings and Landscapes* 29, no. 1 (2022): 94–107.

Hamlin, A. D. F. *A Text-Book of the History of Architecture.* New York: Longmans, Green, 1896.

Hamlin, Talbot. *The American Spirit in Architecture.* The Pageant of America 13. New Haven, CT: Yale University Press, 1926.

———. *Greek Revival Architecture in America: Being an Account of the Important Trends in American Architecture and American Life Prior to the War Between the States.* New York: Oxford University Press, 1944.

Hohmann, Heidi. "Theodora Kimball Hubbard and the 'Intellectualization' of Landscape Architecture, 1911–1935." *Landscape Journal* 25, no. 2 (2006): 169–86.

Hosmer, Charles B., Jr. *Presence of the Past: A History of the Preservation Movement in the United States Before Williamsburg.* New York: G. P. Putnam's Sons, 1965.

———. *Preservation Comes of Age: From Williamsburg to the National Trust, 1926–1949.* Charlottesville: University of Virginia Press, 1981.

Howard, Hugh. *Dr. Kimball and Mr. Jefferson: Rediscovering the Founding Fathers of American Architecture.* New York: Bloomsbury, 2006.

Kimball, Fiske. *Domestic Architecture of the American Colonies and of the Early Republic.* New York: Charles Scribner's Sons, 1922.

———. *Thomas Jefferson, Architect.* Cambridge, MA: Riverside Press, 1916.

———. "What Is Modern Architecture?" *The Nation* 119, no. 3082 (July 30, 1924): 128–29.

Kimball, Fiske, and George Edgell. *A History of Architecture.* New York: Harper & Brothers, 1918.

Kimball, Marie. "The Furnishing of Monticello, Part I." *Magazine Antiques* 12, no. 5 (1927): 380–85.

———. *Jefferson: The Road to Glory, 1743–1776.* New York: Coward-McCann, 1943.

———. *Jefferson: The Scene of Europe, 1784–1789.* New York: Coward-McCann, 1950.

———. *Jefferson: War and Peace, 1776–1784.* New York: Coward-McCann, 1947.

———. "Jefferson's Four Freedoms." *Virginia Quarterly Review* 19, no. 2 (1943): 204–21.

———. "Thomas Jefferson's French Furniture." *Magazine Antiques* 15, no. 2 (1929): 123–28.

Lahendro, Joseph. "The Architecture of Fiske Kimball at UVa." Presented at Fiske and Marie Kimball: Shaping Our Experience of Buildings and Objects, virtual conference hosted by the Robert H. Smith International Center for Jefferson Studies, March 20, 2021. https://www.youtube.com/watch?v=GZ7xIOfS48E& list=PLjRnhUjPwbM3nmDfex_uZUKfR0V3ynN19&index=14.

———. "Fiske Kimball, American Renaissance Historian." Master's thesis, University of Virginia, 1982.

Langlois, Charles-Victor, and Charles Seignobos. *Introduction to the Study of History.* Translated by G. G. Berry. New York: Henry Holt, 1904.

Leepson, Marc. *Saving Monticello: The Levy Family's Epic Quest to Rescue the House That Jefferson Built.* New York: Free Press, 2001.

MacDougall, Elisabeth Blair, ed. *The Architectural Historian in America: A Symposium in Celebration of the Fiftieth Anniversary of the Founding of the Society of Architectural Historians.* Studies in the History of Art 35. Washington, DC: National Gallery of Art, 1990.

Malone, Dumas. *Jefferson and His Time.* 6 vols. Boston: Little, Brown, 1948–77.

Nelson, Mark, William H. Sherman, and Ellen Hoobler. *Hollywood Arensberg: Avant-Garde Collection in Midcentury L.A.* Los Angeles: Getty Publications, 2020.

Peterson, Merrill D. *The Jefferson Image in the American Mind.* New York: Oxford University Press, 1960. Rev. ed., Charlottesville: University of Virginia Press, 1998.

Prown, Jules David. "Mind in Matter: An Introduction to Material Culture Theory and Method." *Winterthur Portfolio* 17, no. 1 (1982): 1–19.

Psarra, Sophie. *Architecture and Narrative: The Formation of Space and Cultural Meaning.* Abingdon: Routledge, 2009.

Roberts, George, and Mary Howland Roberts. *Triumph on Fairmount: Fiske Kimball and the Philadelphia Museum of Art.* Philadelphia: J. B. Lippincott, 1959.

Sloan, Herbert. "The Cosmopolitan and the Curator: Gilbert Chinard, Marie Kimball, and Jefferson Biography in the Mid-Twentieth Century." In *Thomas Jefferson's Lives: Biographers and the Battle for History,* edited by Robert M. S. McDonald, 200–218. Charlottesville: University of Virginia Press, 2019.

Stavitsky, Gail. "The A. E. Gallatin Collection: An Early Adventure in Modern Art." *Philadelphia Museum of Art Bulletin* 89, nos. 379–80 (1994): 4–47.

Stubbendeck, Megan. "A Woman's Touch: Gender at Monticello, 1945–1960." In *Entering the Fray: Gender, Politics, and Culture in the New South,* edited by Jonathan Daniel Wells and Sheila R. Phipps, 118–35. Columbia: University of Missouri Press, 2010.

Taylor, Michael R., et al. *Marcel Duchamp: "Étant donnés."* Exhibition catalogue. Philadelphia: Philadelphia Museum of Art, 2009.

Urofsky, Melvin I. *The Levy Family and Monticello, 1834–1923.* Charlottesville, VA: Thomas Jefferson Foundation, Inc., 2001.

Watkin, David. *The Rise of Architectural History.* London: Architectural Press, 1980.

Wood, Elizabeth B. "Pots and Pans History: Relating Manuscripts and Printed Sources to the Study of Domestic Art Objects." *American Archivist* 30, no. 3 (1967): 431–42.

Zigrosser, Carl. *A World of Art and Museums.* Philadelphia: Art Alliance Press, 1975.

CONTRIBUTORS

LAUREN WEISS BRICKER is Professor Emerita of Architecture, California State Polytechnic University, Pomona, where she also served as an Interim Dean and Director of ENV Archives–Special Collections. She holds a doctorate in the history of art and architecture from University of California, Santa Barbara. She was Clarkson Visiting Chair in Urban Planning, University at Buffalo (March 2019). Her primary research areas are American architecture, the historiography of architecture, and historic preservation. She is the author of *The Mediterranean House in America* (2008) and her upcoming volume focuses on the Western environmental movement and the modern house.

MARIE FRANK is the founding director of the Architectural Studies Program at the University of Massachusetts Lowell; she received the university's Faculty Award for Excellence in Undergraduate Teaching in 2020. Her book, *Denman Ross and American Design Theory,* focused on one of Fiske Kimball's teachers at Harvard University and received the Henry-Russell Hitchcock Award from the Victorian Society in America. She has written a series of articles on Fiske Kimball as an educator, scholar, and architect. Her current research includes two projects on the urban revitalization of Lowell in the late twentieth century, after the departure of the mills.

GARDINER HALLOCK is the Thomas Jefferson Foundation's Senior Vice President for Preservation and Operations. Since joining the Foundation in 2011, he has helped preserve its internationally significant historic architecture, collections, and landscapes. Before Monticello, he served as the Restoration Manager at George Washington's Mount Vernon and was the Director of Architectural Research at James Madison's Montpelier. A native of Albemarle County, Virginia, Gardiner has published and lectured on eighteenth- and early nineteenth-century architectural and landscape history as well as conserving and restoring early American architecture.

SUSAN KERN is Associate Professor and Director of the Historic Preservation Program at the University of Maryland School of Architecture, Planning and Preservation. Her book, *The Jeffersons at Shadwell,* won the 2011 Abbot Lowell Cummings prize from the Vernacular Architecture Forum. She served as national president of the Vernacular Architecture Forum. Her current work on landmark preservation projects of the early twentieth century and their role in setting standards for what visitors expect from museums and historic sites has been supported by research fellowships from the International Center for Jefferson Studies, Library Company of Philadelphia, and Winterthur Museum and Library.

CARL R. LOUNSBURY, from 1982 to 2016, was the Senior Architectural Historian at the Colonial Williamsburg Foundation, where he was responsible for major research and restoration projects in the historic area. Since 2002, he has been Adjunct Associate Professor of History at William and Mary, where he teaches courses in British and early American architectural history and the practice of fieldwork. He has published a number of books, including *An Illustrated Glossary of Early Southern Architecture and Landscape* and *The Courthouses of Early Virginia.* He is the coeditor of and a contributor to *The Chesapeake House* and *The Material World of Eyre Hall: Four Centuries of Chesapeake History.*

ANN M. LUCAS is Senior Historian Emerita at Monticello. Her work there included serving as the NEH Research Fellow for the 1993 exhibition and catalogue *The Worlds of Thomas Jefferson at Monticello.* As Director of Research, she initiated the planning and design of the Jefferson Library and contributed to the founding of the Getting Word Oral History project. More recently, she has recorded oral histories for the 2023 centennial of the Thomas Jefferson Foundation and produced lectures and podcasts on the Foundation's history. She is the coeditor of *Thomas Jefferson's Granddaughter in Queen Victoria's England: The Travel Diary of Ellen Wayles Coolidge, 1838–1839.* She received her master's in Architectural History and Certificate in Historic Preservation from the University of Virginia School of Architecture.

JOHN H. SPRINKLE JR. is a lecturer at the University of Maryland's School of Architecture, Planning, and Historic Preservation. After a decade as a private sector consultant, Sprinkle served as a historian at the headquarters of the National Park Service for over twenty years. Since 2014 he has written three books on the evolution of American historic preservation practice. *Crafting Preservation Criteria* traces the origins of conventions adopted by the National Register of Historic Places. *Saving Spaces* describes the relationship between the land conservation, recreation, and historic preservation movements. *Heritage Conservation,* which presents the story of the first generation of the New Preservation after 1966, received the Organization of American Historians Leopold Prize in 2024.

JOHN VICK is the Executive Director of Andalusia Historic House, Gardens & Arboretum, where he leads ongoing preservation efforts, expanding public access and research into more than two centuries of life on the property. Previously, he spent thirteen years at the Philadelphia Museum of Art, curating and contributing to more than twenty exhibitions and books on diverse topics. He worked on the 2018–19 exhibition *The Essential Duchamp*, which traveled to Tokyo, Seoul, and Sydney, and wrote for its catalogue, and he oversaw the creation in 2021 of new galleries of early American art, a component of the Core Project by Frank Gehry.

DANIELLE S. WILLKENS is Associate Professor in the Georgia Institute of Technology School of Architecture. She is the author of *The Transatlantic Design Network: Thomas Jefferson, John Soane, and Agents of Architectural Exchange* (2024) and *Architecture for Teens: A Beginner's Book for Aspiring Architects* (2021). She has extensive experience in the digital documentation and interpretation of heritage sites, with research support from the Sir John Soane's Museum Foundation, the International Center for Jefferson Studies, the American Philosophical Society, Dumbarton Oaks, the American Institute of Architects, the National Park Service, and the National Center for Preservation Training and Technology.

RICHARD GUY WILSON is the Commonwealth Professor in Architectural History at the University of Virginia. A frequent lecturer for universities, museums, and professional groups and a television commentator for A&E and PBS, particularly A&E's *America's Castles,* he has served as a curator for major museum exhibitions and published widely. His sixteen books include *The American Renaissance; McKim, Mead & White, Architects;* and *Edith Wharton at Home.* He directs the Nineteenth Century Summer School in Newport, RI. He received the University of Virginia's Outstanding Professor award in 2001.

INDEX